David Roberts

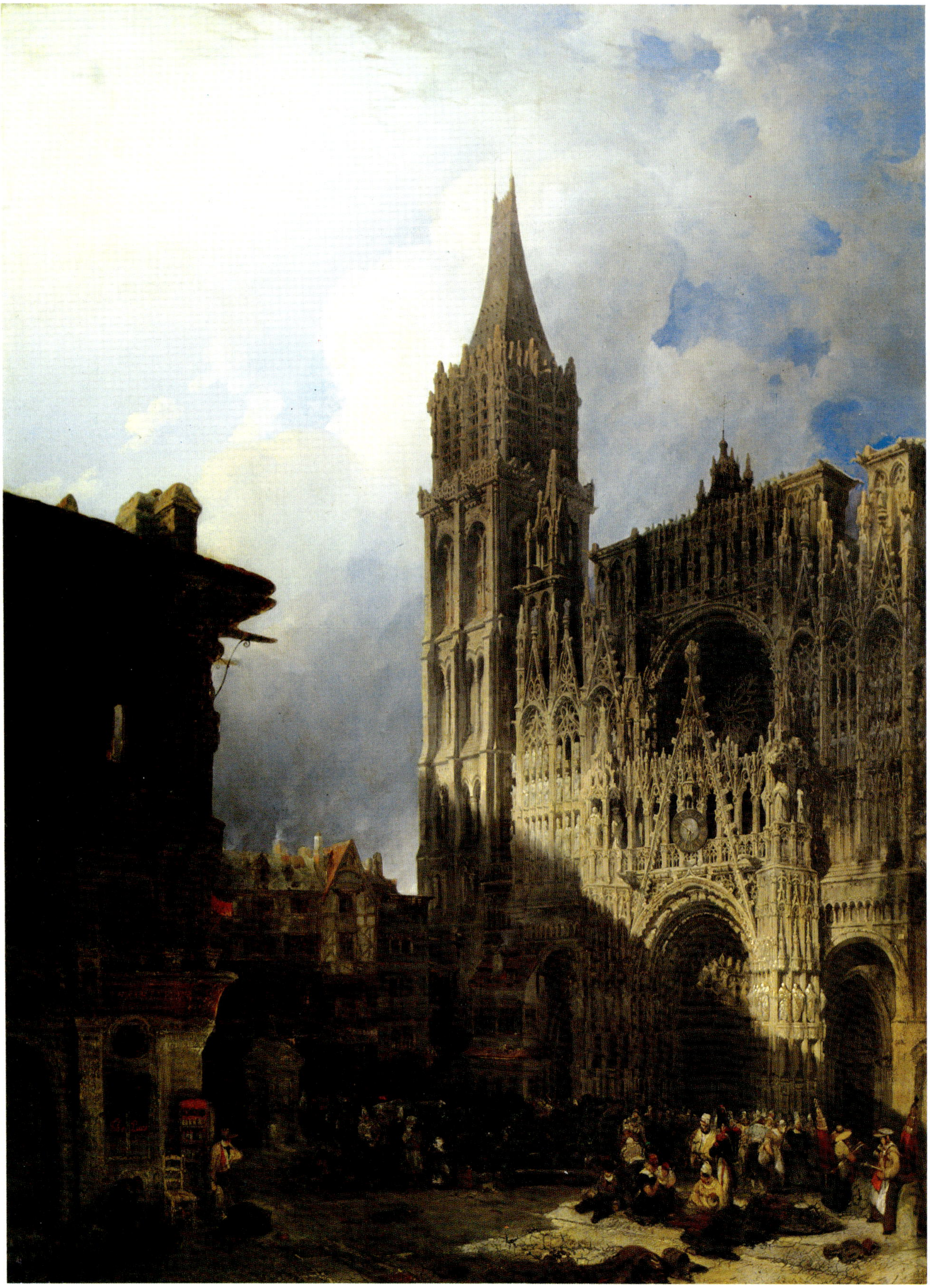

Grand Entrance to Rouen Cathedral, 1831, Grundy Art Gallery, Blackpool. Cat.65.

David Roberts

Compiled by
Helen Guiterman and Briony Llewellyn

Phaidon Press and Barbican Art Gallery

Published for the exhibition *David Roberts* held at
Barbican Art Gallery, London, 6 November 1986–4 January 1987

Phaidon Press Limited, Littlegate House, St. Ebbe's Street, Oxford OX1 1SQ

First published 1986

British Library Cataloguing in Publication Data
Roberts, David, *1796–1864*
David Roberts.
1. Roberts, David, *1796–1864*—Exhibitions
I. Title II. Guiterman, Helen III. Llewellyn, Briony
IV. Barbican Art Gallery
759.2'911 ND497.R6

ISBN 0-7148-2466-6
0-7148-2467-4 Pbk

Printed in Great Britain by Balding + Mansell Limited

Acknowledgements

We would very much like to thank the following for their help in locating and documenting works by David Roberts, and for facilitating the loan of works to the exhibition: Richard and Christopher Kingsett, Gabriel M. Naughton, and W. C. Plomer of Thos. Agnew & Sons, Ltd.; Bill Thomson, of the Albany Gallery; Philip Hook, of Christie's; Niall Hobhouse, of Eyre & Hobhouse Ltd.; Tony Carroll, of the Fine Art Society; the Leger Galleries Ltd.; Martin Leggatt, of Leggatt Brothers; Alan Cowie, of Robert Holden Ltd.; David Moore-Gwyn, of Sotheby's; Mrs Sandra de Laszlo, of Spink & Son Ltd.; and Miss P. M. Baker, of the Sterling Library, University of London.

We would also like to thank the following for their assistance during our research: Jenny Elkan; Mrs Matilda Hall; Ralph Hyde, Keeper of Prints and Maps, Guildhall Library; Dr T. I. Rae, of the Dept. of Manuscripts, National Library of Scotland; Rodney Searight; Peter Stocks; and Tanya Szrajber. Dr Pieter van der Merwe, Michael Pidgley, and Ian Gow, as well as contributing to this publication, have given us much valuable information.

Finally, we are greatly indebted to Charles Newton; to the descendants of David Roberts, David Bicknell, Frank Bicknell, Mrs Martin Fraser, Arthur Stanton, Mrs John Stanton, and Mr and Mrs Mitford Slade; and to Brigitte Lardinois and Krystyna Matyjaszkiewicz, of Barbican Art Gallery.

H. G. & B. L

Contents

Foreword 7

House-painting and Architecture 9
Ian Gow

Roberts and the Theatre 27
Pieter van der Merwe

Travel, Topography and Prints 47
Michael Pidgley

Roberts's Pictures of the Near East 69
Briony Llewellyn

Notes 88

Note on Roberts's Patrons and Friends 89

David Roberts – A Chronology of his Life and Related Events 92
Helen Guiterman

Catalogue 97

Bibliography 127

Lenders 127

Photographic Acknowledgements 127

Index 128

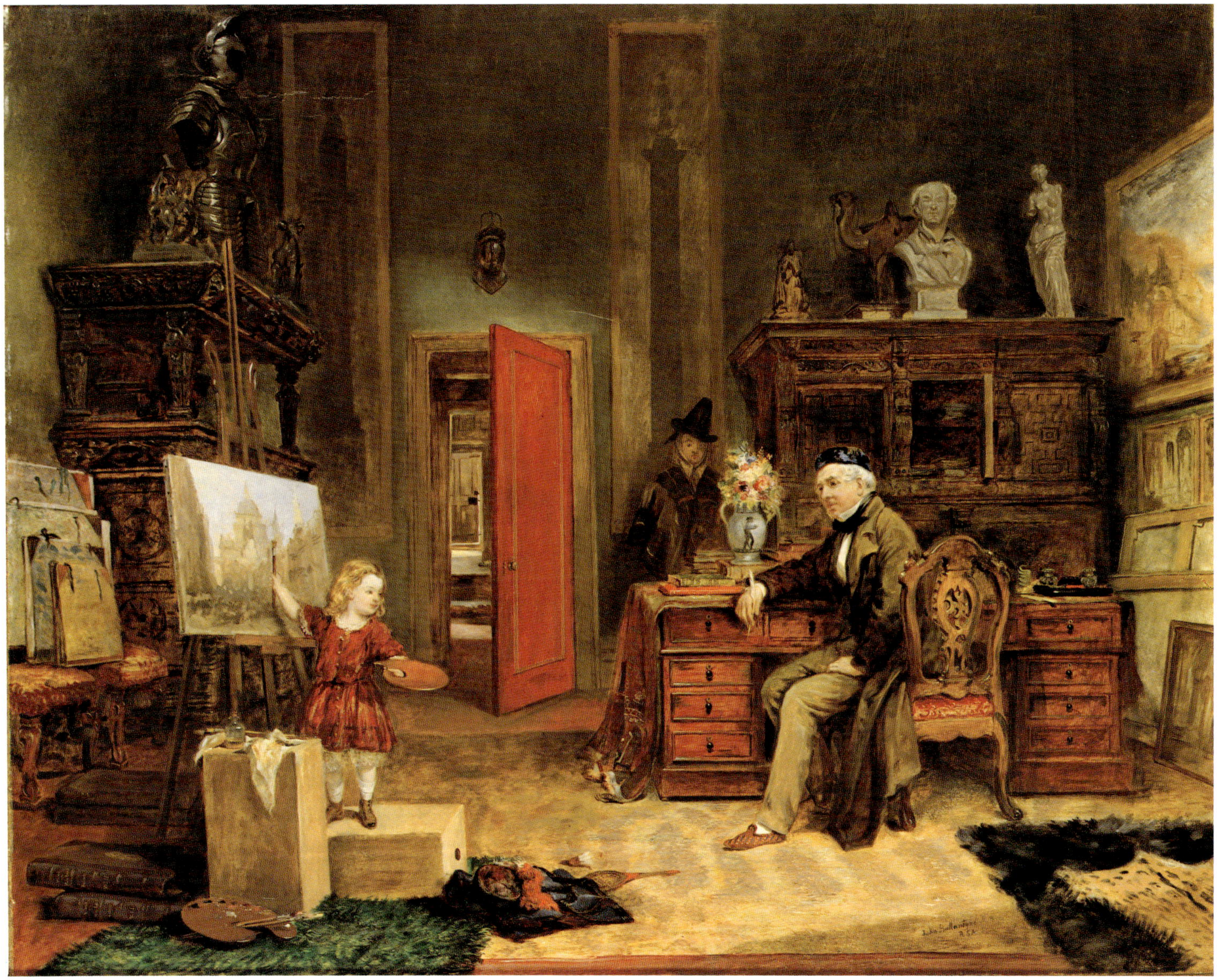

1. John Ballantyne, *Roberts in his Studio*, *c*.1862, The Fine Art Society, London. Cat.213.

Foreword

The re-emergence of interest in particular artists as evidenced by large, retrospective exhibitions is a curious phenomenon encouraged by a variety of coincidental factors. These might be historical, social, aesthetic, financial or even geo-political. With David Roberts, this is particularly so and this exhibition in the City of London comes about through a combination of these factors.

To begin with, Roberts, a Scotsman, found fame in London, initially as a theatrical scene-painter at Drury Lane and Covent Garden during the 1820s. With fellow-Scot Clarkson Stanfield he adapted to southern trends, working on panoramas and dioramas, a form of popular entertainment that originated in London and that combined in a contemporary art form the Georgian and Victorian enthusiasms for travel and spectacle.

Yet while Roberts found success in London and the city provided him with a domestic base and market outlets, such as the Royal Academy and the Society of British Artists, his work always required travel. Following the example of so many British artists before him, Roberts regularly travelled in Europe in search of new subjects, but what set him apart from his British contemporaries was his daring and obduracy in venturing to parts of North Africa and the Middle East that were rarely penetrated by Christians and even more rarely seen through artists' eyes. The speculative interest in this geographical area shown by Europeans during the late eighteenth and early nineteenth centuries, following Napoleon's invasion of Egypt and the establishment of overland trade routes to India, opened up hitherto unvisited countries to French and British archaeologists and artists, and Roberts was among the first of these to visit Morocco, Egypt, Palestine and Lebanon.

The success that followed the publication of Roberts's six volumes of lithographs, *The Holy Land, Syria, Idumea, Arabia, Egypt and Nubia* (1842–9) illustrates the Victorians' fascination for scenes of far-off lands, something that is now paralleled by the present-day interest of the inhabitants of that same region for scenes of their own homelands. Oil wealth from the Arab States has affected art market prices and the home interest in Roberts has correspondingly become revived. The Scots re-acknowledged him in an exhibition that travelled to London in 1981 and the Barbican exhibition accompanies the first major publication on his life and work since 1866.

Compiled by Helen Guiterman and Briony Llewellyn, this book is a prelude to the forthcoming Roberts *catalogue raisonné*, and a summation of Miss Guiterman's lifelong interest in the artist. Without her dedication and hard work, this exhibition could not have taken place and the Corporation of London, already the recipient of a generous gift of works from Miss Guiterman's private collection, is again indebted to her as well as to many lenders who have so kindly released their works for the exhibition.

John Hoole
Curator, Barbican Art Gallery

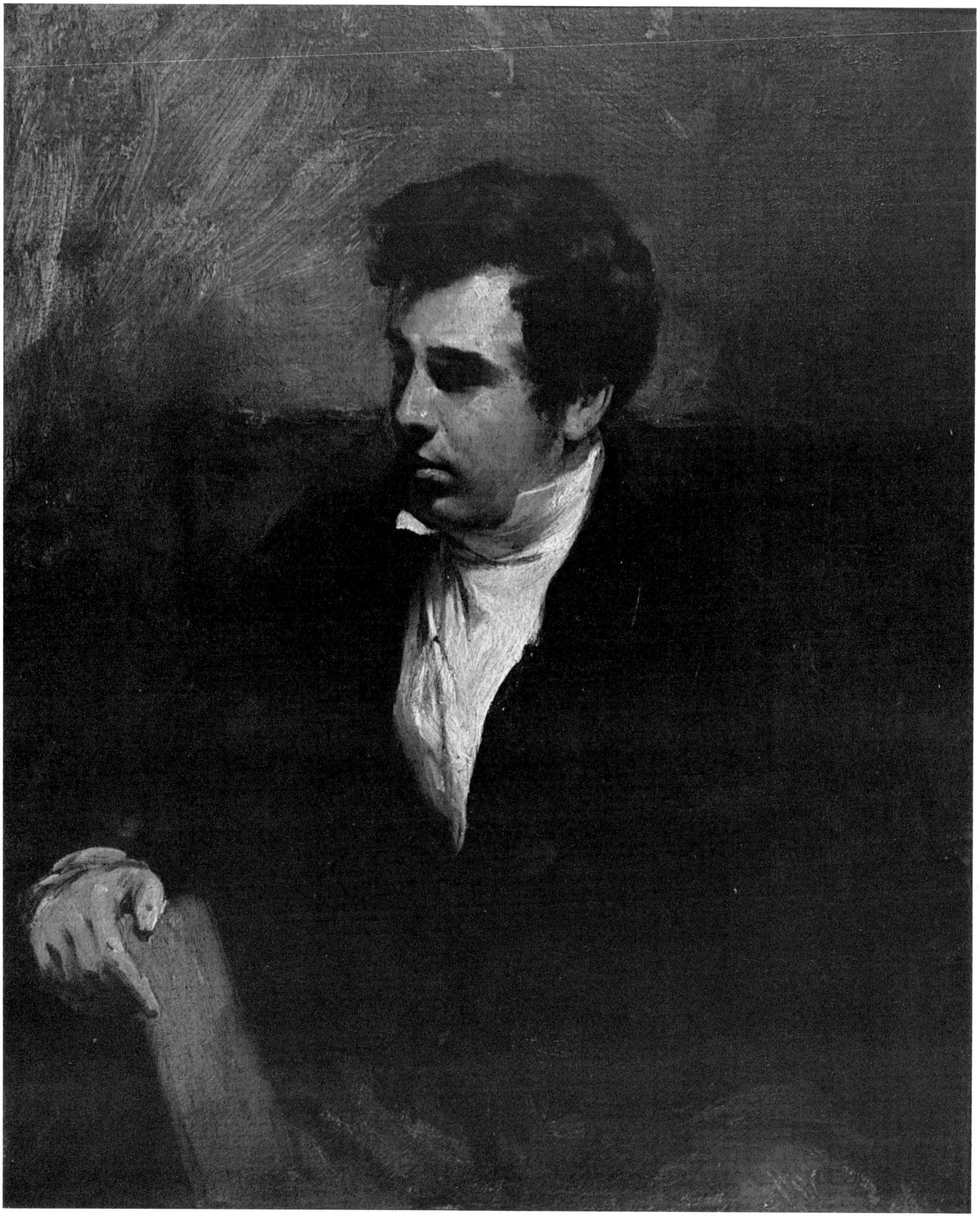

2. Robert Scott Lauder, *Portrait of Roberts as a Young Man*, *c.*1820, Mrs S. M. Fraser. Cat.212.

House-painting and Architecture

IAN GOW

David Roberts, like fellow Scottish artists Horatio McCulloch, John Phillip, William Leitch and William Bonnar, had to work as a house-painter before moving to the 'higher' spheres of fine art. His biographers have highlighted the humdrum character of this period to contrast with his later success in London. The years which Roberts spent in the trade, however, coincided with a phase of intense experiment and innovation in house-painting, which culminated in a major revolution brought about by David Ramsay Hay, a fellow apprentice and life-long friend. Throughout his life Roberts retained an interest in interior decoration and a tremendous sympathy for the house-painter's lot. Always a prolific correspondent and memorialist, his writings are an important source for the student of historic decoration.

Hard economic fact dictated that Roberts should take up house-painting. His family circumstances were humble. Having displayed an early talent for sketching, some of his drawings were shown to John Graham, Master of the Trustees Academy in Edinburgh, who advised 'that as the parents of the boy were poor, he had best be apprenticed to a house-painter, where he might still practice drawing, and learn an art by which he could earn his living.'[1] This might seem harsh in view of Roberts's undoubted abilities, but in fact his apprenticeship to the Edinburgh house-painter, Gavin Beugo, showed a measure of indulgence: it was better than following his father as a shoemaker.

Very little is known of Beugo's work and no accounts from his firm have been traced. On his death in 1822 his debts included sums owed by professional men. He had also been in charge of a few sizeable government contracts, such as those for the Excise Board and the Post Office. A sum of £200 owed by Sir John Marjoribanks, the Lord Provost, suggests that the firm may have been fashionable.[2] Roberts's own account of his apprenticeship concentrates, understandably, on the rough treatment that he received from Beugo rather than on the firm's jobs. The 'wareroom' in West Register Street was sited strategically between the Old and New Towns. Like many prosperous Edinburgh firms at this period, Beugo probably benefited from the New Town's rapid expansion.

As contemporary bills from other firms show, clients were beginning to demand more elaborate effects from the house-painter. In the late eighteenth century, neo-classical architects, with their predilection for plain colour-washed walls and white woodwork, had made few demands on the house-painter's abilities. As a result the 'slushers', as they were colloquially called, had sunk in the hierarchy of the trades. Their lowly station was further reduced by their association with evil smells and reputation for sharp practice. Since most painting was done

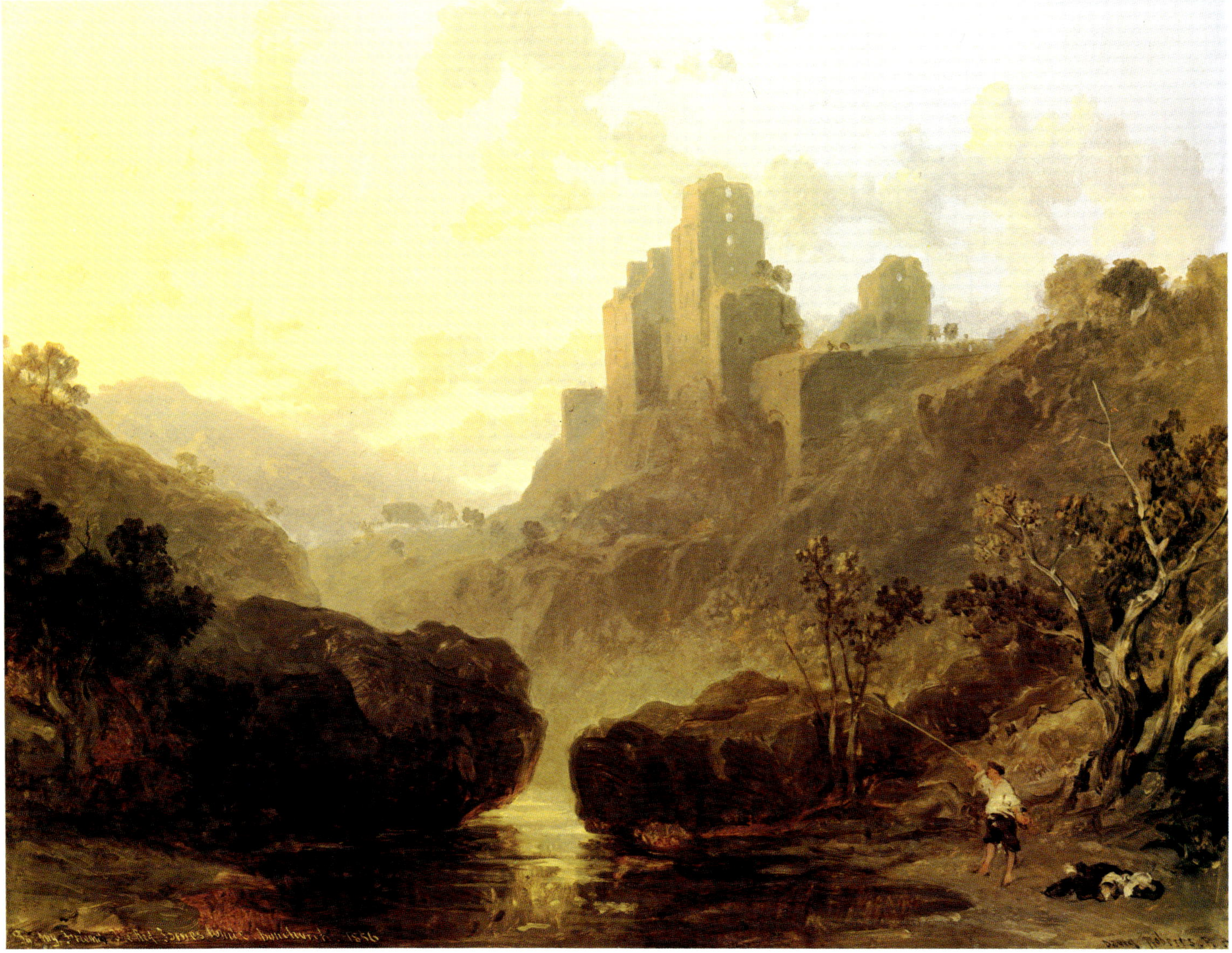

3. *Roslin Castle*, 1856, Private collection. Cat.36.

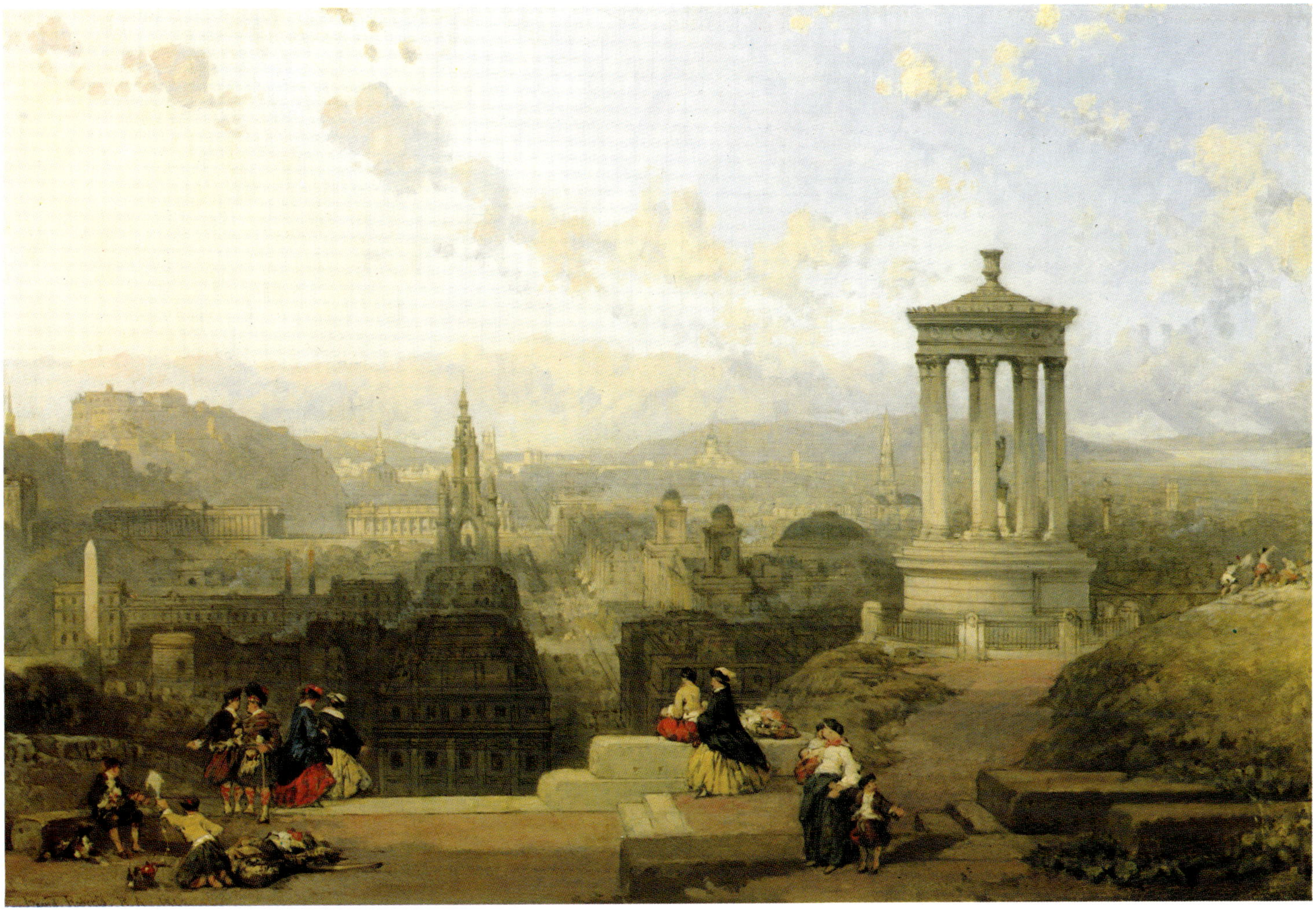

4. *Edinburgh from the Calton Hill, Looking West*, 1863, Guildhall Art Gallery, City of London. Cat.23.

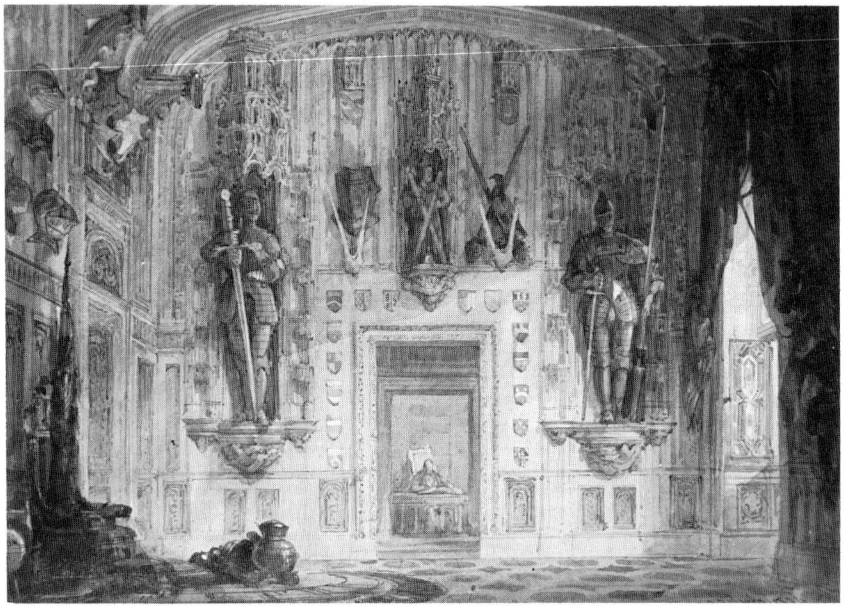

5. *Abbotsford, the Hall*, 1834, Private collection. Cat.17.

while a family and their architect were away from home, it was all too easy for the unscrupulous to omit one of the coats specified in the estimate or to adulterate raw materials in order to increase the profit margin.

During the short span of Roberts's house-painting years this state of affairs changed. Two of the houses where Roberts was employed after his apprenticeship, Scone Palace and Abercairney Abbey, were Picturesque essays in Gothic-revival style. To create a convincing feeling of antiquity, Roberts had to transform the glaring white gimcrack plaster vaults and beamed ceilings of these houses by painting imitations of dressed ashlar stonework and 'old oak'. Alas, Abercairney is no more, while Scone has been repainted, but the effect can be seen in other houses, such as Dunninald, which retains its original paintwork. Here, nothing is what it seems: the opulent 'marble' staircase and pavements are in reality made of humble sandstone, while the dining-room's handsome traceried panelling is a flat wall, which, like the golden stair-rail, has responded to the house-painter's 'Midas' touch.

Unlike the earlier practice of 'graining' and 'marbling', which had aimed merely at decorative effect, the whole point of the imitative painting in these houses was to fool the eye. Such counterfeit required not inconsiderable skills, and Roberts wrote that his 'imitations of woods and marbles were much commended', citing the library at Francis Jeffrey's Craigcrook Castle, where he had matched successfully the fictive oak graining of the plaster vault and walls to the antique patina of one of the famous carved-oak 'Stirling Heads' given place of honour over the chimney.

Such new-found talents on the house-painter's part were to have two important results. Firstly, such decorations have an obviously strong theatrical element, and it was through the medium of stage scenery that Roberts was to make his escape from house-painting (see *Roberts and the Theatre*, pp. 27–45). Secondly, the architect's dependence on these skills was to be the means of raising the house-painter's status and earnings. The traveller and writer James Skene, writing on house-painting in the *Edinburgh Encyclopaedia*, correctly predicted that:

> It is obvious from the very beautiful and correct imitations of the varieties of wood, so much in use at present, that there is far from any want of capacity, were it directed to the many excellencies of which the art is susceptible. And the present seems a favourable moment, when the practice is undergoing a change, to endevour to lead it into a still more extensive field of improvement. It would be a means of obtaining for

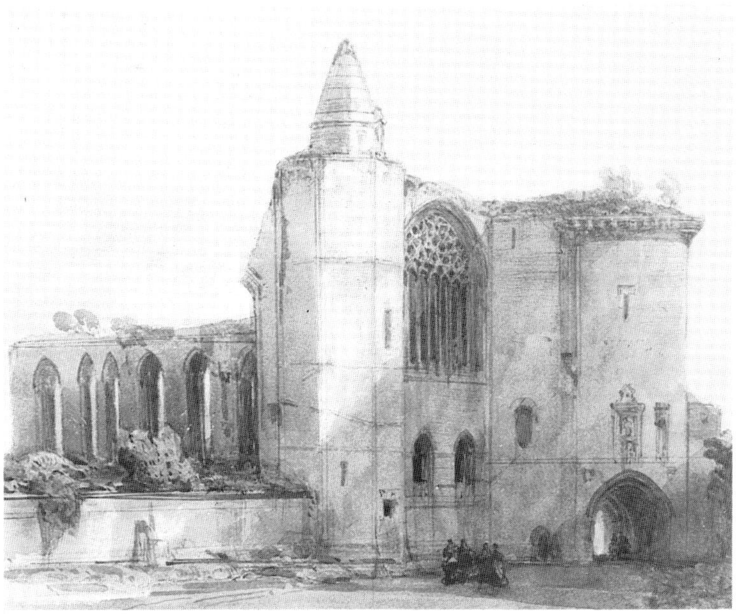

6. *Dunfermline*, Whitworth Art Gallery, University of Manchester. Cat.19.

> the art itself a higher place in the scale from what it now holds, as a mere trade, where the skill and assiduity of a handicraftsman is all that is considered necessary.[3]

This spirit of change and self-improvement was certainly not lost on either Roberts or Hay during their Beugo years. Hay was ultimately to personify Skene's wildest imaginings during the 1830s, when his business embraced an 'ornamental department' where 'artists', even more highly paid than his 'grainers' and 'marblers', could tackle anything from altar-pieces to a re-creation of Pompeii.[4] Roberts's house-painting years, seen against this background, were therefore far from time wasted, even if they were more prolonged than he wished.

Roberts retained his interest in decoration even after he was established as a famous artist in London. He numbered among his friends the house-painters J. G. Crace and John Clarke, as well as D. R. Hay, and took great pains to secure employment for any out-of-work house-painter who came to his notice. As late as 1862 he 'furnished a pattern for the colouring of the great hall of [South Kensington] Museum'.[5]

Like Roberts, Hay had no intention of remaining a mere house-painter after his apprenticeship at Beugo's, and he attempted to make a career in art. His paintings attracted the attention of Walter Scott, but the 'Wizard of the North' soon divined that his protégé was no second Wilkie, and counselled Hay to relinquish the uncertain prospects of an artist with a slender patrimony in favour of the secure future of a house-painter. As an inducement he offered Hay his newly built house, Abbotsford, as his first commission. With Scott's enthusiastic backing, Hay and his firm, D. R. Hay and Co., was soon established as the most innovative decorator in the British Isles.[6] In 1845, looking back over Hay's 'improvements' with a fellow house-painter's insight, Roberts wrote to his friend:

> I ought to have written before to acknowledge receipt of your last work on 'Ornamental Design' which will add another wreath around the brow of the most accomplished and intellectual of all *House-painters*. The only wonder is how you find the time out of all the numerous calls you have upon it, to devote it to so abstruse a pursuit. Poor Norrie has taken his last gill and there I suppose has gone the last of the Auld Reekie Slushers. He was a jolly dog but a *true conservative* and how different from yourself—a greater revolution has not been worked by Mehemet Aley himself in the land of the Pharohs than you have worked in that of the science of slushery

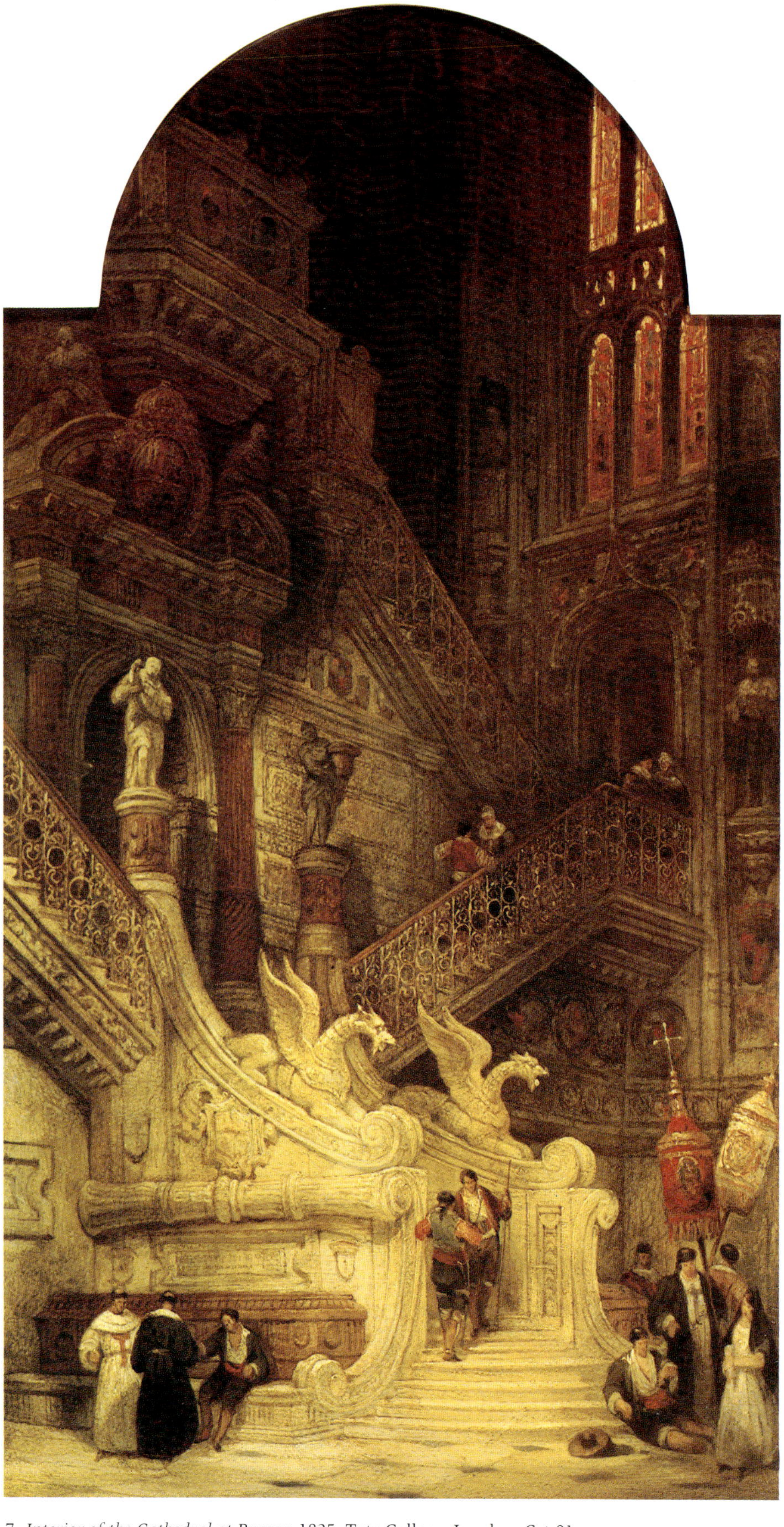

7. *Interior of the Cathedral at Burgos*, 1835, Tate Gallery, London. Cat.81.

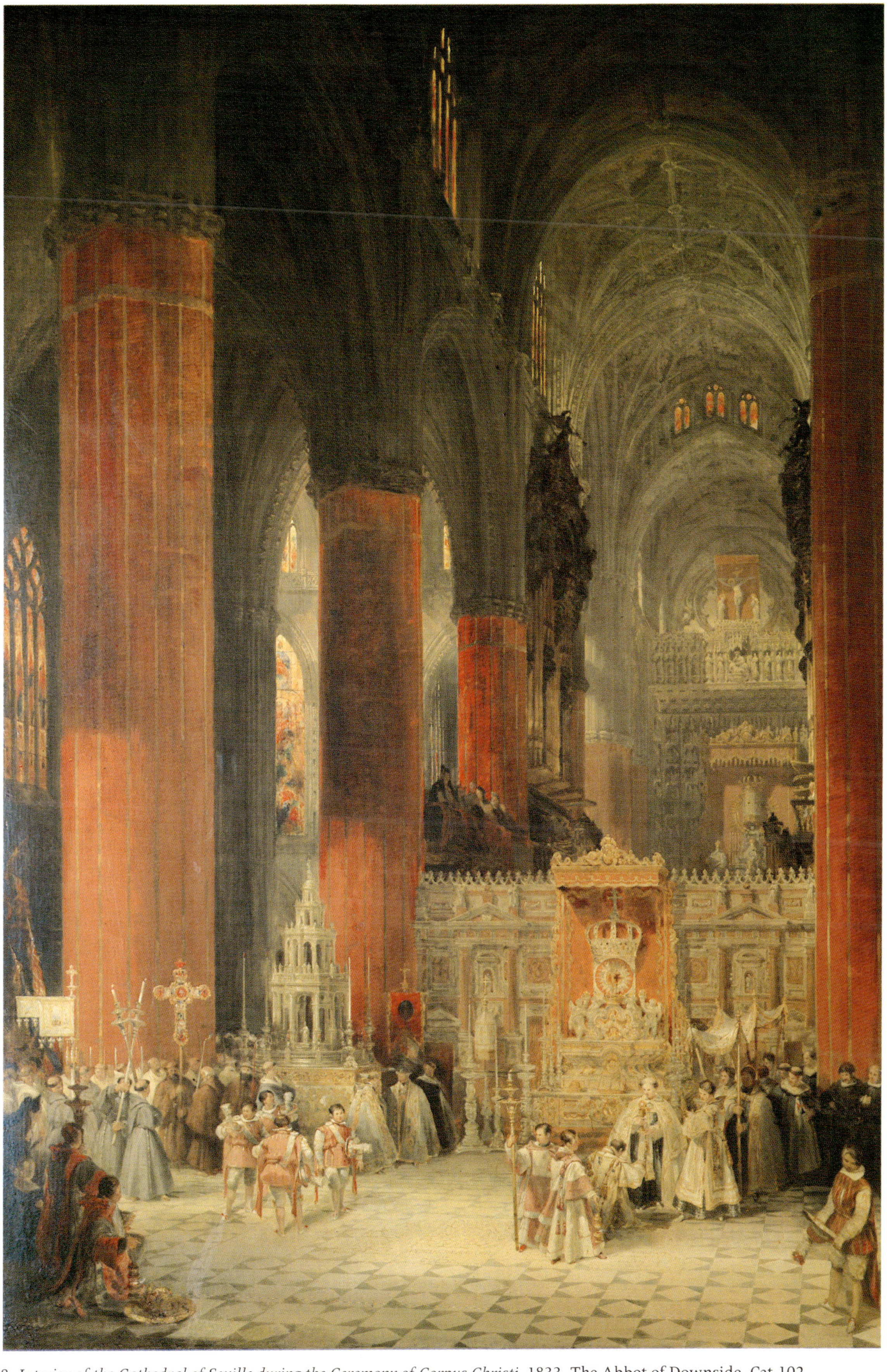

8. *Interior of the Cathedral of Seville during the Ceremony of Corpus Christi*, 1833, The Abbot of Downside. Cat.102.

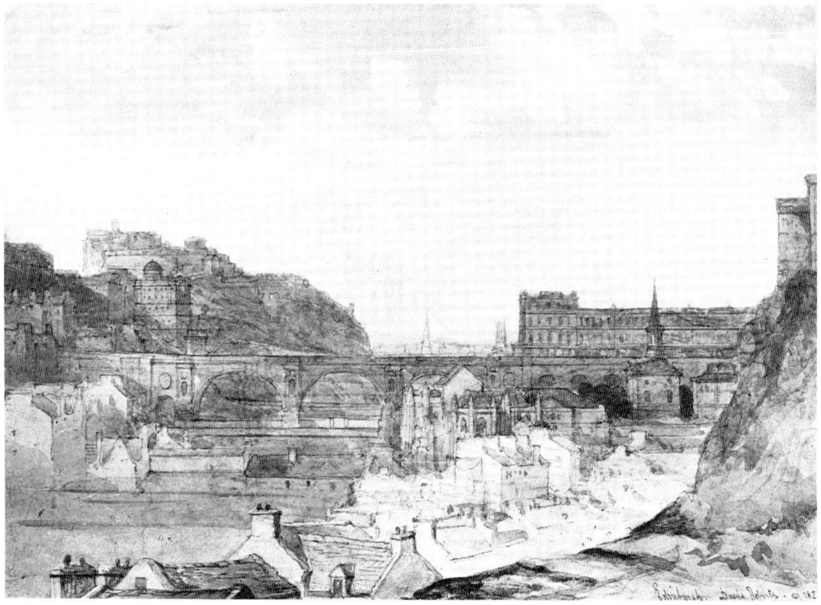

9. *Edinburgh Castle from the New Gaol*, 1821, Thomas Agnew and Sons Ltd., London. Cat.27.

from what you found it when first initiated into its mysteries—viz. stirring up the filthy tubs in Beugo's back shop. Fauch! I fancy I smell it still . . .'[7]

Hay's premises were the antithesis of Beugo's shuttered lock-up wareroom. D. R. Hay & Co. occupied a Palace of Art at 90 George Street, Edinburgh. The firm aimed to attract custom from the carriage trade, and the building was redolent of art and learning rather than permeated by the smell of paint. It was impossible to leave without receiving a 'presentation copy' of the latest treatise on aesthetics by the proprietor and 'sole-partner'. His Saloon, where clients met 'the leader of decorative art in Scotland', was no ordinary shop but the finest private picture gallery in Edinburgh. His prosperity had allowed him to build up an important collection of the emergent Scottish School and it must have given him great satisfaction to be numbered among Roberts's patrons. As befitted a pioneer interior decorator, Hay was keenly interested in the most advantageous means of displaying works of art and the centre-piece of the top-lit gallery with its claret-coloured walls was Roberts's large canvas of the *Interior of the Cathedral of Seville* (Plate 8), which had cost Hay £300. Hay's firm also developed a picture-framing department and he prided himself on its elegance and sophistication. D. R. Hay and Co. was thus both Roberts's Edinburgh agent and framer.

Inevitably, in the face of Hay's relentless enthusiasm for his newly established profession, Roberts in turn found that he became the London agent for Hay's firm. In the late 1820s, for instance, he tried somewhat reluctantly to sell Hay's patent for 'Imitation Damask' to selected London house-painters while, more congenially, he happily scoured Wardour Street so that Mrs Ramsay's hall at Barnton Castle could bristle with sufficient ancient weaponry. As both an old friend and sometime 'slusher', he was uniquely well placed to comprehend the importance of Hay's long line of publications on practical design and decoration, and enthusiastically extolled them in London. As a friend of both the influential architect, Charles Barry, and President of the Royal Academy, Charles Eastlake, Roberts did everything in his power to manoeuvre D. R. Hay & Co. into the New Palace of Westminster, the decorative prize of the century. However, at a critical moment he disastrously filed away Hay's 'learned dissertation upon "First Principles"' after he himself had read it, not realizing that it was meant for circulation among influential interested parties.

At other times, Hay benefited profoundly from Roberts's advice and criticism, which was often bluntly expressed. After inspecting Hay's most important decorative work, in the Hall of

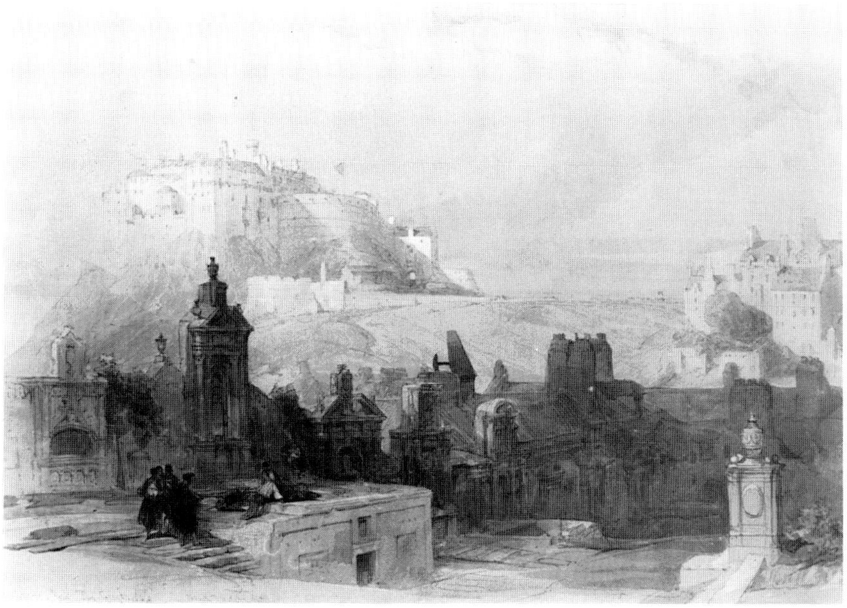

10. *Edinburgh Castle from Greyfriars Churchyard*, Cecil Higgins Art Gallery, Bedford. Cat.26.

the Society of Arts in London, Roberts wrote a critical review in 1846, which ended: 'I think if you had not been looking too much at the House of Lords you never would have introduced the armorial bearings—which I think are clap traps that you could well have dispensed with.'[8]

Hay and Roberts collaborated on at least one occasion when they decorated the temporary pavilion designed by their friend Thomas Hamilton for a dinner to honour Earl Grey at Edinburgh in 1834, although Roberts nobly wrote to Hay that he felt that the newspapers had exaggerated his own contribution.

It is ironic that the decoration in the style of Watteau assigned to David Roberts in Edward Croft-Murray's *Decorative Painting in England* can actually be firmly documented as belonging within the repertory of improvements practised by the 'ornamental department' of D. R. Hay & Co.[9] Both Hay and Roberts would have greatly relished the joke of this mistaken identity.

Roberts's involvement with architecture went deeper than the surface decoration involved in house-painting. His travels in Europe and the Near East brought a rich harvest of dramatically captured images of architectural remains, which held the same powerful fascination for the architects of the nineteenth century as the monuments of ancient Greece and Rome had exerted on those of the eighteenth. In analysing these structures for his art, Roberts became an extremely competent architectural critic, while his technique became the envy of every architect struggling to realize an 'artist's impression' in order to capture the heart and release the purse-strings of a client. Among Roberts's friends were leading architects of the day like Thomas Hamilton, William Playfair, and George Angus in Scotland, and the London lions, Charles Cockerell and Charles Barry, while another architect, William Burn, became a lifelong enemy.

Following Sir Walter Scott's death, a competition was held for a suitable monument to him, to which some fifty leading British architects submitted designs. Roberts not only entered the debate, he also submitted a design of his own: 'as it is to be Gothic I think without assuming too much to myself—I am quite as competent to make a design as any of the names you mention', he wrote to Hay.[10] His commitment to the preparation of designs may have owed a great deal to Hay's encouragement. Many of the details of Roberts's scheme remain to be established. Only one drawing survives (Plate 13) and its precise place in the evolution of the design is unclear. He was bitterly disappointed at losing the competition, and it was small satisfaction to know that his ideas had provided the matrix for George Meikle Kemp's solution.[11]

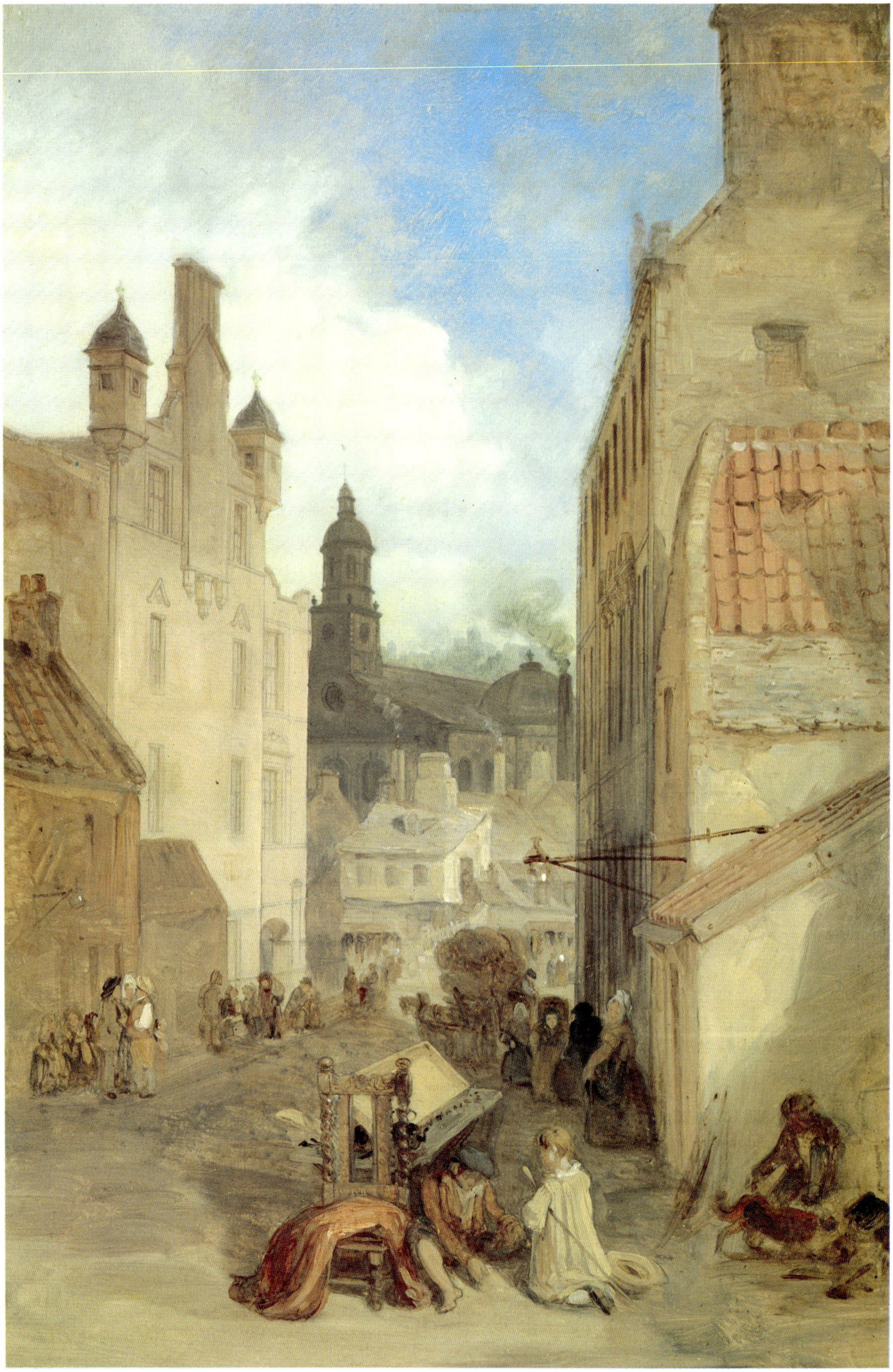

11. *Street in Edinburgh*, *c*.1819, Private collection. Cat.28.

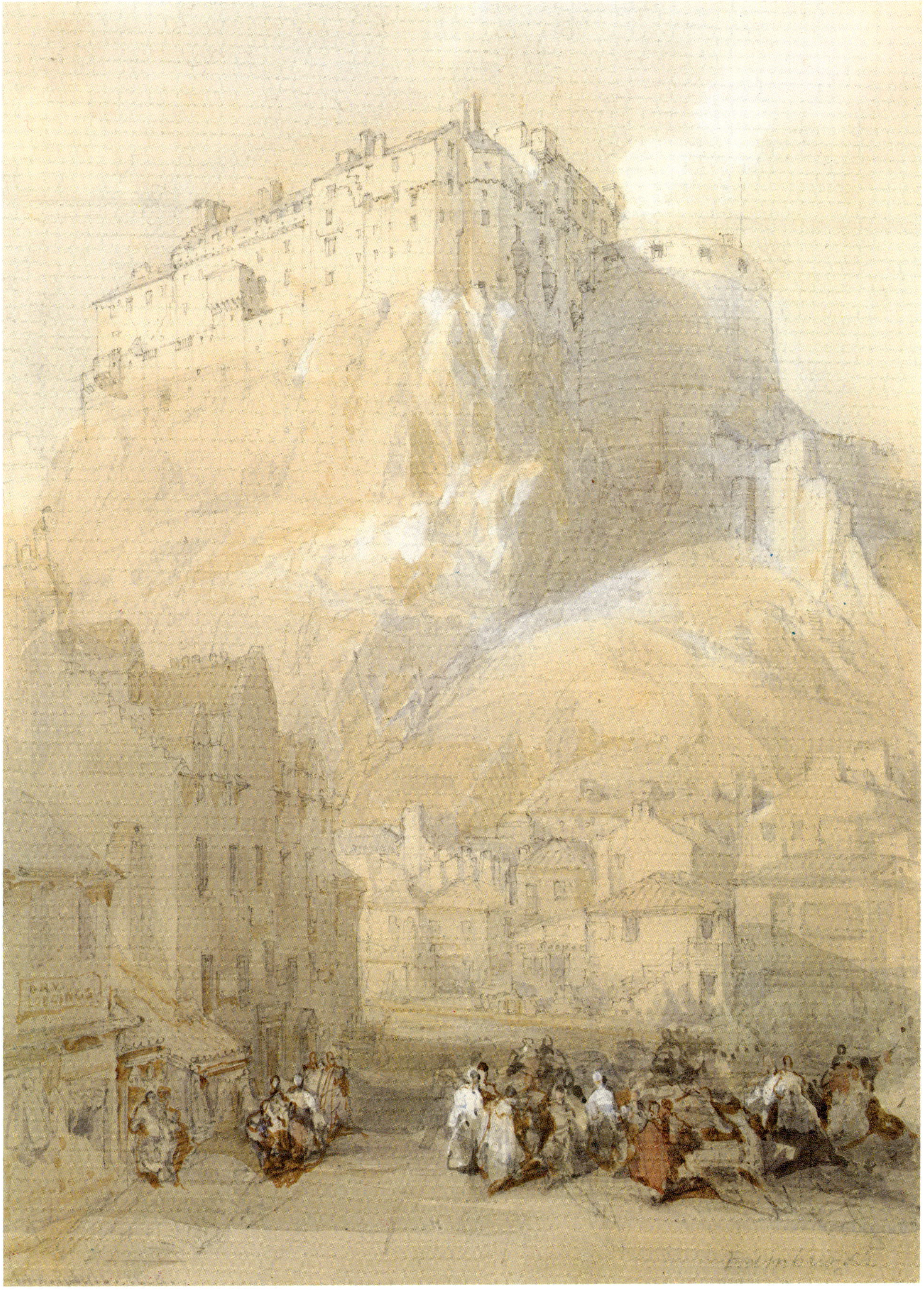

12. *Edinburgh Castle from the Grassmarket*, 1828, Family collection. Cat.24.

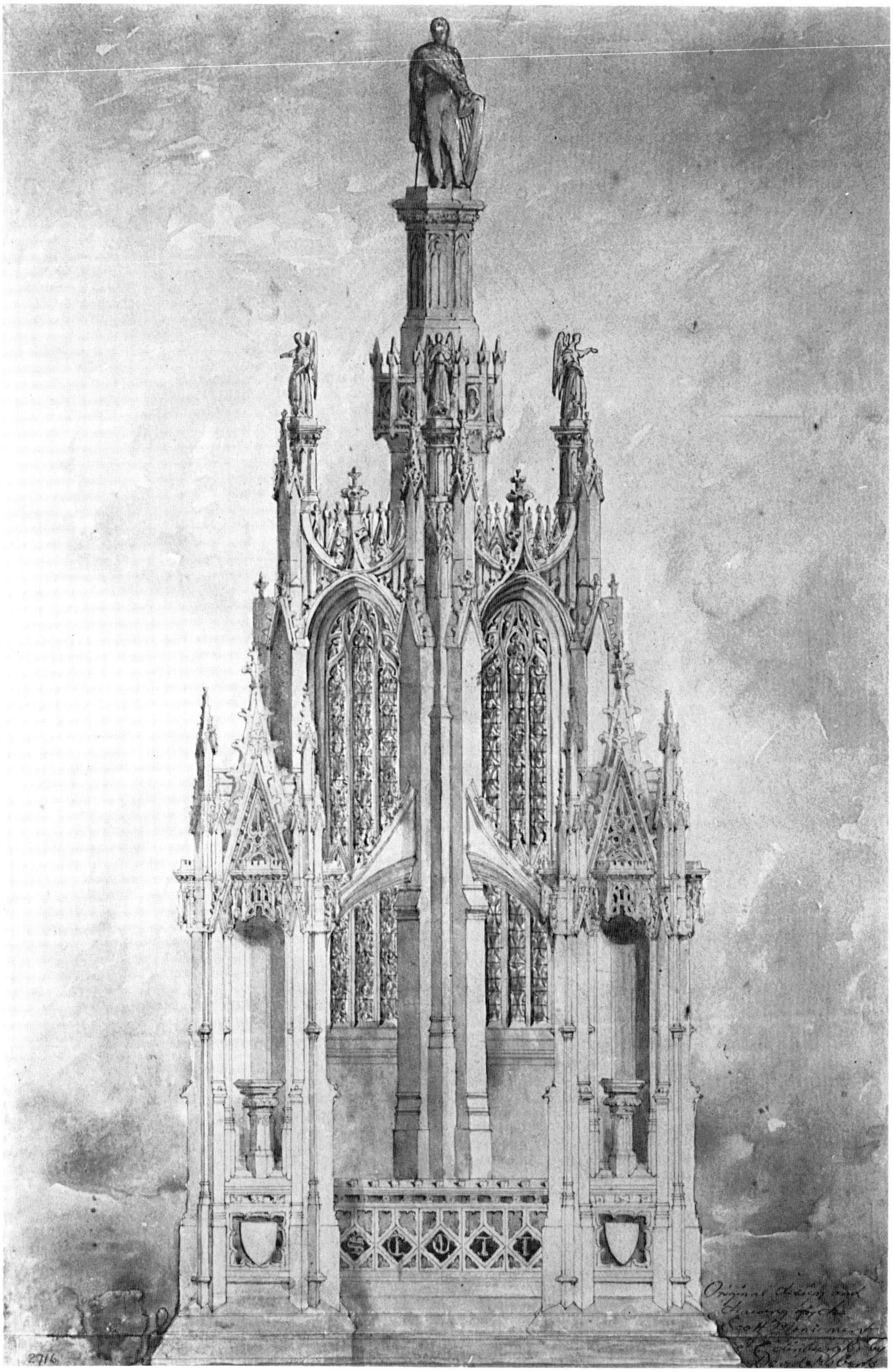

13. *Design for the Scott Monument*, (?)1834, National Galleries of Scotland, Edinburgh. Cat.13.

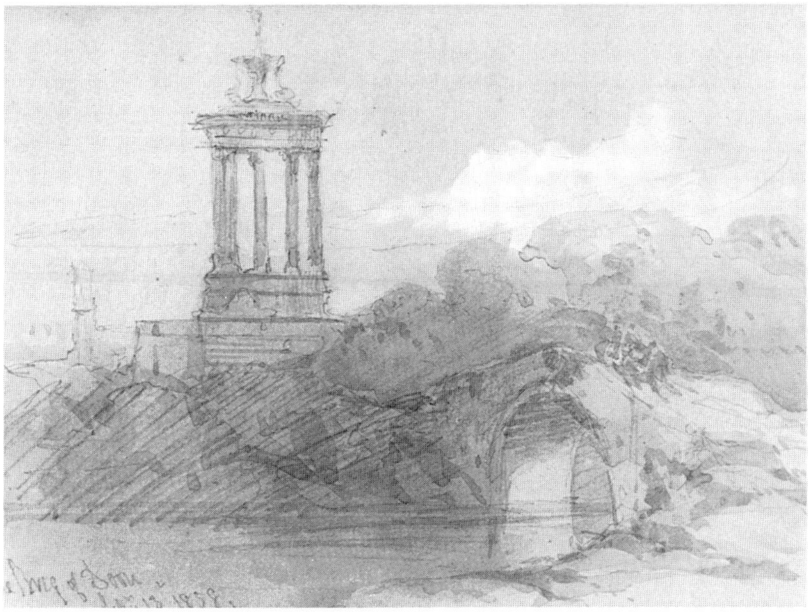

14. *Brig o' Doon*, 1858, Private collection. Cat.18.

The monument was to remain a sore subject, but Roberts never lost interest in its fortunes. After Kemp's death in 1844 he fought to preserve it in the face of a threat from the railway, while in 1854 he magnanimously designed stained-glass windows for its Museum Room, which were executed by his friend James Ballantine.

In turning architect, Roberts was following the model of Alexander Nasmyth, an artist whom he held in high esteem (see p.36). Both Nasmyth and Roberts drew on their experience as designers for the stage in their architecture. It had been an obvious transition for Nasmyth, under the sway of Picturesque ideas, to turn landscape gardener and use his pictorial skills to compose vistas glimpsed from the house; thence he turned his attention to the buildings, to arrange them so that they would not spoil the picture.

The problems of relating architecture and landscape on Picturesque principles were nowhere more acute than in Edinburgh, the 'Athens of the North'. Roberts's boyhood had been marked by a series of clashes between commercial developers, keen to profit from speculation, and those who rated the natural beauties of the area higher than any promised architectural splendours. The most celebrated debate concerned the proposed development of the Calton Hill and the victor was the brilliant architect, William Stark, who had suggested that the buildings must take a subordinate place to the trees and crags. After Stark's tragically early death in 1813 his pupil, William Playfair, went on to realize his design.

In Scotland the most successful architectural practice was that of William Burn. Schooled in the rigid discipline of the Greek revival under Smirke, Burn had the knack of finishing buildings on time, within budget and to his clients' precise instructions. These skills were to make him the leading country-house architect in Britain. But he was weak on Picturesque, which was his rival William Playfair's strongest card. Playfair ran an idiosyncratic and high-minded practice on uncommercial lines, which perhaps gave him a moral authority over Burn. Edinburgh's Whig sophisticates found that Burn's somewhat prosaic work failed to satisfy their Romantic yearnings; accordingly, they promoted Playfair, and architecture became polarized around the Burn and Playfair camps. It was perhaps inevitable that Roberts, in siding with Playfair's party, headed by Lord Cockburn, should range himself against Burn. The enmity had as much to do with politics and personalities as with architecture. Their long-running quarrel cannot easily be unravelled today, but exerts a certain fascination, for though Burn is recognizable as a bully, Roberts was otherwise a very kind and generous man.

Roberts took exception to Burn's support of the illustration of *The Baronial and Ecclesiastical*

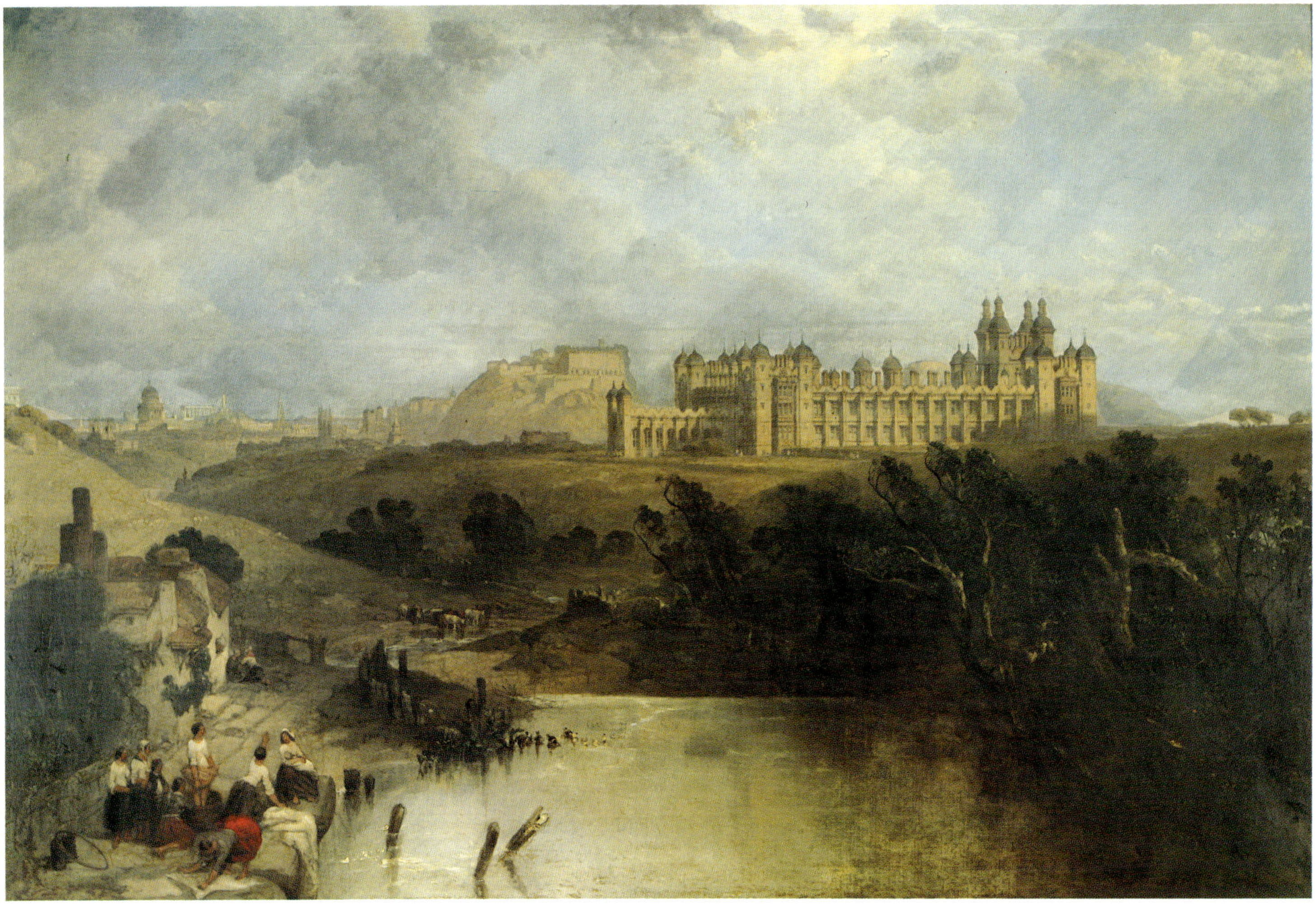

15. *The Donaldson Hospital, Edinburgh,* 1851, The Donaldson Trust, Donaldson's School for the Deaf, Edinburgh. Cat.21.

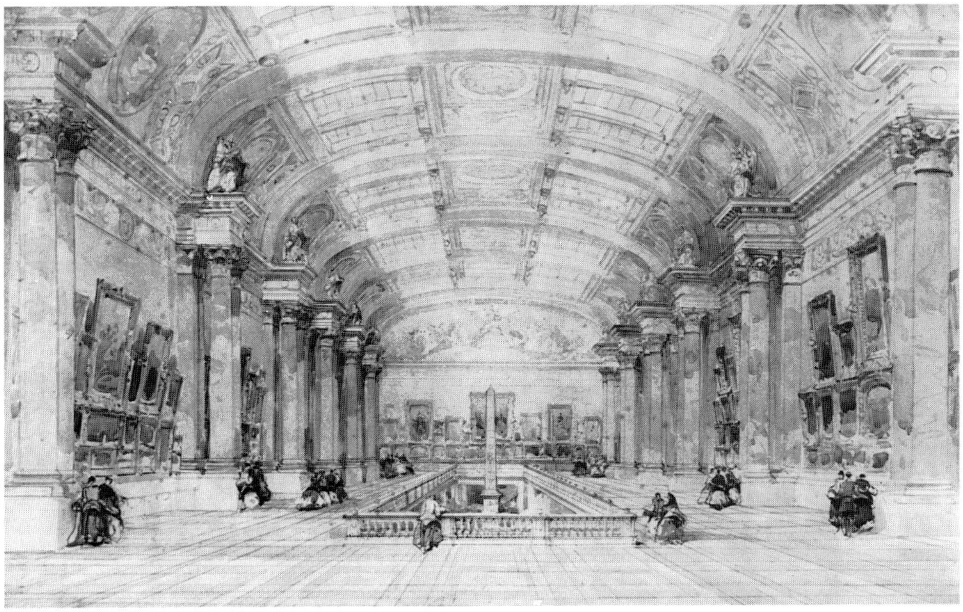

16. *Design for a New National Gallery: Interior View*, c.1856, Family collection. Cat.16b.

Antiquities of Scotland by the English architectural illustrator, Robert Billings. Published in 1845–52, it became the bible of the Scottish baronial revival. 'Who is Billings!', he wrote to Hay, and went on to say of the portrayal of the monuments 'that their overthrow in the days of Knox was not worse than that their illustration will be in such hands'.[12] While Roberts would unquestionably have made a more artistic job than Billings's factual reportage, it would have been impossible to fit such a project into his programme of wandering in Europe and the Near East, and residing in London.

As a campaigner on behalf of architecture, Roberts fought valiantly for the preservation of threatened antiquarian remains. He pulled influential strings to save John Knox's house and threw himself with an especial enthusiasm into opposition to anything that threatened his beloved Roslin Chapel.[13]

Established as a successful artist in London, Roberts found that he was invited to give expert advice to the government in both artistic and architectural matters, as when he was asked to help with the decoration of the New Palace of Westminster and to judge the competition entries for the new Public Offices in Whitehall. His decision to prepare designs for the National Gallery was a more personal matter, and he rightly considered that he was uniquely well qualified to design a building worthy of its precious contents. His design is highly creditable, but its magnificent interior (Plate 16) was unlikely to be built in the financial and political conditions that prevailed in Britain. The richness of Roberts's design forms a fascinating contrast with Playfair's austerely rational design for a building to accommodate both the Scottish National Gallery and the Royal Scottish Academy, in which Architecture seeks no relief whatsoever from the sister arts of Painting and Sculpture. In recognition of Playfair's new building, Roberts presented his large painting of Rome (Plate 45) to the Royal Scottish Academy in 1857. It is shaming to record that the Scots have exiled this handsome present to a dark corridor in Parliament Square.

More important, and perhaps surprising, was that Roberts was directly concerned with producing drawings for architects in the 1830s. Under the influence of the Picturesque and the development of public competitions, huge stakes were risked on a single 'artist's impression' which had to sell the design at a glance to a building committee and the public. It was no longer a matter of a presentation portfolio containing a design in the abstract diagrammatic form of plans and elevations in Indian ink wash; now a single, realistically coloured, perspective view was demanded, showing the building as it would appear in 'life'. Since architects were not trained to

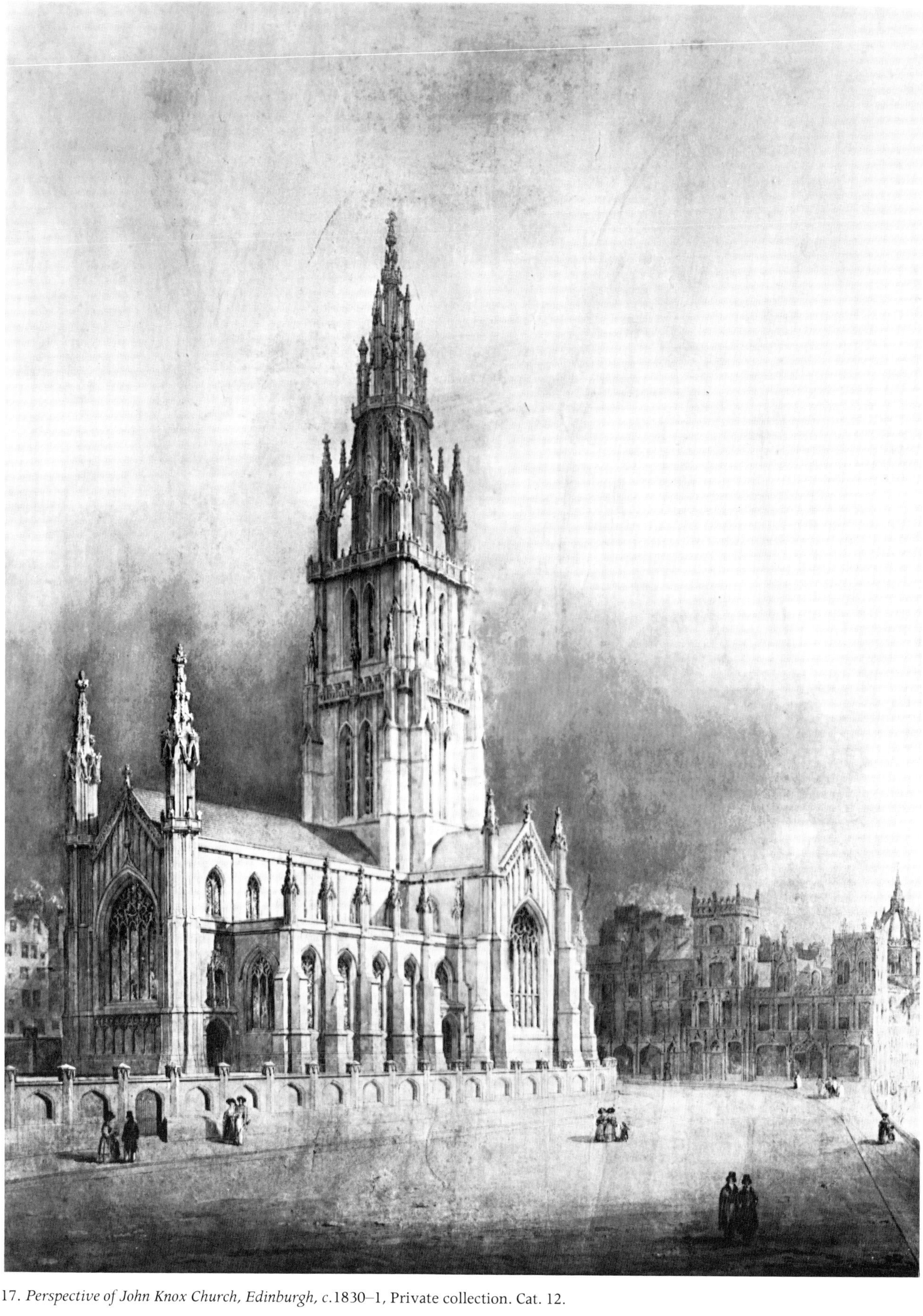

17. *Perspective of John Knox Church, Edinburgh*, c.1830–1, Private collection. Cat. 12.

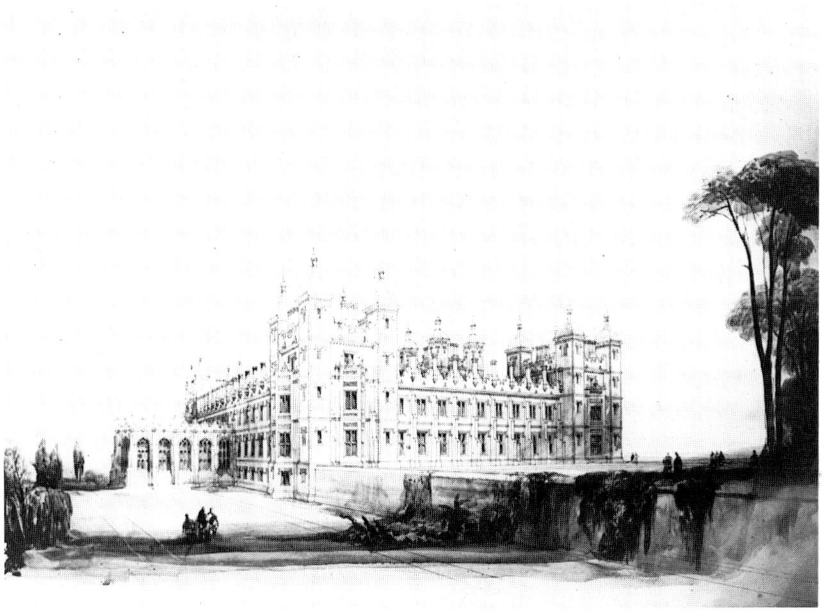

18. *Perspective of the Donaldson Hospital, Edinburgh*, c.1838, whereabouts unknown.

draw figures and trees, still less skies, it was a short step to the creation of perspectives that were almost certainly the work of artists and not made by the architects who signed them.

The architects were at pains to ensure that such 'ghosting' was not documented, so the discovery that Roberts was involved in such work on two occasions makes the accounts worth quoting in full. On 30 March 1831 Roberts wrote to Hay: '. . . by the by—"between you and me and the wall". There is a Drawing of *Knox's* Kirk—which with the exception of the outline—is by your humble servant. Let me know in your next what you think of it. Mind this is in confidence as I wish the architect who is a very worthy fellow to have what little credit may be attached to it.'[14] Since his friend Thomas Hamilton's design for the church had been accepted and was under construction (though never finished) when this Exhibition Drawing (Plate 17) was shown, any deception was above board.

The following is a clearer case of skulduggery. On 18 March 1838 Hay wrote to Roberts:

> My reason for writing you today is this. Mr Playfair the architect has just called to say that the Managers of the Donaldson Hospital (a building that I believe is to cost about £70,000 to £80,000 and for which he formerly made designs and a model) have lately come to the resolution of again opening the competition and he has consequently made a new design or rather modified and altered the former one. Now he is most anxious to be successful in this competition, and is aware that there is no artist living whose magic pencil could so enhance the effect of his drawing and thereby give him an additional chance of success. He has applied to me to ask if you would have the goodness to colour lightly two perspective drawings for him. They will be accurately drawn in outline and all that you would require to do would be to give an effect. Now my dear Roberts, Mr P has been and still is a particularly kind friend to me, and you therefore could not confer a greater favour on me than to do *him* this service. He would cheerfully pay whatever charge you might make but I said that I believed it to be one of those things that unless you would do it as a favour there was no hopes of your doing it for payment.[15]

As a result of Roberts's secret involvement, Donaldson's Hospital arose to Playfair's design. To thank Roberts, Playfair commissioned a view of his finished masterpiece in 1851 (Plate 15). The transition from imagined to real to painted architecture at Donaldson's exemplifies one of the central threads in Roberts's career.

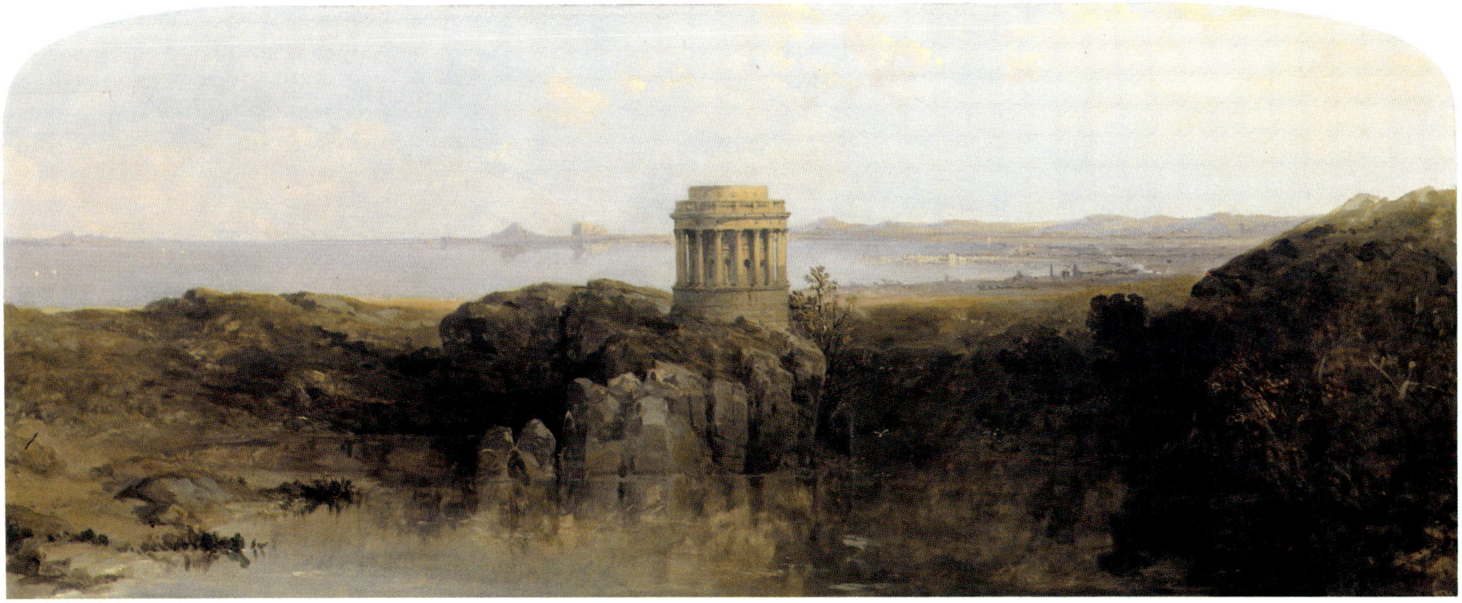

19. *A Proposed Restoration of the Temple of the Sybil at Tivoli on a Rock called Drumsapie, on Arthur's Seat, with a Distant View of the Bay of Aberlady*, 1853, The Forbes Magazine Collection. Cat.15.

Roberts and the Theatre

PIETER VAN DER MERWE

> The scenery of the olden time cannot be compared with the present; they had no David Roberts, Stanfield, Grieves, Telbin or Beverley . . . The scenic effects in these modern times are astounding—the people have become so elated and transported that they think only of the *scene-painter*, and demand his presence. Then the artist enters and receives the plaudits of admiring thousands while the author is left to chew the cud of his disappointment in gloom and solitude.[1]

David Roberts's scenic career began in 1816 and ended in 1830. In those fourteen years he became famous, both on his own merits, and as the other half of the artistic double-act 'Stanfield and Roberts', an association which, despite the fact that it existed largely in the public mind rather than in any formal sense, became a talisman for scenic excellence on the London stage.

Assessment of Roberts's work quickly runs into a common problem: none of his scenery survives. Some was overpainted deliberately, but even without this none would have outlasted normal use for more than a few years. Moreover, neither Roberts nor Stanfield are represented by any great body of surviving designs. Roberts's reputation is supported by a sole unquestioned example (Plate 25), although playbills, reviews and other written sources provide a record of what he did.

Nevertheless, Roberts has another, undervalued, importance, as 'abstract and brief chronicler' of the profession in which he worked. His account is incomplete but valuable, as none of the dozens, if not hundreds, of other scene-painters working in his lifetime wrote anything similar. There is only one nineteenth-century manual of English scene-painting,[2] while the few other articles and memoirs by, or relating to, scene-painters say little beyond generalities. In contrast, Roberts, a compulsive writer of letters and journals, was still involved with the theatre when he began to write his memoirs in 1829.[3] The result is unique, immediate, and as informative of his own role and character as of contemporaries, exemplars and rivals. It also charts how he rose from near the bottom of the provincial heap to the top of the metropolitan one.

Institutionally, the theatre which Roberts joined in 1816 comprised three broad elements and held two traditions of painter, an old division between those granted the status of 'artists', like James Thornhill or Philippe de Loutherbourg, and those who were basically artisans, without pretension to easel reputation. In London, the two Theatres Royal, Drury Lane and Covent Garden, held a legal monopoly to perform 'the drama'—the spoken word—granted by

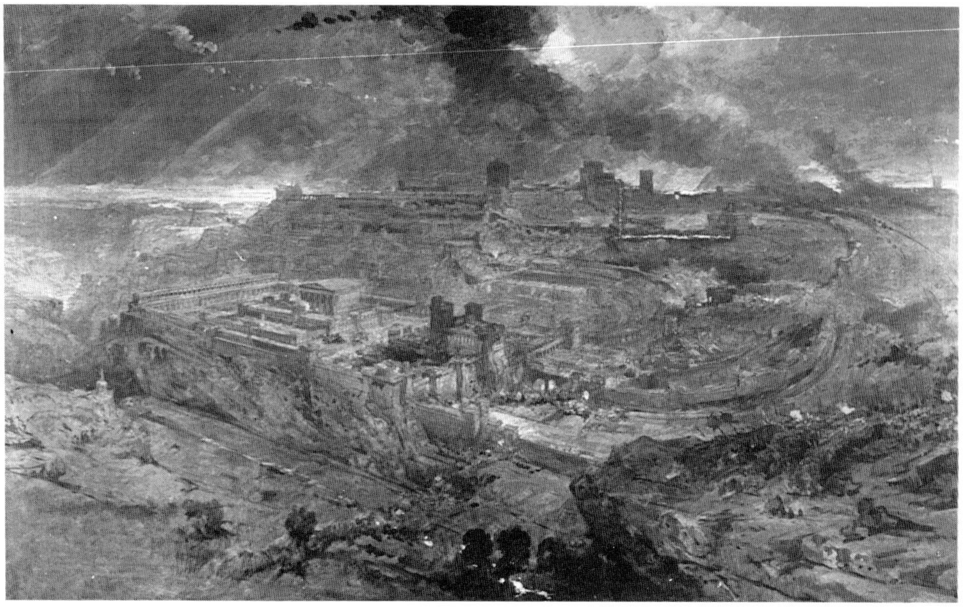

20. *Study for 'The Destruction of Jerusalem by Titus'*, c.1849, Williamson Art Gallery and Museum, Wirral Borough Council. Cat.166.

seventeenth-century Royal Patents. This monopoly, though hotly defended, was under assault from the second element, 'minor' houses, operating under local magistrates' licences to perform musical dumbshow (the original 'melodrama'), 'sub-operatic' pieces, variety and animal acts. In all of these, scenic spectacle soon became a vital common factor of popularity. While London had only nine theatres in 1800, twenty-one more appeared before the abolition of the Patent theatre monopoly in 1843, indicating the demand generated by the capital's early nineteenth-century population boom. In the provinces—the third estate—an analogous situation prevailed. Theatres Royal existed in the main towns, often at the centre of a circuit which extended their privileges to further venues. Other companies, usually strollers of various standards, plied their trade at the risk of apprehension, or at least poor treatment, as rogues and vagabonds.

Minor provincial companies could rarely afford a full-time scene-painter and in his first job Roberts was one of many who were also required to act; the reverse could also apply to actors of pictorial bent. While Roberts frankly confessed to being a 'ham' performer, he noted that his scenic superior, Dearlove (or Deerlove), doubled as a singer, as well as being 'an ingenious man' in making stage properties.

In the artisan tradition of the London theatres matters were different. Here scene-painting was a full-blown craft, a specialist occupation in which masters trained apprentices, either as father to son or by taking pupils who paid the master a 'premium'. The Frenches and Orams, practising in the mid-eighteenth century, are two of the earliest-known English scene-painting families; the Greenwoods, Whitmore and Phillips were some of those holding the high ground at the turn of the century; the Grieves, who subsequently seized it and held a virtual thirty-year possession of the Covent Garden scene-room, led the profession across three generations, from the Regency to around 1880.

As in other crafts, apprenticeship was the key means of controlling entry and limiting competition. However, the high demand for painters in the early-nineteenth-century theatrical boom gave talented unknowns like Roberts their chance. How the 'legitimate' artisan school, as they called themselves, regarded 'artist' importations is unknown. Their resentment was perhaps limited by the fact that such people were often 'scenic directors' rather than executants. The most notable late-eighteenth-century example, Philippe de Loutherbourg (at Drury Lane from 1773 to 1781), and to a certain extent his contemporary John Inigo Richards at Covent Garden both provided designs and supervision but did little or no actual painting.

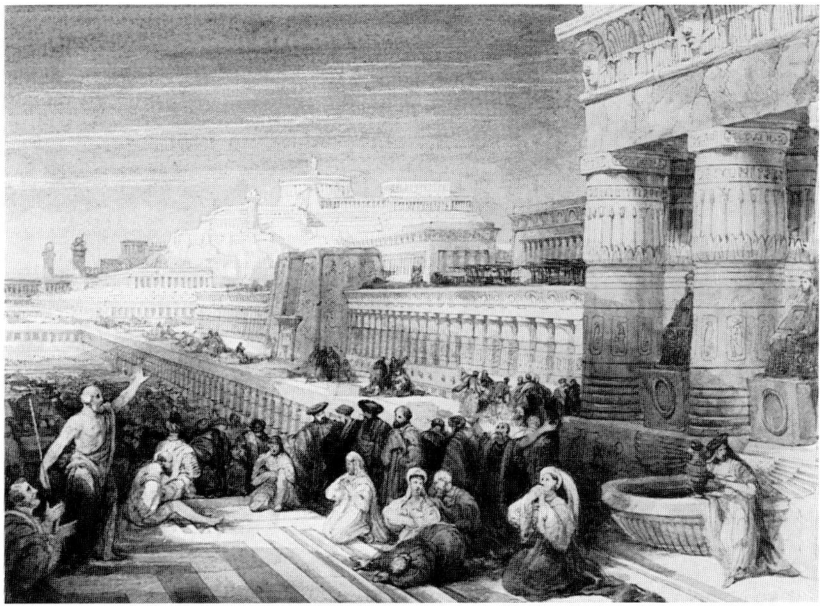

21. *Aaron Delivering the Message of the Elders of Israel*, c.1827, Williamson Art Gallery and Museum, Wirral Borough Council. Cat.115.

Roberts had little trouble regarding 'legitimacy'; by the time he reached London his provincial experience seems to have counted as suitable entrée. His friends John 'Jock' Wilson (1774–1858) and Clarkson Stanfield (1793–1867) were less lucky. Wilson, also a Scot and a house-painter who worked his way into theatre, was sneered at for his background by the 'legitimate' school. Roberts, who called him 'the father of a race of scene-painters', considered his prime contribution as being 'the first to break through the boundary that separated the old legitimate style of Scene-painting from real art—that is by Painting Pictures and exhibiting them',[4] something Wilson had been doing prolifically at the Academy from 1807. Stanfield, who began work in London in 1816 with even less qualification than Wilson, received even shorter shrift from his first colleagues, who refused to let him work with them or even warm 'his size-kettle (a most essential thing in scene-painting) in their room'.[5]

The ambience of the system is summed up in Roberts's passage about his early bugbear, Dearlove, who would:

> . . . boast of advantages to which I could make no pretension—that of being 'regularly bred' was his own term 'at the Theatre Royal Covent Garden'. This carried immense weight with it as no one at that time could be allowed any pretensions to talent who had not been regularly apprenticed to some of the great painters, as they were then termed at Drury Lane and Covent Garden. Phillips, Whitmore, Pugh, Hollogan etc. at Covent Garden and the Greenwoods at Drury Lane were the standards of art—and on such good terms with themselves that it was said of Thom. Greenwood [jun., that] his usual boast was that Drury Lane might do without Kean (then at his zenith) but it could not do without Greenwood; unfortunately he lived to see it could do without them both.

Roberts goes on to provide telling confirmation of how after 1800, under pressure for a rapid turnover of spectacular novelty, the old restrictive traditions gave way:

> Old Grieve [John Henderson Grieve, 1770–1845] was the first to break through this long standing rule—being sent from Astley's Theatre where he was scene-painter to assist in getting up the spectacle of Timour the Tartar at Covent Garden. The managers then found that a scene might be painted in a day equally effective with

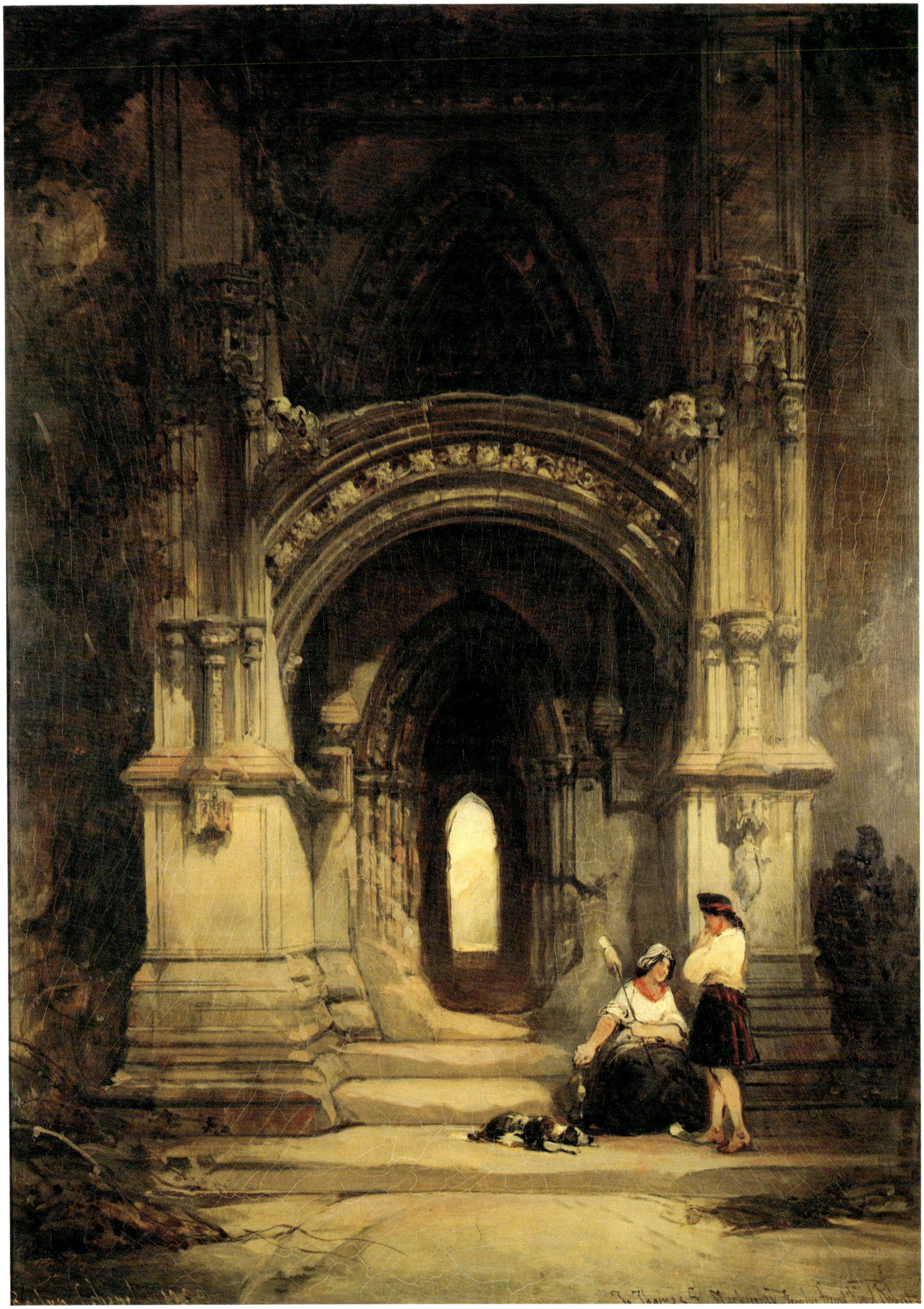

22. *Porch of Roslin Chapel*, 1845, Blackburn Art Gallery and Museum. Cat.35.

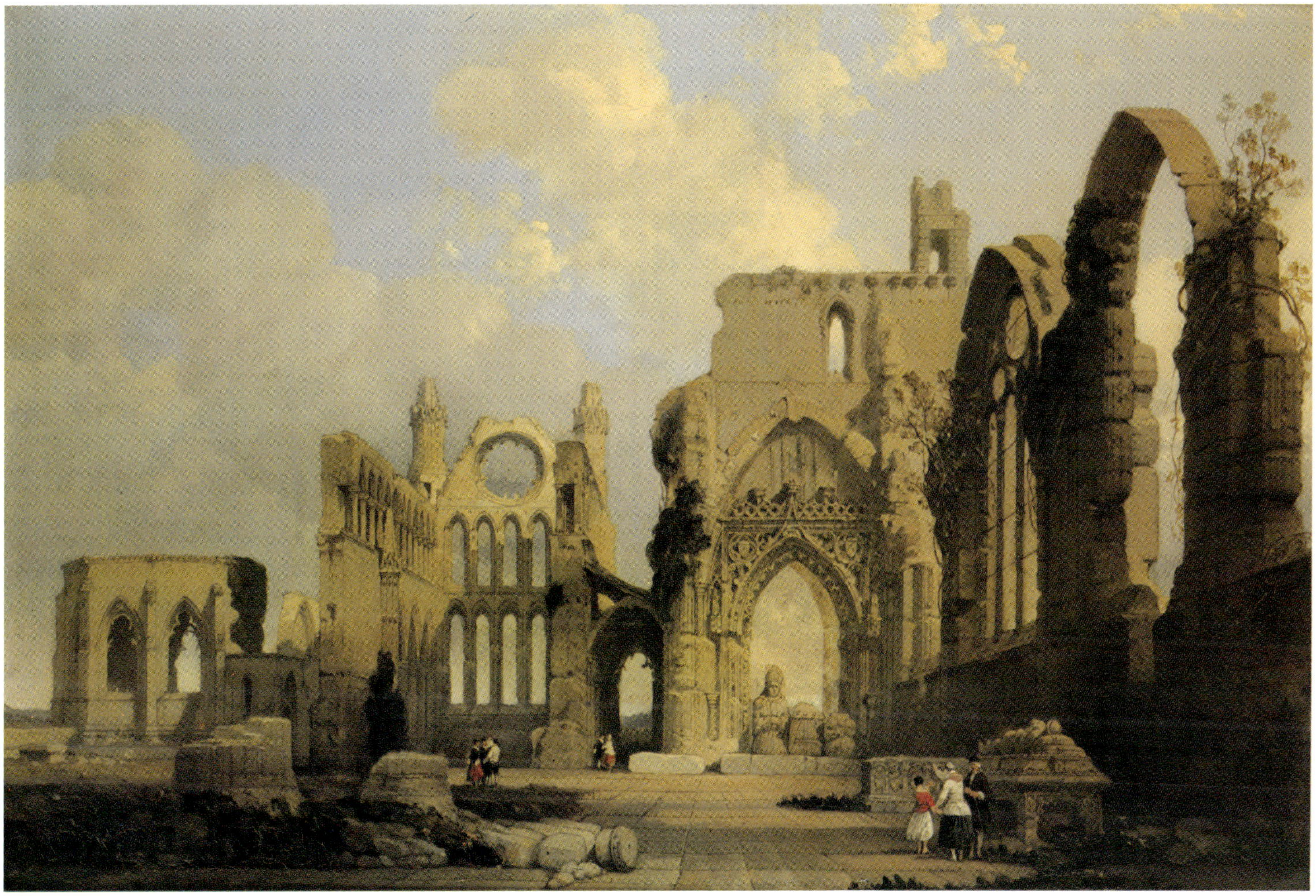

23. *Ruins of Elgin Cathedral*, 1853, Victoria and Albert Museum, London. Cat.30.

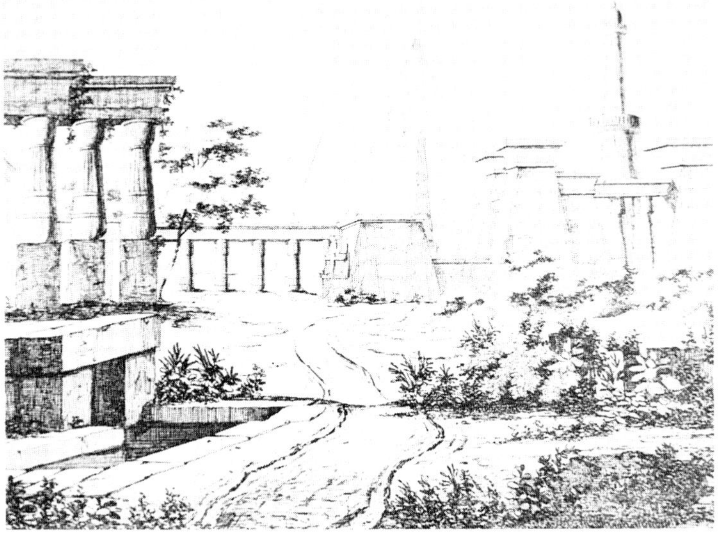

24. *A Romantic Landscape in the Suburbs of Memphis . . .*: a toy theatre scene derived from one by Roberts, published by Hodgson in *Zoraster*, Drury Lane, April 1824.

> those that had taken a month or perhaps more—and that a spectacle might be produced in a couple of weeks—at a fourth of the expense and equally effective with that used to occupy the greater part of a season. Stanfield and myself followed up the same principle at the other house [Drury Lane] and completed the overthrow of the race of legitimate scene-painters.[6]

The importance of the passage lies in its indication of the new methods of working pioneered by John Grieve, copied by Stanfield and Roberts, and passed on, among others, through Grieve's sons, collaborators and successors Thomas (1799–1882) and William (1800–44). These included the invention of a glaze which lent depth to painting viewed under gaslight. Although universally adopted to supplement the previous sole use of opaque colours, enemies at first called it Grieve's 'Scotch wash' in contempt.[7] However the real key to the success of the new style was its cost effectiveness, the bold broad effects it introduced and the impact these had under the new gaslight, which from 1817 concentrated unprecedented brilliance and public interest on the scenes and from which the Roberts, Stanfield and Grieve generation was the first to benefit. The actor Joseph Cowell summed up the revolution in describing Old Phillips, Roberts's most admired painter of the old school (*fl.* 1789–1817): 'Though his productions were beautiful specimens of art the elaborate *finish* he bestowed on them rather decreased than added to their effect; and while in the same room, the elder Grieve . . . was every day *splashing* into existence a cottage or a cavern with a pound brush in each hand, Phillips would sit for hours with a rest stick and a camel's hair pencil, shading the head of a nail.'[8]

Roberts claimed that his early knowledge of art was based on the scenes he saw from the shilling gallery of the Edinburgh Theatre Royal, but he seems to have had no burning desire to enter the theatre himself. He simply fell into it through the agency of a friend while out of work as a house-painter in April 1816, finding employment with the strolling company then being set up by James Bannister to expand the activity of his animal and variety circus in North College Street, Edinburgh. The wages were better—thirty shillings a week against eighteen shillings for house-painting—but the change was made without illusions of glamour and with some calculation that the stage might be a means to an end rather than an end in itself. 'Although the drawback of joining a strolling company of actors was in itself anything but a creditable pursuit', he wrote, 'yet it jumped with my wishes . . . to follow the bent of my mind—in drawing pictures on a large scale—which might lead to something even better.'[9]

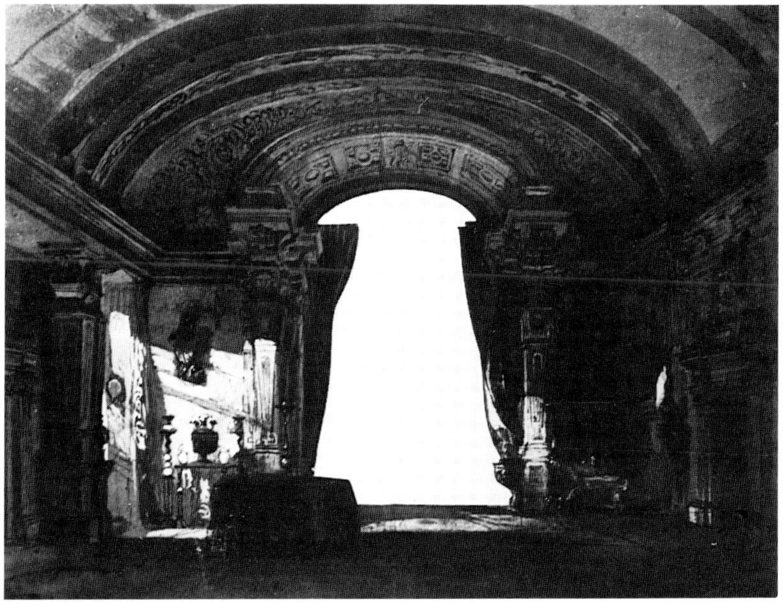

25. *Design for a Cut Scene*, British Museum, London. Cat.2.

This is the first of various scattered clues which hint that as a scene-painter, as in his other work, Roberts's interest and ability lay predominantly with the possibilities of draughtsmanship. He felt his early deficiencies to lie in linear perspective, 'composition, light and shade and aerial perspective',[10] and the absence in his writing of any great concern with colour—which even at the height of his scenic career was sometimes criticized—may be significant. For while Roberts was undoubtedly a master of line and dramatic mass, one has somehow to account for the fact of his almost continual and resented placement as 'runner-up' to Stanfield in scenic ability. If this can partly be accounted for by the other man's doing much 'more and more various work',[11] it may also be due to his greater range in terms of colour. The fact that, today, the economy, clarity, and even the abstraction of Roberts's style is often more agreeable is as much due to changes in taste as to his being intrinsically the better draughtsman.

Despite the success of his first trial for Bannister—some small pieces painted on the latter's dining-room floor—Roberts found that 'to attack a scene itself and this to one who . . . still had everything to learn . . . was no joke!!!'[12] This was at Carlisle, the company moving on to Newcastle, Hull and York before returning for a winter opening in Edinburgh in January 1817. At Newcastle, Roberts benefited from seeing and copying scenes by Cornelius Dixon (*fl.* 1783–1821), a perspectivist, who vied with Old Phillips as 'the best painter in England of architectural scenery'.[13] He also learned a valuable first lesson in atmospheric effects from the work of a man called Wallace that he saw backstage at the Theatre Royal, York.

By May 1817, however, he was back house-painting, and fretting for the stage. Bannister had gone into partnership with N. Corri to convert the latter's music hall, Corri's Rooms, into a circus theatre to be called the Pantheon. The speculation rapidly collapsed, but in July 1818 Corri's composer-nephew, Montague Corri, was able to reopen with a resident company, which included Roberts engaged as assistant to Dearlove at twenty-five shillings per week. Because there was no scene-room, work had to be executed overnight and between shows on the stage itself. This gave Roberts's efforts 'great rapidity and decision', even though he invariably saw his work ruined by his superior's insistence on working over his best effects.

His salvation came with Dearlove's exhaustion through acting by day and painting by night during preparations for a piece called *The Silver Swan*. While 'it pleased God to visit [Dearlove] with a most profound and comfortable snooze',[14] Roberts managed to paint and secrete a spectacular scene of the forum of Trajan in Rome. This burst on an astonished first-night audience as something quite beyond Dearlove's capacity and led to Roberts's engagement next

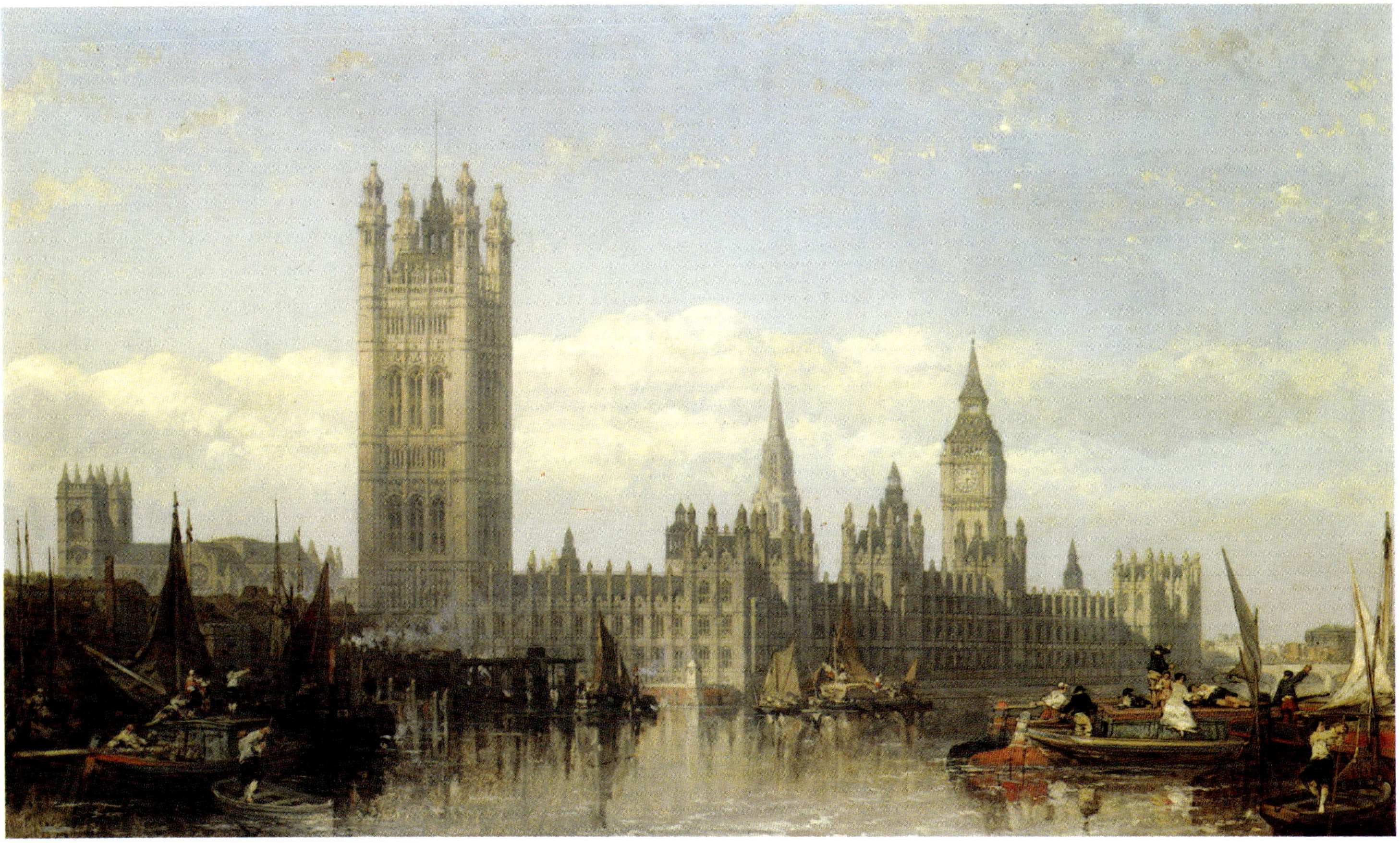

26. *The New Palace at Westminster from the River,* 1861, The Worshipful Company of Goldsmiths. Cat.40.

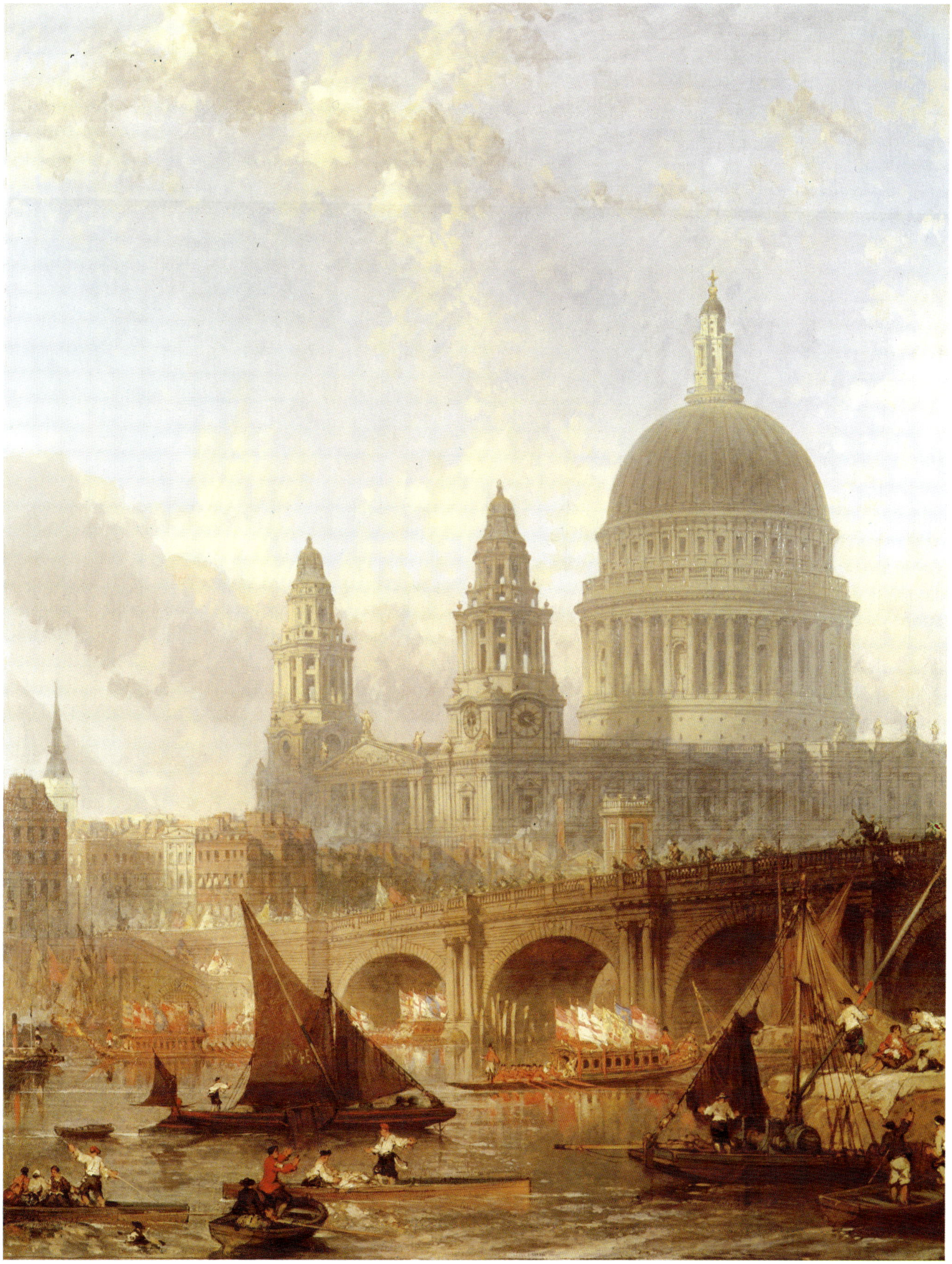

27. *St. Paul's from Blackfriars,* 1862, The Worshipful Company of Goldsmiths. Cat.42.

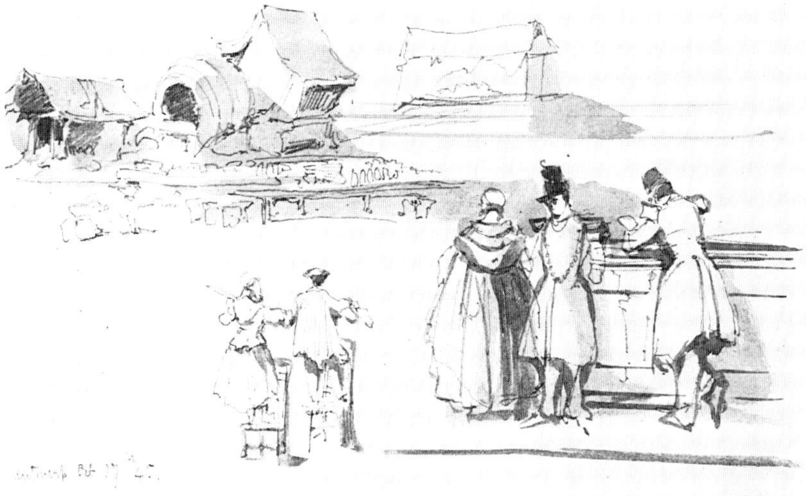

28. From an *Antwerp Sketchbook*, 1845, National Galleries of Scotland, Edinburgh. Cat.67c.

season as principal painter to Mason's company at the Glasgow Theatre Royal, with a welcome return to thirty shillings per week. Roberts found the theatre stocked with the splendid works of Alexander Nasmyth (1758–1840) and his family. He later claimed to have formed his own style on these, though W. L. Leitch, who knew both artists' Glasgow work, was more struck by the contrast between Roberts's breadth and Nasmyth's meticulous realism.[15]

At Glasgow Roberts began to widen his circle of professional contacts, among whom were the well-respected lessees of the Edinburgh Theatre Royal, William Murray and his sister Mrs Henry Siddons. At their request Roberts made a brief excursion to decorate *The Heart of Midlothian* in Edinburgh and, following ructions with Mason in July 1820, accepted an offer of £2 a week to work as principal there from October. His final work for Mason was at Ayr and Dumfries, whence he walked seventy miles to Edinburgh, somewhat light on cash (Mason had failed to pay him) but with an important letter in his pocket. This was an introduction from the Glasgow prompter to his son, Clarkson Stanfield, who was due in Edinburgh as scene-painter to the company visiting the Pantheon from Astley's Amphitheatre, London. 'This was my first introduction—a sincere and intimate friendship took place and which has with one or two interruptions ever since continued.'[16]

> . . . his scenery at the opposition theatre . . . made an immense impression so much so that before the following spring he ultimately superceeded me at the Theatre Royal—and in a new piece—in which I had painted the whole of the scenery, some of the principal were cut out to make way for his . . . in a way that cut me to the quick and which quite opened my eyes as to what I might trust to in that quarter . . . But which after all invariably turned out for the best—in this instance it proved so. I was placed alongside of a man who has proved a colossus in art but particularly in scene-painting—hitherto I had been groping my way in the dark as well as I could. I had seen none paint but myself—as to real works of art. I had had little or no opportunity seeing any. Here was a man that had . . . only seen the first specimens of scene-painting in the Metropolis . . . and no inconsiderable artist himself in Oil Painting . . . I profited much from his acquaintance.
>
> Whilst painting at both the [Edinburgh] theatres Stanfield did not neglect his oil pictures several of which he painted and exhibited at the Spring Exhibition of 1821. At his suggestion I commenced a Picture [in oil] for the first time and had the vanity to

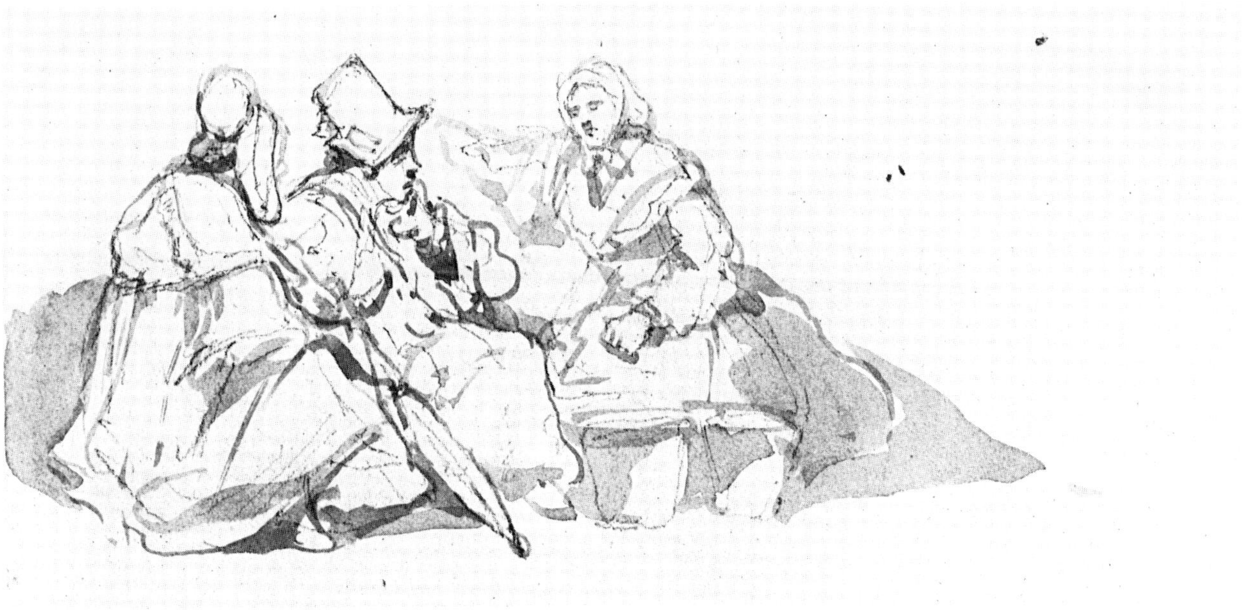

29. From an *Antwerp Sketchbook*, 1845, National Galleries of Scotland, Edinburgh. Cat.67a.

> send it to the Exhibition . . . and had the mortification of having it turned out as unworthy whilst that of my *rivals* was the talk of the town.[17]

But Roberts was not discouraged and soon found the study of oil pictures 'of immense service to me in my scenic career'. At the 1822 exhibition he had three works accepted and sold two.

By now, though, Roberts's future was being decided elsewhere. The Astley's company returned to London in March 1821, Stanfield and its manager William Barrymore, an expert in spectacular staging, reverting to their mother house, the Royal Coburg Theatre (now the 'Old Vic') in Lambeth. Here, Stanfield fell under the covetous gaze of R. W. Elliston, the 'Great Lessee' of the Theatre Royal, Drury Lane. At Christmas 1821 Barrymore did further work with Roberts in Edinburgh and subsequently invited him south, primarily as a stalking horse to draw Elliston off Stanfield. However, Roberts had married in 1820 and, now with a wife and child to care for, 'looked with dread as to the chance I might have [in London] where even the painter of one of the smallest theatres . . . had shown himself so much my superior.'[18] But Murray gave him notice of a long lay-off in the summer of 1822, and in August that year Roberts sailed for London.

Here, the first work he did was on the Coburg's *Guy Fawkes* with Stanfield, but he quickly realized that he would stand a better chance, away from such competition, at Drury Lane, 'where the scene-painters Marinari and Andrews [were] both old men'.[19] At the end of September he had a trial for Elliston, painting two scenes of Old and New St. Paul's (later used in the Drury Lane Christmas pantomime *Gog and Magog*). Typically, however, Elliston left Roberts dangling, until the painter forced his hand by re-engaging himself to Murray for two months up to Christmas. Elliston then promptly signed him on a three-year contract from 1 January 1823 at five guineas per week, rising to six after a year. Well pleased, Roberts went north.

However, when he returned in mid-January, having been delayed three weeks by bad weather at sea, he found 'that the very thing I had most dreaded had occurred': Stanfield was already installed ahead of him at the Lane, also on a three-year contract and at the higher sum of £8 per week. The cause was a series of disasters combining managerial collapse at the Coburg, the death of Andrews at Drury Lane, and the failure, and then brilliant resurrection by Barrymore and Stanfield, of Elliston's Christmas pantomime as *The Golden Axe*.

Elliston, with characteristic luck, had had everything fall into his lap, securing the basic team of Stanfield, Roberts and Barrymore with whom he was to create a major challenge to Covent

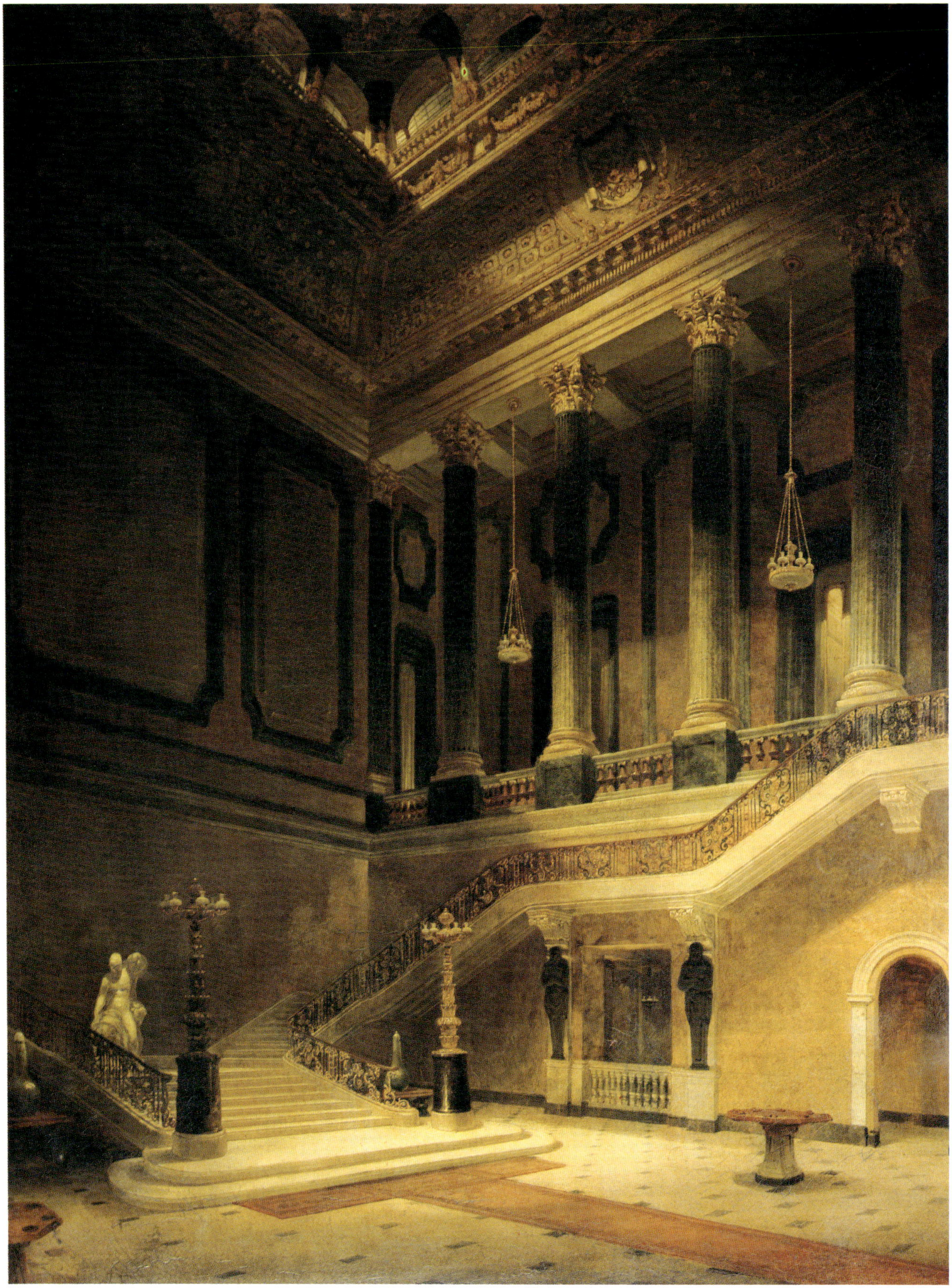

30. *The Staircase at Stafford House*, 1832, Government Art Collection. Cat.47.

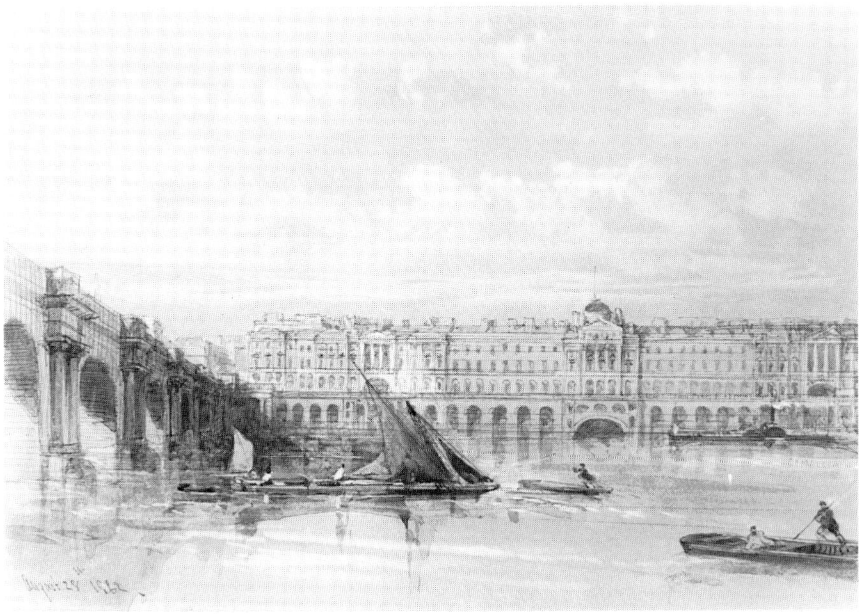

31. *Somerset House and Waterloo Bridge*, 1862, Baring Brothers & Co., Ltd. Cat.46.

Garden's supremacy in spectacle. The improvement was immediate. 'Spectacles have of late been dull affairs at Drury Lane', wrote a critic in April 1823 of *The Chinese Sorcerer* (31 March), 'but the house is making an effort to redeem its character in that department . . . The illuminated marine pavilion (moonlight) by Roberts, is a very delightful performance; and the grand harbour (Stanfield) is of a still higher order . . . This production will certainly do away the idea that splendid and effective scenery cannot be got up at Drury Lane.'[20]

For the next four years Roberts and Stanfield were to be in increasingly acrimonious, if successful, proximity. Roberts wished to pursue his architectural forte but that was also the speciality of their senior, Gaetano Marinari, who had first choice. Since Marinari and Stanfield did not compete in this, the former probably favoured Stanfield (who certainly painted his portrait). Roberts thus found that:

> . . . the refuse of both . . . fell to my share and my having to dabble in all sorts of subjects while at the Edinburgh theatre was of great service to me—had it been otherwise I must have gone to the wall.
>
> Stanfield . . . [soon] . . . decidedly got the lead of Marinari and notwithstanding the indifferent subjects that fell to my lot, my name was mostly . . . associated with his. But . . . I approached much too near him for him to be comfortable . . . I will take no notice of the numerous petty jealousies and bickerings that took place betwixt us and which was ultimately the cause of my withdrawing from the theatre altogether. One good it certainly did me and that was in making me turn serious attention to my oil pictures.[21]

He also made a head start on the important business of foreign sketching tours when in 1824 he visited France with John Wilson.

The first major clash between Roberts and Stanfield came just before his departure abroad. Late in 1823, Roberts again worked briefly at the Edinburgh Theatre Royal and, after Christmas, spent two weeks painting at the Dublin Theatre. As a result he had a number of provincial invitations, of which he only accepted one, in Birmingham for June 1824. He was furious when Stanfield stepped in and undercut his price. But he had his revenge. They had together agreed to paint an exhibition hall panorama of the Bombardment of Algiers (1816) for a Mr J. B. Laidlaw, for touring on the Continent. Roberts made a point of having most of the work finished before Stanfield returned to town and it was from him that Laidlaw in 1825 requested two extra

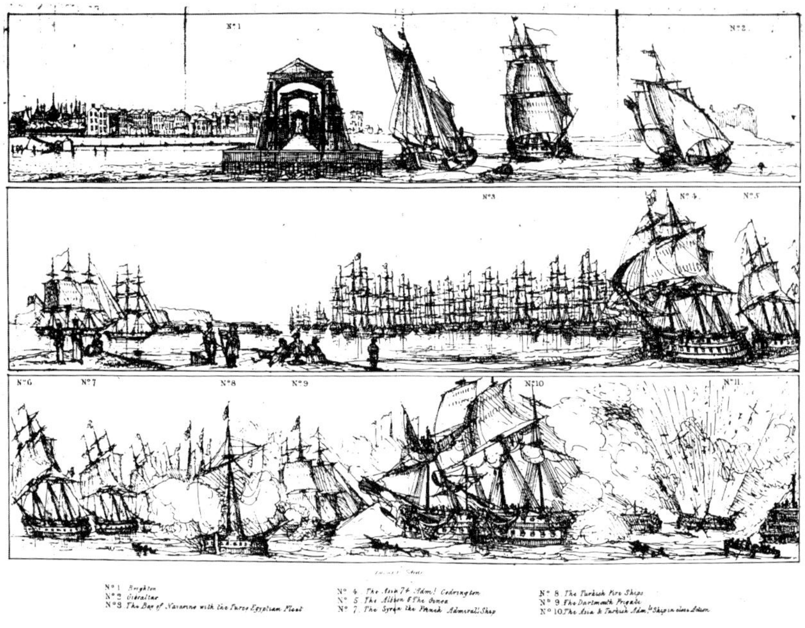

32. Lithographic Key to Roberts's *Grand Panoramic Naumachia* in *Harlequin and Number Nip*, Covent Garden, 1827, Family Collection. Cat.4.

scenes of the burning of the *Kent* Indiaman, to add to the exhibition at Liverpool. It subsequently toured to Rotterdam, Amsterdam and Cologne.[22] In late 1827, both artists collaborated with others on a sequel showing the naval Battle of Navarino (20 October 1827), which did a similar European tour.[23]

In 1826, however, Elliston's extravagances—including the large material costs of scene-room competition—brought his management to an end. Roberts greatly resented current rumours of his being 'meanly jealous' of Stanfield, a denial not helped by his declining to serve with Stanfield that year on the exhibition committee of the Society of British Artists. On 18 April, Roberts resigned from Drury Lane and in August took up an unusually generous offer from the Covent Garden management. Happy by now to draw any of the rival house's scenic teeth, they were prepared to pay him £10 per week for a six-hour day (or pro rata), and all on the part-time basis that Roberts now considered essential for pursuit of his other work.

The sequel suggests that Roberts's avowed distaste for 'the intrigue and tact'[24] required in a large theatre was perhaps a covert confession. It is certainly hard to see how such an individualist as his later career showed him to be would fit into a large organization for long. At Covent Garden he found his problems with Stanfield were nothing compared to the hostility of the Grieves, despite his respect for the patriarchal John. The first insult was also the greatest. For having spent the eighteen months to November 1827 getting up single-handed all seventeen scenes for the first London production of Mozart's *The Seraglio*, 'without assistants (a thing perhaps unknown in the great theatres and . . . not likely to occur again)', these were 'totally obliterated within six weeks after its production' at the Grieves' orders. It did not help that Roberts thought them the finest scenes he ever painted.[25]

By comparison, absence from Stanfield made the heart grow fonder. In October 1827 they joined up to paint four successful transparency pictures for Thomas Hamlet's 'British Diorama' at the Queen's Bazaar, Oxford Street, Roberts's contribution being views of Tintern Abbey and St. George's Chapel, Windsor. These were ready for February 1828 and a second quartet followed for April 1829, Roberts doing the interior of St. Sauveur, Caen, and the Temple of Appollinopolis, Egypt. Unfortunately, one of Stanfield's pictures caught fire during a performance in May 1829, destroying all eight and the Bazaar.[26]

There is a case for saying that Roberts's career as a regular scene-painter ended in 1826. His London work was not large overall compared to others and most of it was concentrated in his time at Drury Lane. Here he was credited with 105 scenes in some twenty-five shows.[27] If one

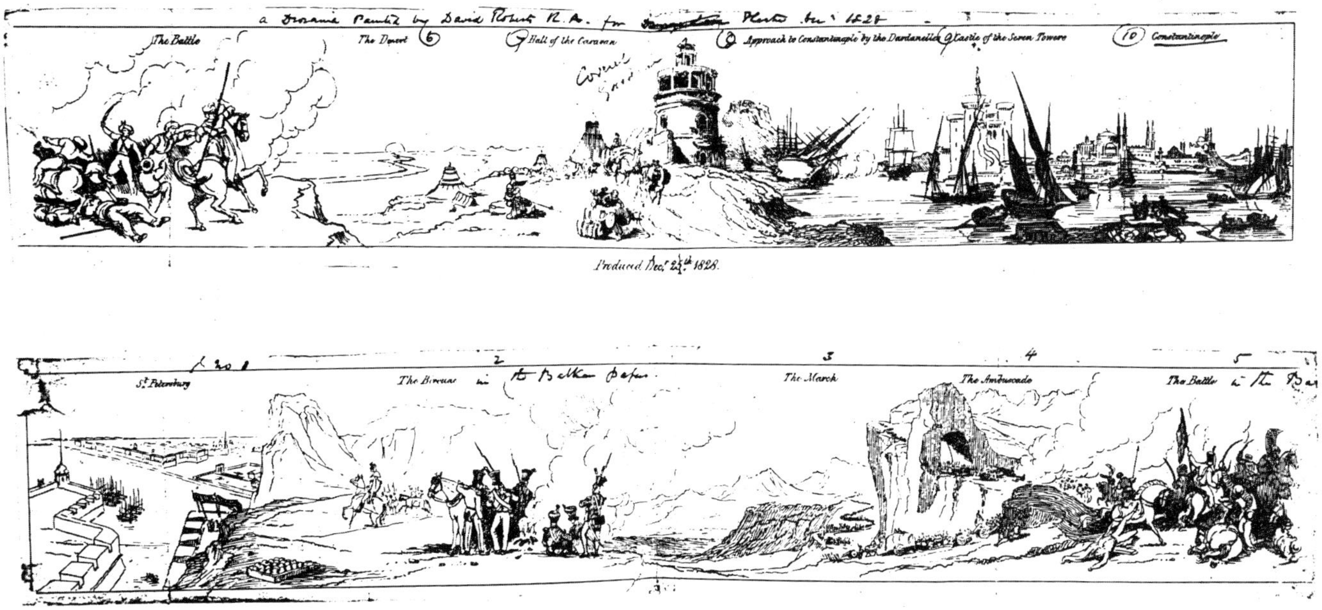

33. Lithographic Key to Roberts's *Moving Panorama of the Grand Russian Army's March to Turkey* in *Harlequin and Little Red Riding Hood*, Covent Garden, 1828, Family collection. Cat.5.

excludes *The Seraglio*, in the brilliance of which Roberts 'certainly left even Stanfield behind him',[28] his unusual terms as part-time star of Covent Garden were sustained by contributions to only seven other shows during his engagement. Among these were the Christmas pantomimes of 1827–9, in which he attempted, though with only partial success, to challenge Stanfield's supremacy in the dioramic field.

Almost all the pieces for which he painted were ephemeral spectacles in which scenery was a main attraction and for which comments like 'Stanfield and Roberts have again proved themselves masters in the art of scene-painting'[29] became routine. Shakespeare received but slight benefit from Roberts's work[30] and otherwise the only significant pieces of opera or drama were Weber's *Der Freischutz* (1824), *William Tell* by Knowles (1825), and *The Seraglio*. A poor version of *Faustus* by Soane in 1825, however, had such splendid scenic effects by both artists as to attract the praise of Delacroix.[31] In the same year, Roberts capitalized on his earlier French visit with scenes of Rheims cathedral, 'drawn beautifully and coloured with clearness and spirit',[32] while other criticism of the time praised his topographical accuracy and 'great knowledge and aerial perspective'.[33]

Leitch, in commenting on Roberts's earlier work in Scotland, had 'found that especially in architectural scenes, the simple beauty of his outline, combined with the masses of light and shade gave them a grand and most impressive effect',[34] and with this every comment of later years agreed. 'Perhaps our finest architectural scenic draughtsman,' wrote John Timbs in 1829, 'although his landscapes fall short of those by Stanfield.'[35] There were one or two more informatively critical comments in other areas. His Temple of Shakespeare act-drop for Covent Garden in October 1828 drew the usual praise for fine perspective but, added *The Times*, 'the drawing of the figures appeared . . . rather clumsy and harsh and the colouring rather dingy'.[36] This was elaborated at Christmas in consideration of his second Covent Garden diorama, of the Russian army's march to Turkey. Although critics praised its topographical views of St. Petersburg and Constantinople they drew the line at figures imitated from other artists, 'ill-drawn and worse coloured'. 'The clouds of brickdust intended to represent "the sulphurous canopy" of the combat are also exceedingly objectionable',[37] while 'the sunset [is] not only stolen from Danby but disfigured'.[38] While this is perhaps worse than anything Roberts received for his easel painting, echoes and reflections of his scenic qualities can also be picked out in that field, as far apart as contemporary comment on his *The Israelites Leaving Egypt* (1829, Plate 62) and the Redgraves' retrospect published two years after his death.[39]

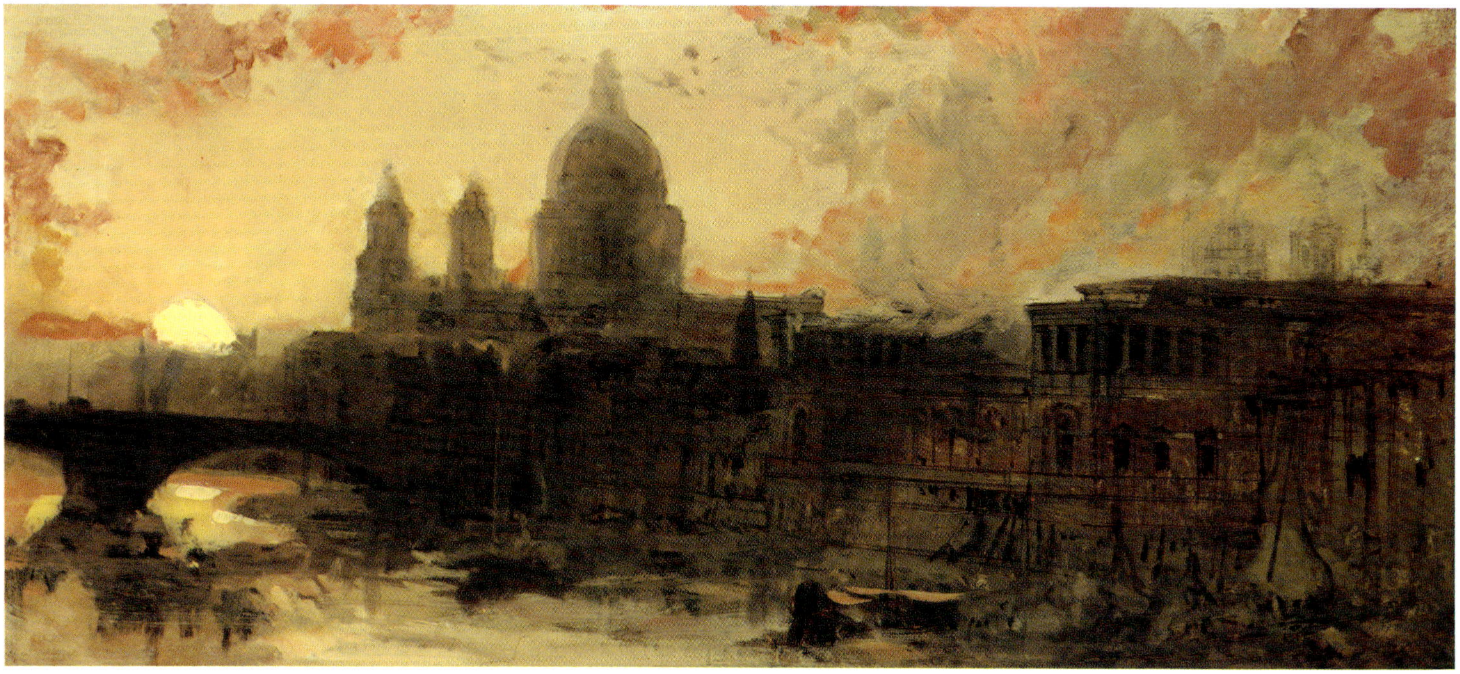

34. *St. Paul's, Sunset*, *c.*1863, Private collection. Cat.43.

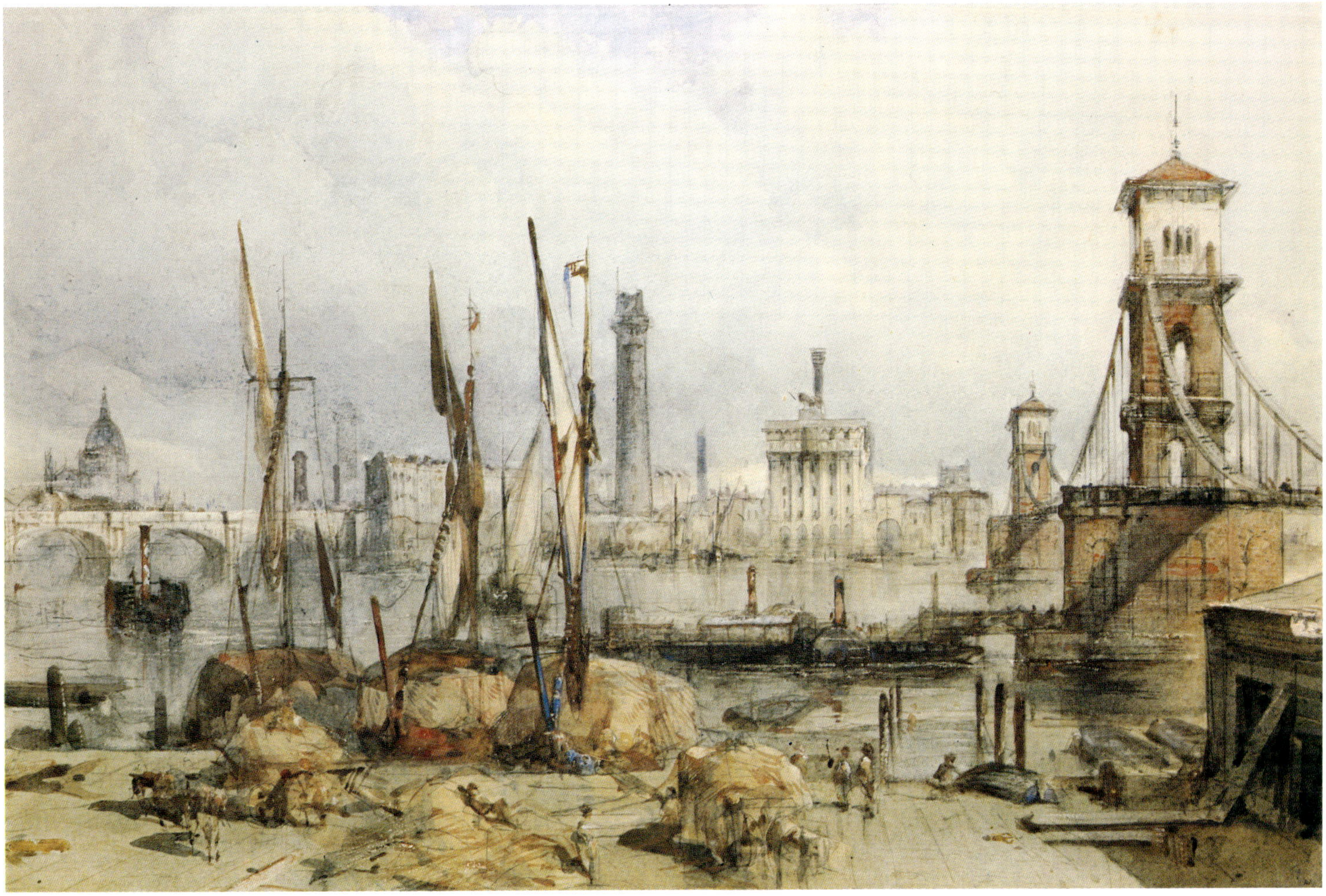

35. *The Thames at Hungerford Bridge*, *c*.1861, Ingram Family Collection. Cat.49.

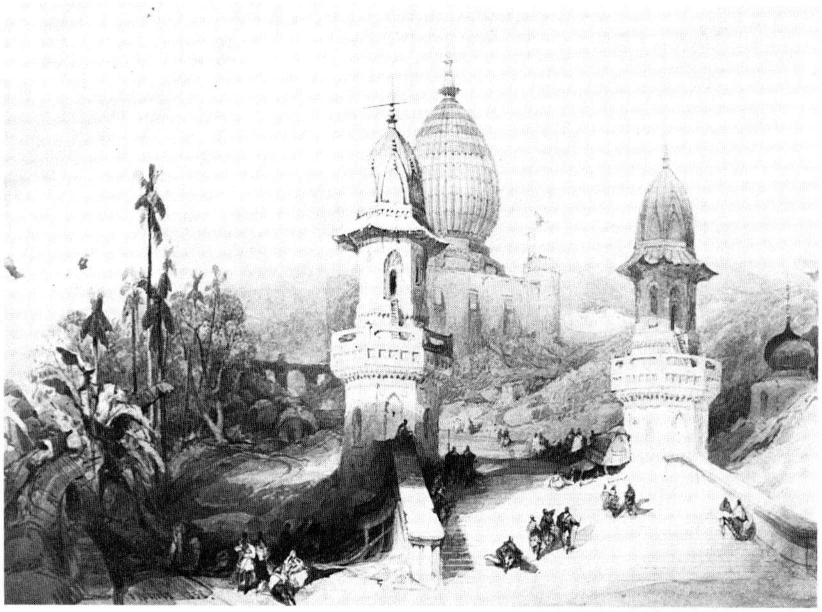

36. *Ghat and Temple at Gokul*, 1838, Private collection. Cat.112.

Roberts's last stage work was at Christmas 1830. Frederick Lloyds later heard him speak of the delight with which he used to look back on his scene-painting days, and the great use they had been to him in his after career',[40] but, unlike Stanfield, he was never persuaded back to the stage and declined the one recorded offer made to him in 1846.[41] He did not, however, give up his theatrical friends and interest, becoming one of the first members of the Garrick Club and, through Stanfield, an occasional member of the Dickens circle. It was in this capacity that he painted his last scene, an act-drop for Dickens's amateur production of *Not so Bad as We Seem* in aid of the Guild of Literature and Art in 1851. His last contribution to the stage was in a similarly charitable vein when, at his suggestion, he and Stanfield commemorated their old rivalry and long friendship in 1860 by funding one of the houses for 'decayed actors' in the new Dramatic College at Maybury.

Roberts and Stanfield occupy an unusual position in early nineteenth-century painting where, as regards their theatre work, it is difficult to consider either in isolation from the other. In 1825 *The Times* noted their scenic excellence as an omen of future Academy distinction,[42] a prophecy soon fulfilled. The key to their early success lay both in the suitability of their picturesque talents to the theatre, and in the concurrent demand for stage spectacle which allowed them to make the most of their gifts. Given their obscure and unprosperous origins, they showed realistic good sense in choosing to enter the scene-room rather than the Schools. Once started, their theatrical success soon promoted and benefited from the parallel growth of their work for gallery and engraver. On the stage, one of them had to be *primus inter pares*. That it was not Roberts in no way detracts from his stature, or from his share of the credit for the promotion of public interest in landscape art which both men effected through their scenery.

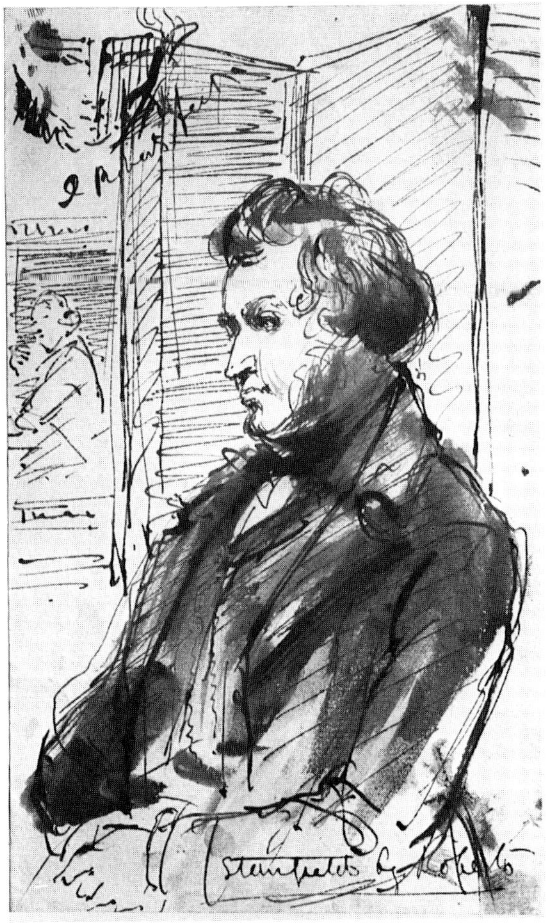

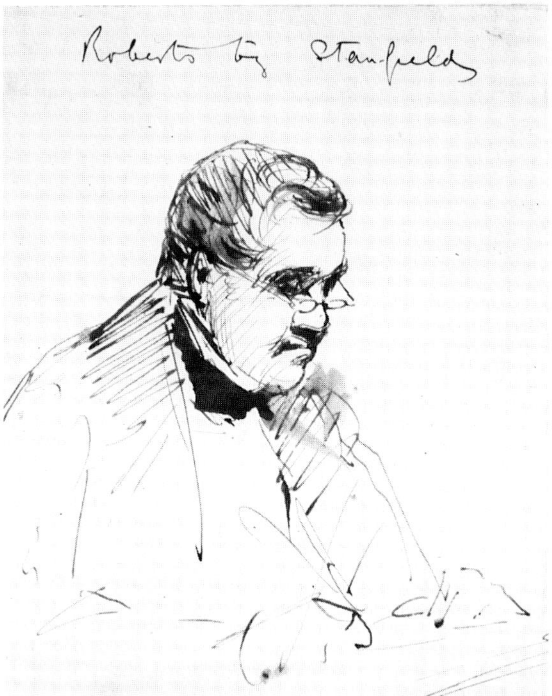

37. Two portrait sketches: *above*, David Roberts, *Clarkson Stanfield*; *below*, Clarkson Stanfield, *David Roberts*. Royal Academy of Arts, London. Cat.215 and 216.

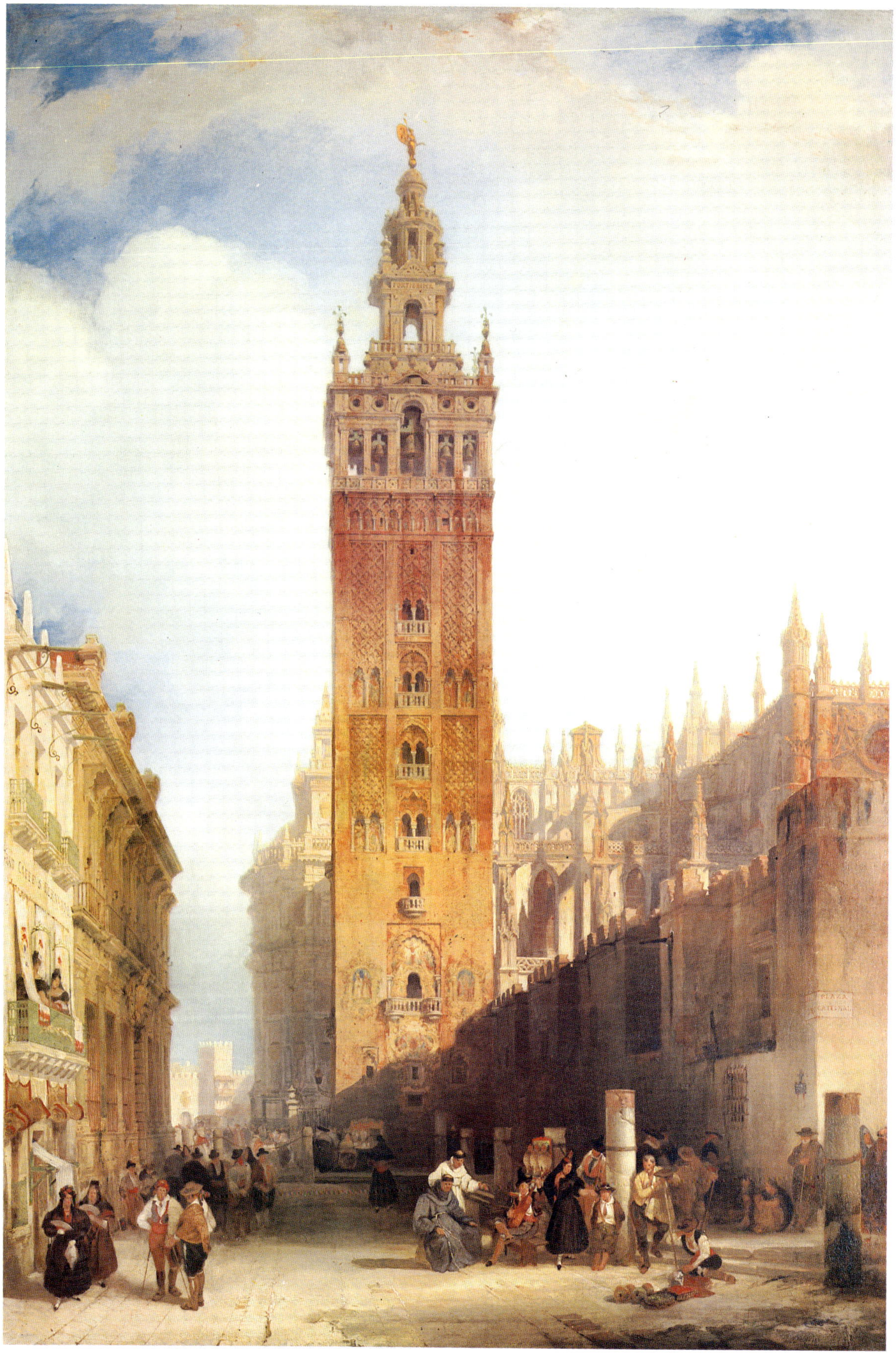

38. *The Moorish Tower at Seville, Called the Giralda*, 1833, The Abbot of Downside. Cat.104.

Travel, Topography and Prints

MICHAEL PIDGLEY

> Mr Roberts is an artist possessing talents of the highest class; in his works profound art and the most scientific display of detail are equally perceptible; not as subservient the one to the other, but as cooperating to produce a perfect whole. He exhibits the breadth and magnificence of architectural subjects with a precision which satisfies the beholders of their truth, and at the same time with a degree of taste and feeling which prevents their taking the character of a dry elevation.

This appraisal of Roberts's talents comes from *The Gallery of Modern British Artists*, published in 1835 in London, Edinburgh, Dublin, Paris, Berlin and New York, which indicates the wide appeal that such a publication then had. No other artist was better represented in the volume than Roberts. His eight architectural subjects comprised four from Scotland, three from Normandy, and an imaginary cathedral interior. They reflected well his achievements to date. The same year saw the publication of the first of four *Landscape Annuals*, all illustrated by Roberts, three of which were devoted to Spain (1835–7), and one to Spain and Morocco (1838). In 1834 had appeared his impressive series of picturesque and dramatic scenes on the Rhine, illustrating Bulwer Lytton's *Pilgrims of the Rhine*. The engravings did much to confirm Roberts's standing among the foremost artist-topographers of his day, and the book gained a reputation as 'one of the most perfect volumes of the pictorial class'.[1]

The influential *Landscape Annual* was first published in 1830, proclaiming its originality as 'a work at once novel and attractive, and widely different in point of design and execution from any of a similar class hitherto announced'. The early volumes were illustrated by J. D. Harding (three on Italy and France), and by Samuel Prout (two on Italy and Switzerland). Prout was widely acknowledged as the originator of the continental Picturesque movement. 'I founded what little I possess on your good works', wrote Roberts to Prout in 1833, and Prout in his turn acknowledged the younger man's 'bright talent'.[2] Prout had acquired his great skill as an architectural draughtsman under the tuition of John Britton, whose many publications educated a new generation in the beauties of Gothic architecture, and gave an added impetus to the cause of topographical delineation. With Britton's energetic promotion it became a respectable activity, demanding of its practitioners very considerable skills.

When he came to write the obituary of one of his most travelled protégés, William Henry Bartlett, Britton put the artist's achievement in the context of recent developments, which included the work of Turner, Roberts, Stanfield, Harding, Cattermole, Allom, and others:

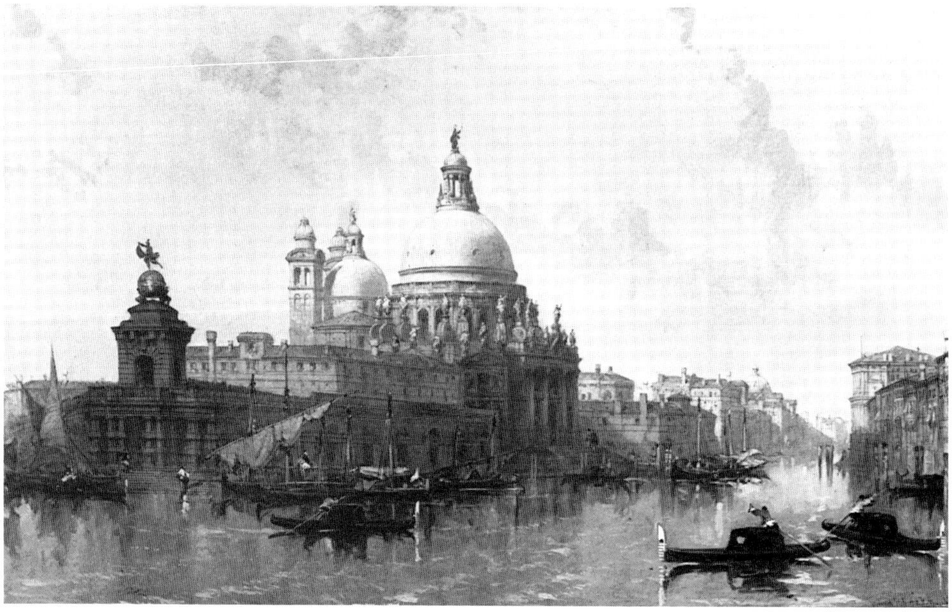

39. *Santa Maria della Salute, Venice*, 1862, Sheffield City Art Galleries. Cat.200.

> All of these, in my opinion, are and were artists of unquestionable talent, many of whose works are not only high in the market value, but in the estimation of the profound and impartial connoisseur. When Fuseli pronounced his cynical dogmas, it was the fashion, it was the practice of artists and writers on Art . . . to decry modern Art, and the artists of such as were based on the principles of truth and daylight and with forms and colours which were referable to the laws and effects of nature.[3]

Henry Fuseli had been Professor of Paintings at the Royal Academy during a period of twenty-five years (1799–1805 and 1810–25), and his tastes did not extend to landscape paintings of any but the most elevated kind.[4] Fortunately, his prejudices had little effect in checking the growth of topographical art, which had begun to take itself very seriously.

In an essay on Roberts written in 1869, F. T. Palgrave wrote: 'Our school of architectural art having once fairly established itself, the extension of its range of subjects was inevitable. For just at the time when Prout and Roberts, Lewis and Harding, had formed themselves, the barrier between England and the Continent was broken up, and modern travelling—an art in itself—began.'[5] The works of these artists became known to thousands in the form of small steel engravings, which appeared in countless 'annuals'. This new taste was well expressed in John Weale's *Quarterly Papers on Architecture* in 1844:

> The introduction of our richly-illustrated ANNUALS administered more and more to that taste for *picture* which had already been excited; and architectural representations soon formed the most prominent attraction of this class of works. Artists and engravers shortly became perfectly competent to delineate every variety of building with all the united charms of accuracy and poetical effect; and, what may be termed the romance of architecture, obtained a considerable influence on the public.[6]

An artist had two main problems: to get his work noticed for its individual style, and also for its individual content. 'We may regard as the great merit of Roberts's style', wrote Palgrave, 'its intelligibility; he leaves one in no doubt of what he thinks worth attention; making his object perfectly clear, and at the same time putting in just enough effect to raise it to the level of a picture.'[7] This was intended as limited praise only, for he went on to say that 'it must be confessed that Roberts omits much which we cannot afford to lose.' There was a sameness in

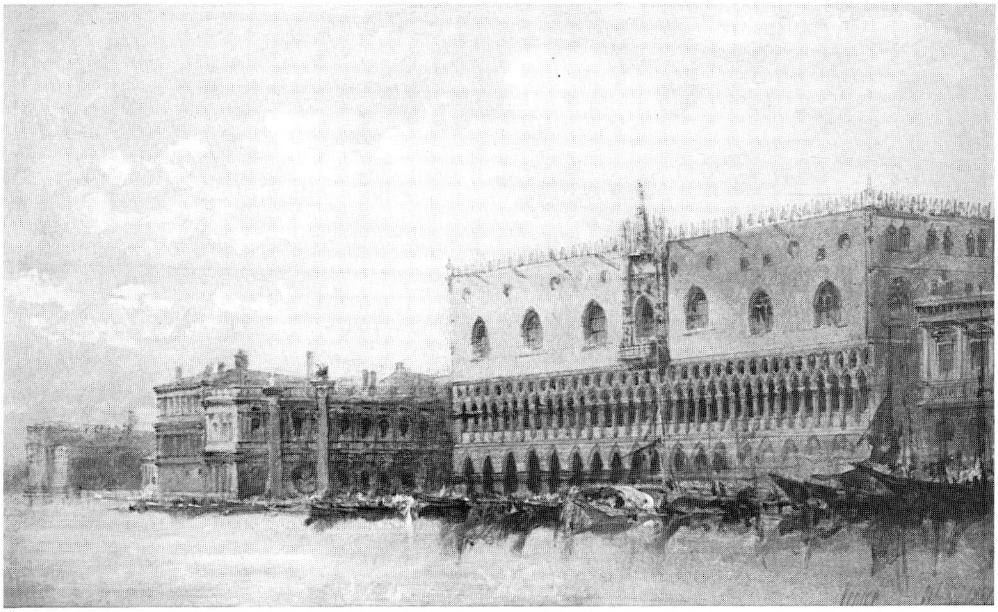

40. *Venice*, 1851, Private collection. Cat.197.

texture and colour, 'no delight in dwelling upon the signs of age', and all his subjects were bathed in 'one sunlight . . . one atmosphere'.

Ruskin had the measure of Roberts's art when he compared him to Prout, who with all his imperfections and mannerisms had 'an appreciation and realization of continental character . . . a locality and life' not seen in the works of others. This was made all the more evident 'after we have been rendered most fastidious by the exquisite drawing and perfect composition of the accomplished Roberts'.[8] The latter was decidedly not an imaginative artist, but his great success lay in recognizing his limitations and making clarity of perception a virtue. His sheer professionalism was the sort that could not fail to be noticed, especially in early Victorian England with its pride in industrious and honest toil. The drawbacks of such an approach were equally obvious, especially when it became the prevailing mode. 'Possibly there is a certain want in Modern art', wrote one critic in 1867, 'and it is too much made up of light and shade, drawing and composition, mechanical power and dexterity; possibly it altogether wants the higher and more spiritual qualities of relationship to man's moral and religious nature.'[9]

Comparisons were inevitable. Turner in Venice and Roberts in Venice resulted in two quite different approaches. Turner's 'rapturous and visionary' approach produced pictures which were 'a dream, a delirium'. 'We left Venice under the persuasion that nature could not rival the extravagance of Turner. Then plain, honest, and somewhat prosaic David Roberts made himself at home on the Grand Canal, and we have to thank his pencil for many noble pictures of Santa Maria della Salute and other equally well-known subjects.'[10] The Redgraves accounted for Roberts's success by defining the appeal of such pictures as their 'onceness, their direct appeal to the eye'.[11] Thackeray coupled Roberts with Stanfield as artists who could not fail to show their evident powers of drawing, but to him their skilful pictures always appeared 'more pleasing in little on the sketching-board than when expanded on canvas'.[12] Among the later admirers of Roberts's studies was the twenty-year-old Roger Fry, who saw those exhibited at the Manchester Jubilee Exhibition in 1887. 'Some . . . small architectural drawings', he wrote, 'delighted me as much as anything in the way of unfinished sketches.'[13]

Roberts's work was well-known in the form of steel engravings, and his style was well-suited to this form of reproduction. His 'admirable designs' were exempted by Thackeray from his general condemnation of the 'trumpery' annuals and their 'paltry subjects'. 'In Roberts's *Annual* the prints are successful; for the artist is skilful, and his drawings are far more easily copied in engraving than subjects of history or figures.'[14] Familiarity, however, soon bred a

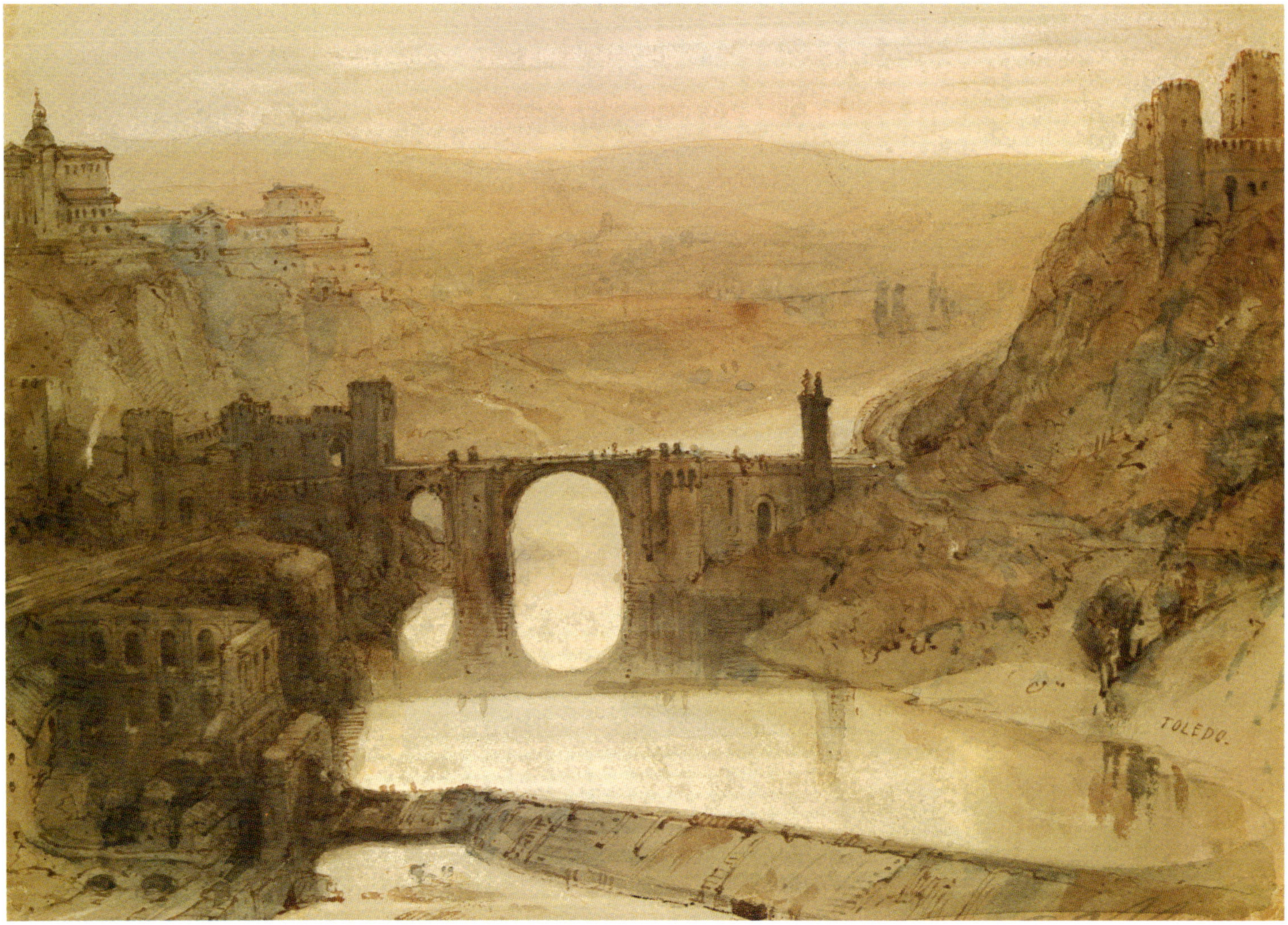

41. *Bridge of Toledo*, *c.*1836, Ingram Family Collection. Cat.106.

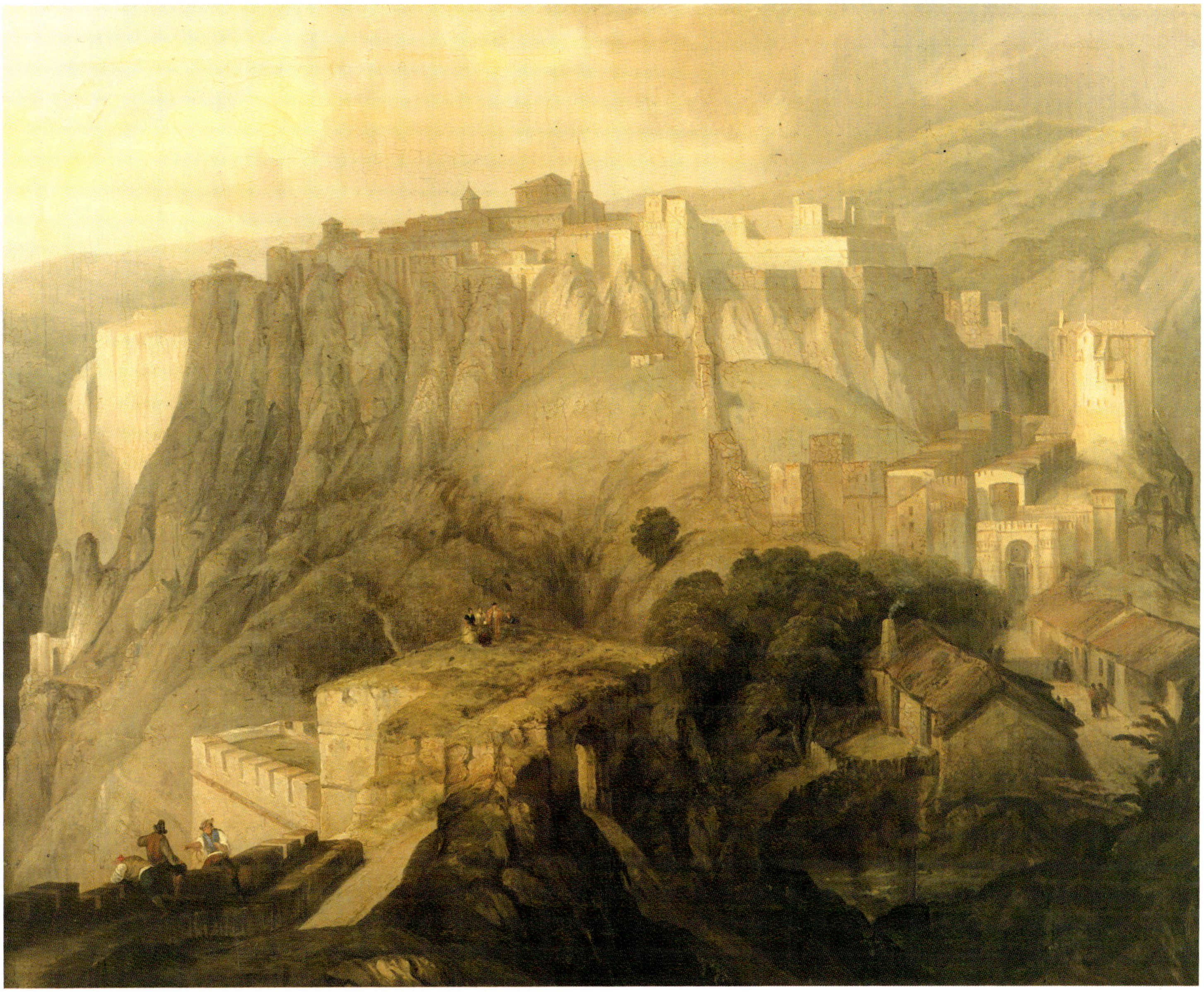

42. *Ronda*, *c*.1835, Revd Canon Ivor Walters. Cat.97.

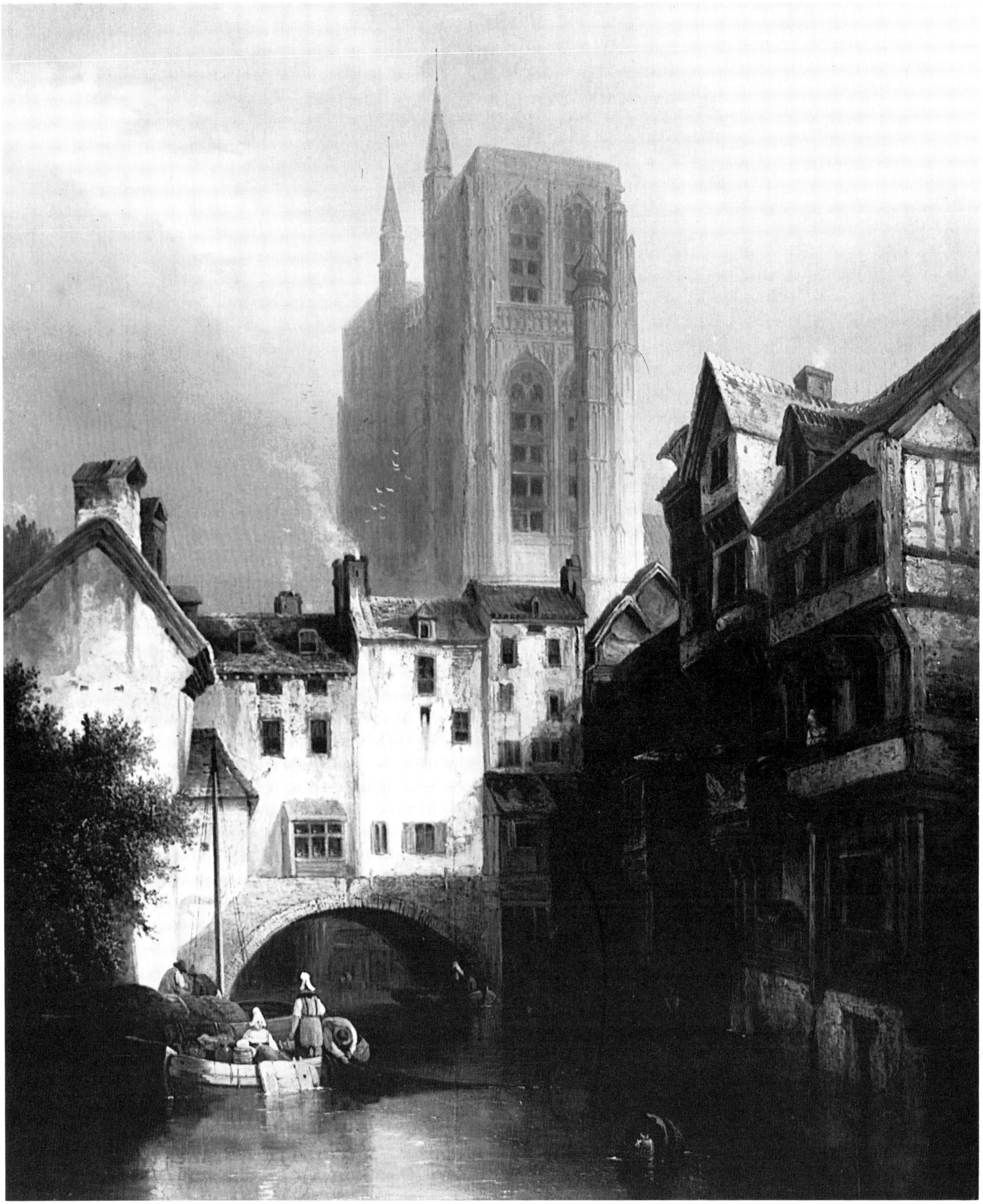

43. *Abbeville*, *c*.1830, The Merchant Taylors Company. Cat.58.

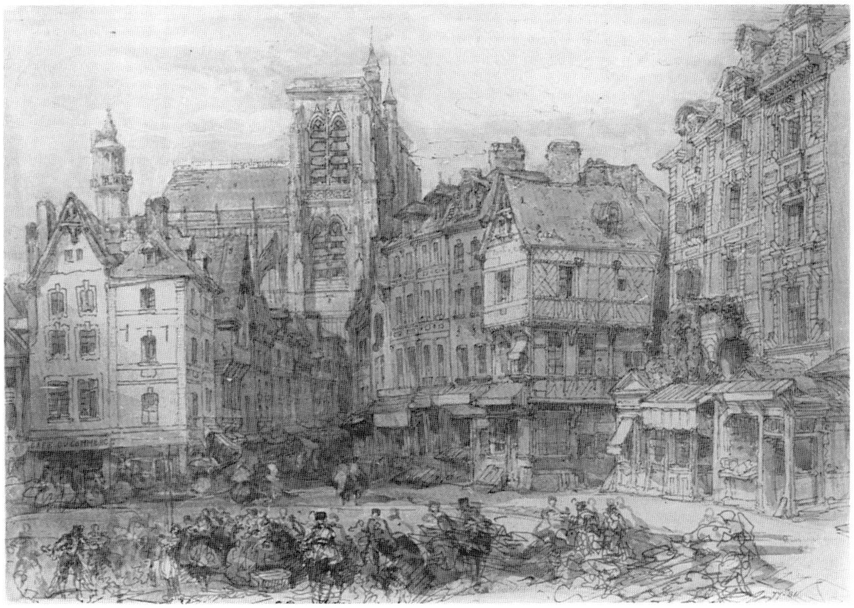

44. *Marché au Blé, Abbeville*, *c*.1824–5, Victoria and Albert Museum, London. Cat.56.

certain indifference, and when the last of the *Landscape Annuals* was illustrated by an artist new to the series, James Holland, Thackeray viewed his drawings as not 'quite so glib and smooth as those from more practical hands', and 'more like nature, and certainly less mannered than the excellent, though exaggerated performances of some of the seniors in the art'.[15]

The great numbers of these annuals, all competing for the same middle-class audience, inevitably led to a sameness. At first, they had been recognized as 'a new though limited source of encouragement' to artists, as Sir Thomas Lawrence, President of the Royal Academy expressed it.[16] One of the promoters of modern art in this period was Samuel Carter Hall, who accorded a significant improvement in taste to these engravings 'after the choicest works of our British painters, executed in such a manner as to educate the eye and give employment to the mind'.[17] Not everyone agreed; John Eagles, writing in *Blackwood's Magazine* in the mid-1830s, expressed considerable doubts about the improvements in engraving, which were, he admitted, 'admirably calculated to represent the works of modern artists, whose aim is more to surprise than permanently to please', but whose efforts to vie with each other ended in a 'gorgeous poverty' of superfluous effects. 'How could I wish', he wrote, 'the improvements never had been invented, when I see how accurately they represent the effects of Turner, his skies—his town views, their stir, and bustle, and vapour.' They astonished too much; *effects* were not landscape.[18]

Many of Roberts's own drawings were engraved by men skilled in interpreting Turner's watercolours, and not a little of Roberts's success with the public was due to the prowess of these same engravers. It was seldom, however, that Roberts allowed himself many Turnerian effects, although when he did the results could be quite dramatic.

One outspoken critic of the period's productions was A. N. W. Pugin. These engravings were to him 'dry and mechanical productions . . . devoid of soul, sentiment and feeling'. They would 'remain an everlasting disgrace on the era in which they were manufactured'.[19] By the time F. T. Palgrave wrote his commentary on Roberts in 1869, taste had changed. 'The value', wrote Palgrave, 'of the exquisite line-engravings . . . which hardly survived the "annual" period, has made itself conspicuously felt in these days of the coarse woodcut and the caricatured fidelity of the frightful photograph.'[20]

Engravings familiarized a new and appreciative audience with the look of foreign places. Poetry books—particularly those of Scott and Byron—containing landscape illustrations on the guidebook principle were so successful that publishers sent artists abroad in increasing

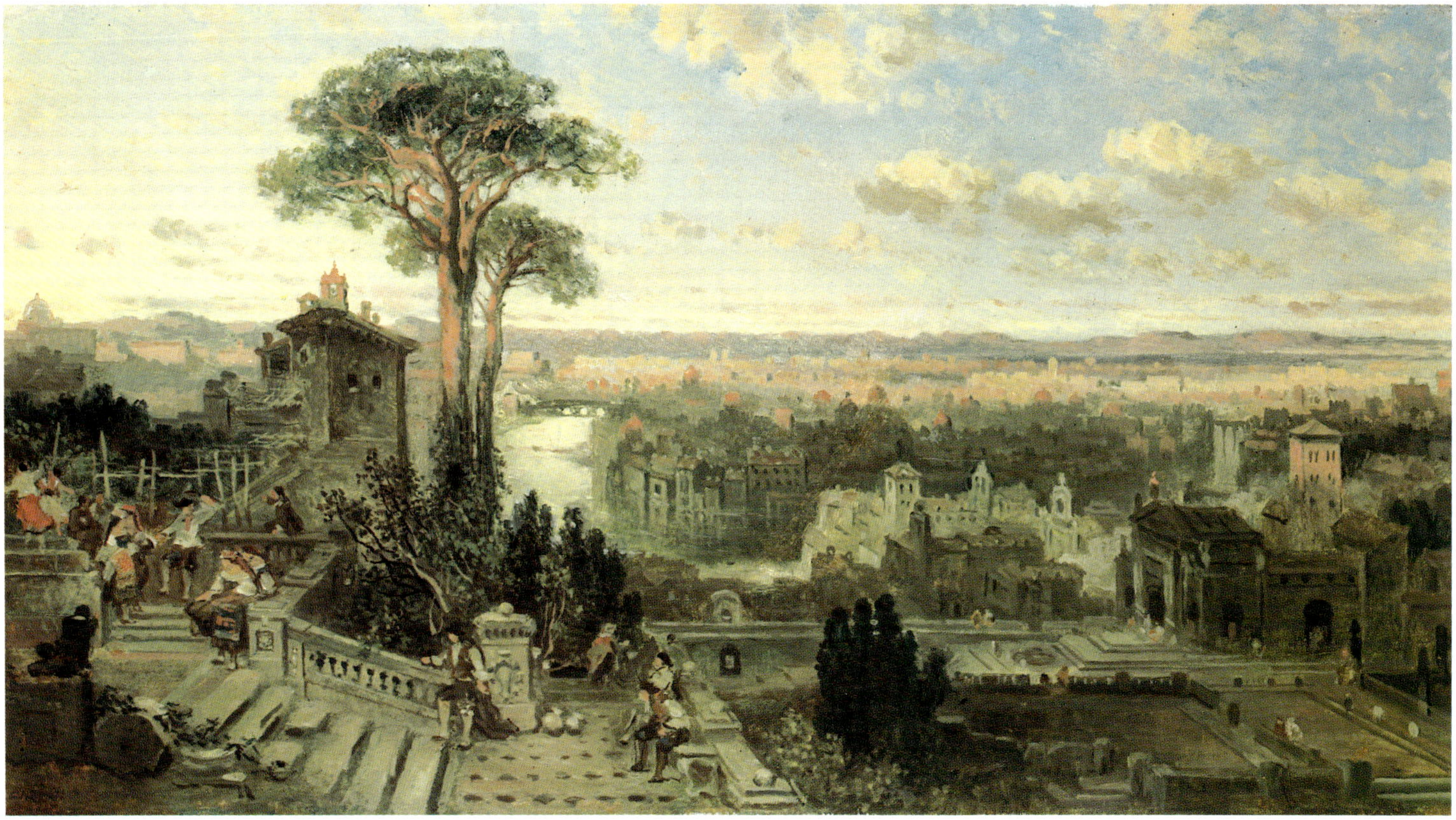

45. *Rome, from the Convent of St. Onofrio, Mount Janiculum*, 1856, National Galleries of Scotland, Edinburgh. Cat.187.

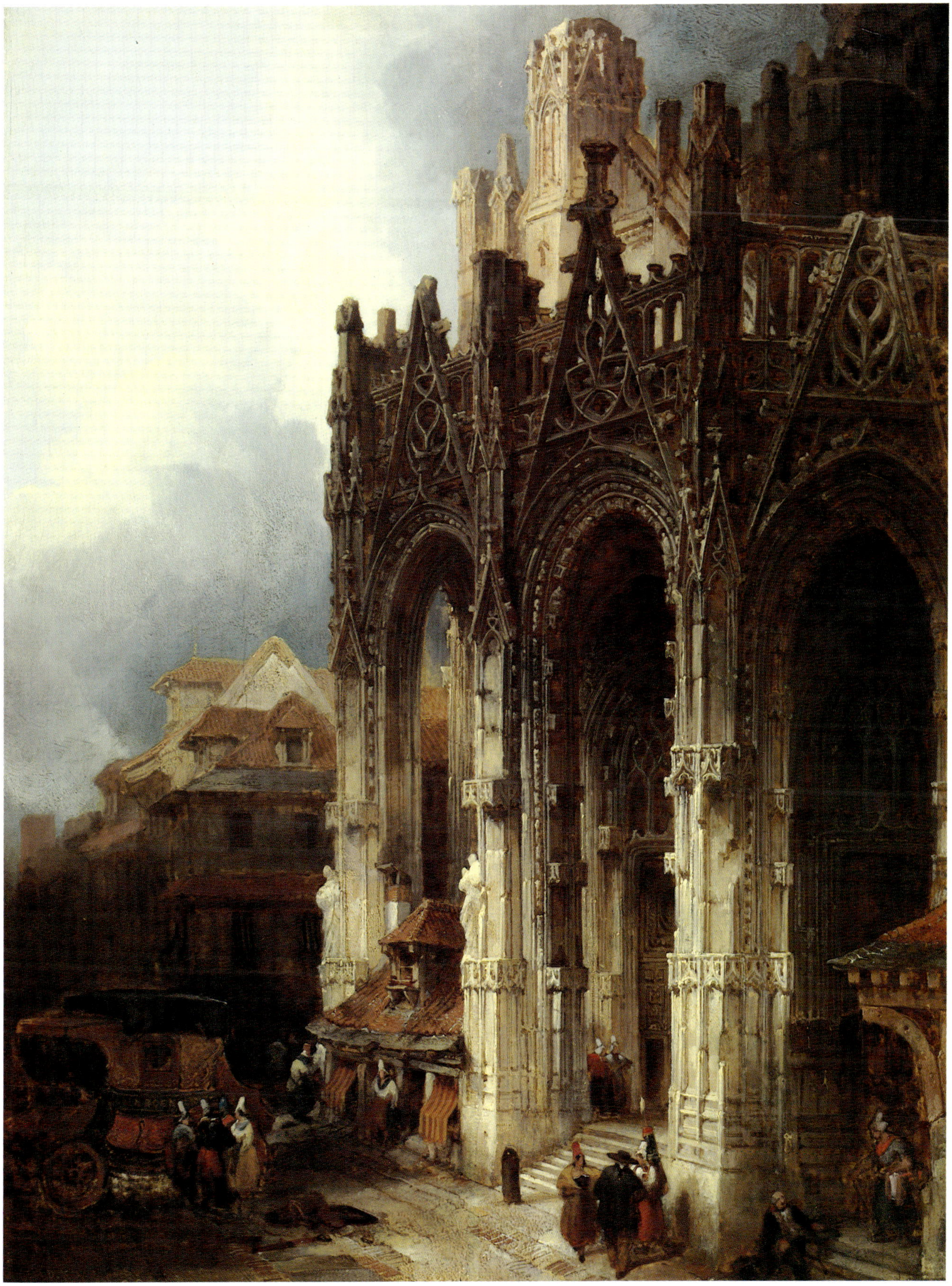

46. *Church of St. Maclou at Rouen*, 1829, Tate Gallery, London. Cat.66.

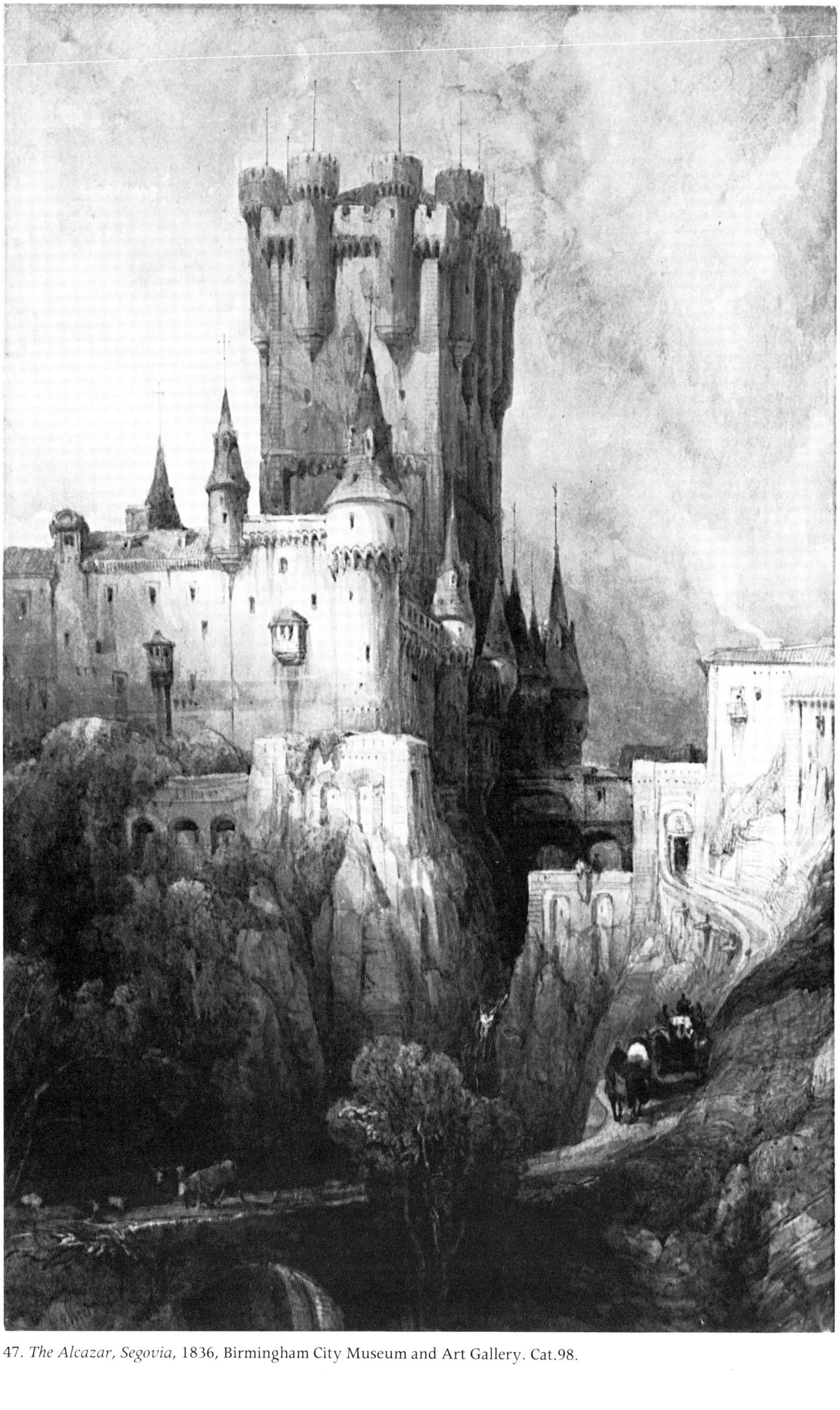

47. *The Alcazar, Segovia*, 1836, Birmingham City Museum and Art Gallery. Cat.98.

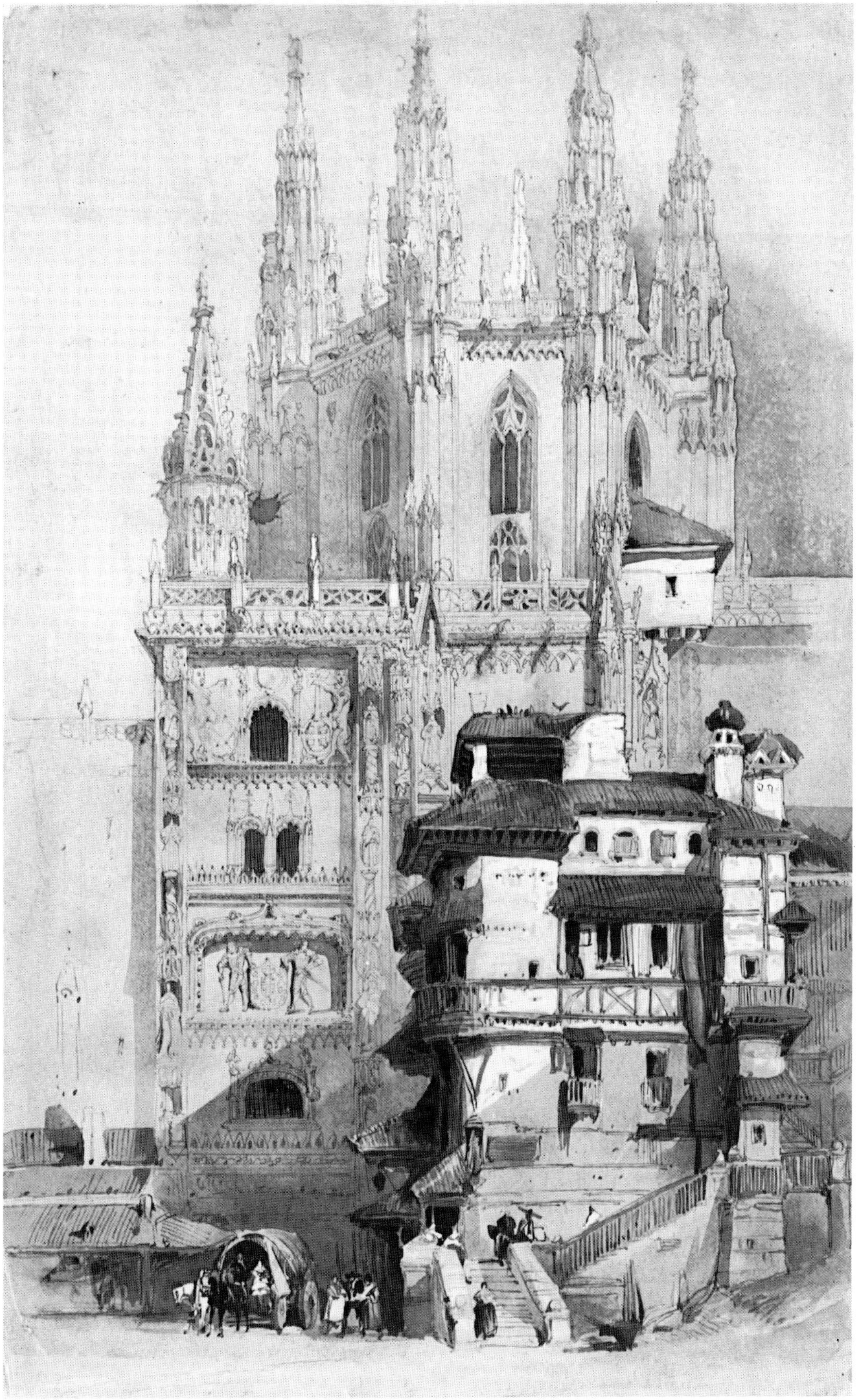

48. *Chapter House, Burgos Cathedral,* (?)1836, Private collection. Cat.84.

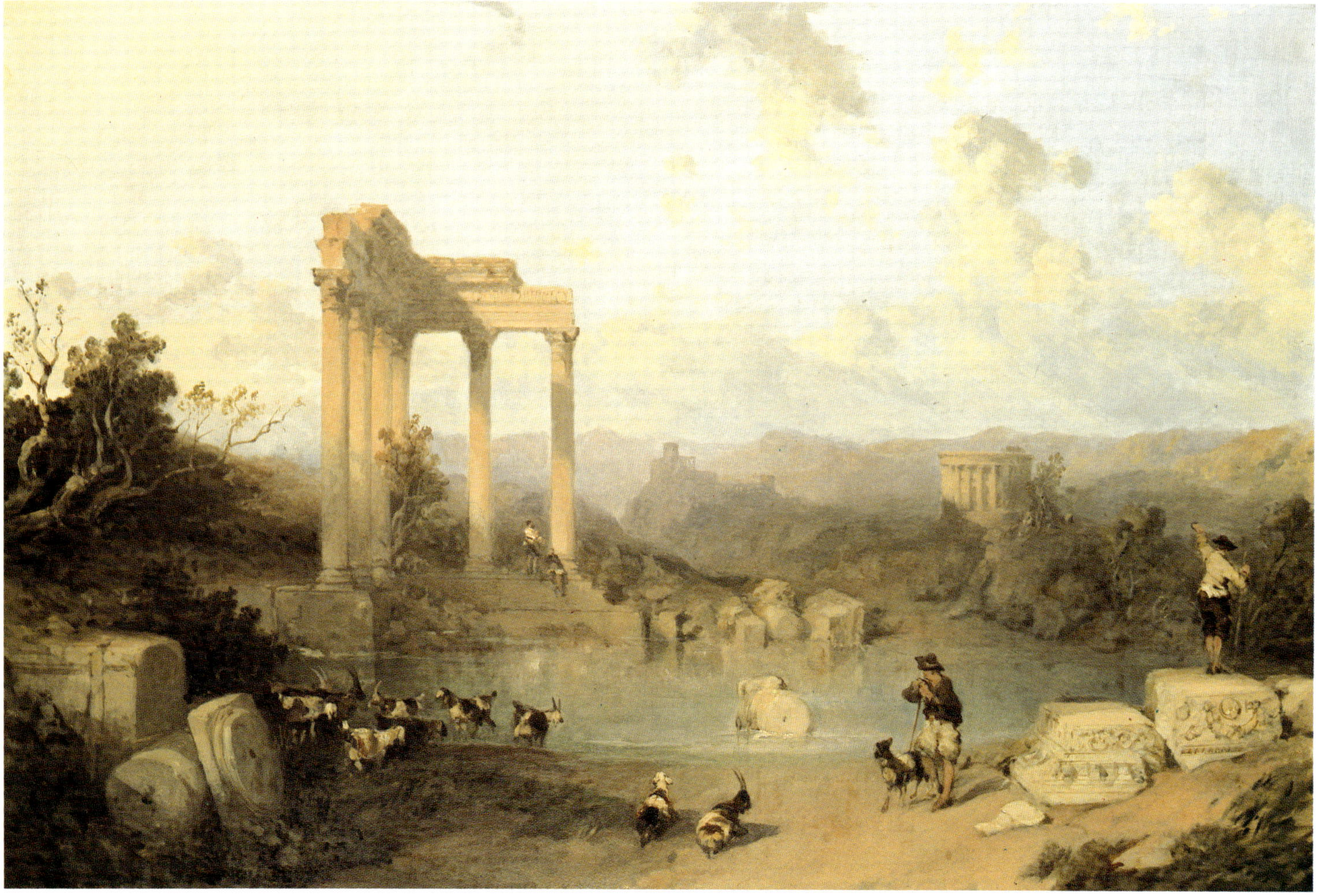

49. *Ruins of the Temple of Neptune, Pozzuoli*, 1858, Private collection. Cat.186.

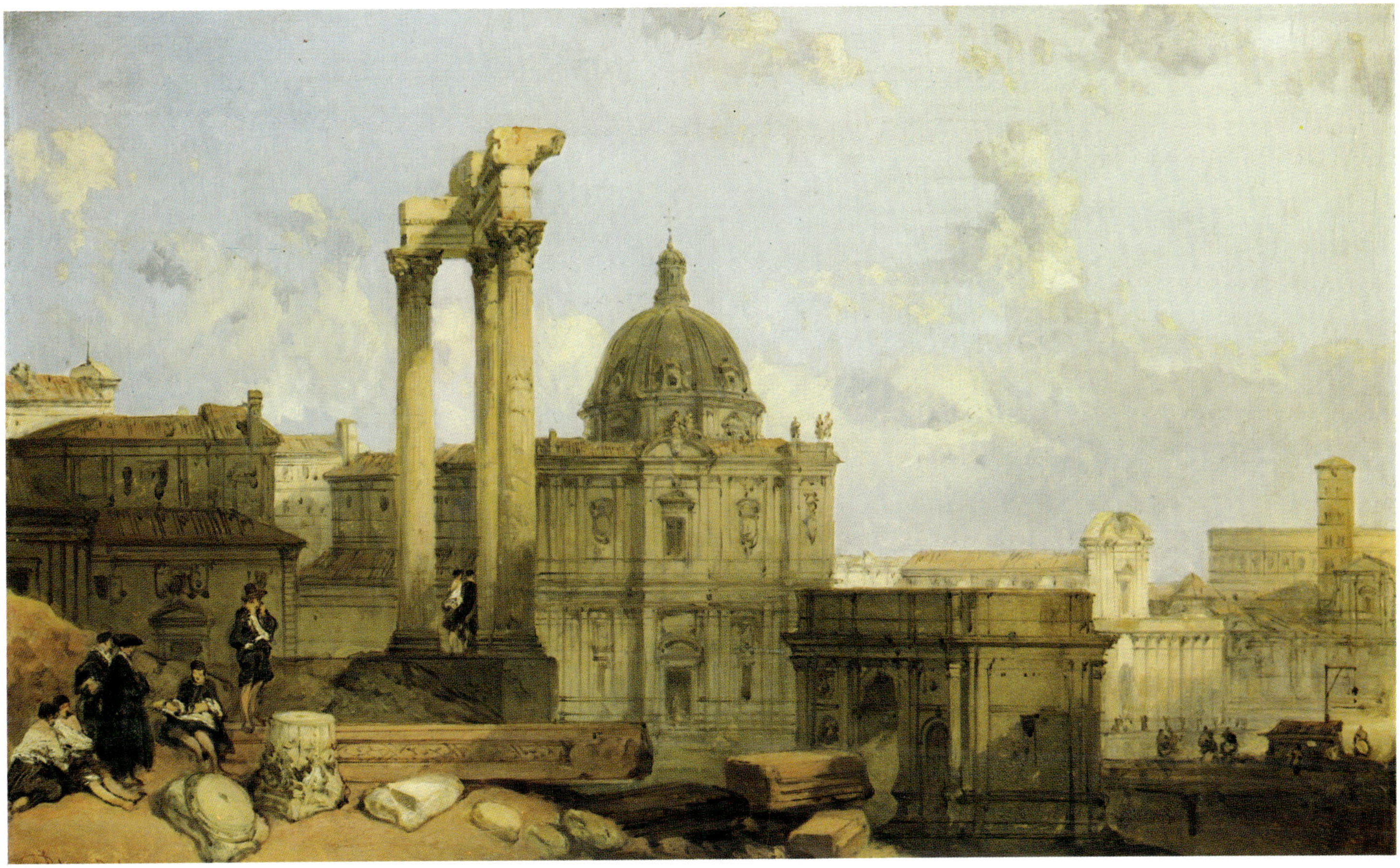

50. *At Rome*, 1859, Wolverhampton Art Gallery. Cat.191.

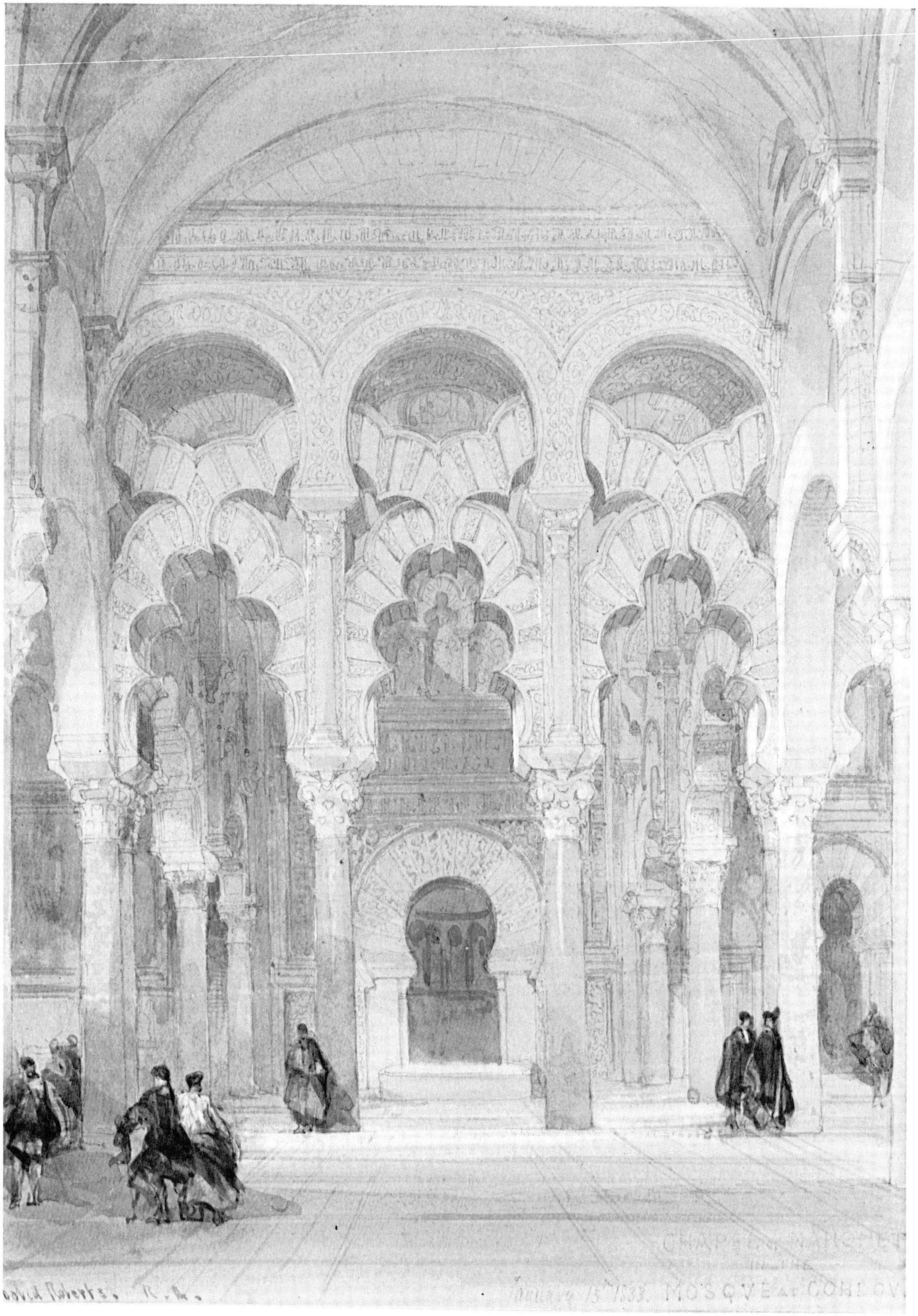

51. *Chapel of Mahomed in the Mosque at Cordoba,* 1833, Private collection. Cat.87.

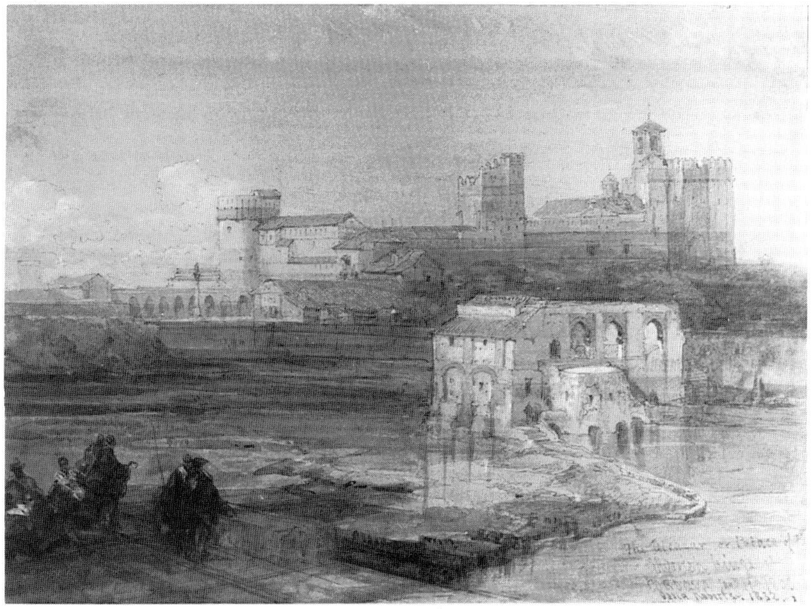

52. *The Alcazar or Palace of the Moorish Kings, Cordoba*, 1833, Dudley Museum and Art Gallery. Cat.86.

numbers. Roberts himself contributed to such books. David Wilkie remarked on 'the craving of the public for variety and of the publishers for new thoughts'.[21]

As well as providing original sketches, artists, including Roberts, were also employed to 'vamp up' sketches by amateur artists. In 1839 Thackeray referred to the illustrations by Thomas Bacon in the *Oriental Annual*: 'Mr Bacon is not, we presume, artist enough to do more than sketch; so Roberts, Stanfield, and others, have been employed to complete the drawings.'[22] Roberts did this on other occasions, for Murray's *Landscape Illustrations of the Bible* (1836), and Commander Robert Elliot's *Views in India, chiefly among the Himalaya Mountains* (1838).[23] The resulting hybrid effect in some of these illustrations was incongruous, and attention was often drawn to this at the time of their publication.

Roberts was soon to travel to the Holy Land himself and sketch some of those places that he had already drawn from the sketches of others. It is for his views of the Holy Land and Egypt that he is now best known, but such was not the case as recently as twenty years ago. Then it was his Spanish sketches that were most admired, and it was with these and with the engravings and lithographs made from them that he first gained true recognition in the 1830s. Wilkie noted in 1835 'a kind of enterprise among the publishers. Roberts and Lewis have been to the south of Spain . . . [and] have produced Annuals and Lithographic Works . . .' He was particularly impressed by the folio-size lithographs. He thought them 'extremely well executed' and remarked that the artists were 'trying to get the impressions coloured. I expect, indeed, that coloured prints will come again into fashion.'[24] The hand-coloured sets cost ten guineas, as opposed to four guineas uncoloured. But they looked remarkably like the original drawings, as was the intention, through touches of blue, scarlet and emerald bodycolour in addition to the more sobre background washes. The highlights in white bodycolour on the original drawings were facsimiled in the actual printing of the lithographs by letting the white paper (sometimes embossed) stand out against the printed, toned background. Roberts actively supported the use of white bodycolour, which was still a controversial practice in the 1830s and followed the innovations of Richard Parkes Bonington, whose reputation had continued to grow and whose influence was felt long after his premature death in 1828. The artist J. C. Horsley recalled a heated argument in which Roberts and Harding 'were supporting feebly the *convenience* of the vulgarising material', while Turner and Linnell opposed its use. As for the new artificial ultramarine Roberts 'seemed hardly able to find words strong enough to express how valuable an acquisition he considered its production to be to artists'.[25]

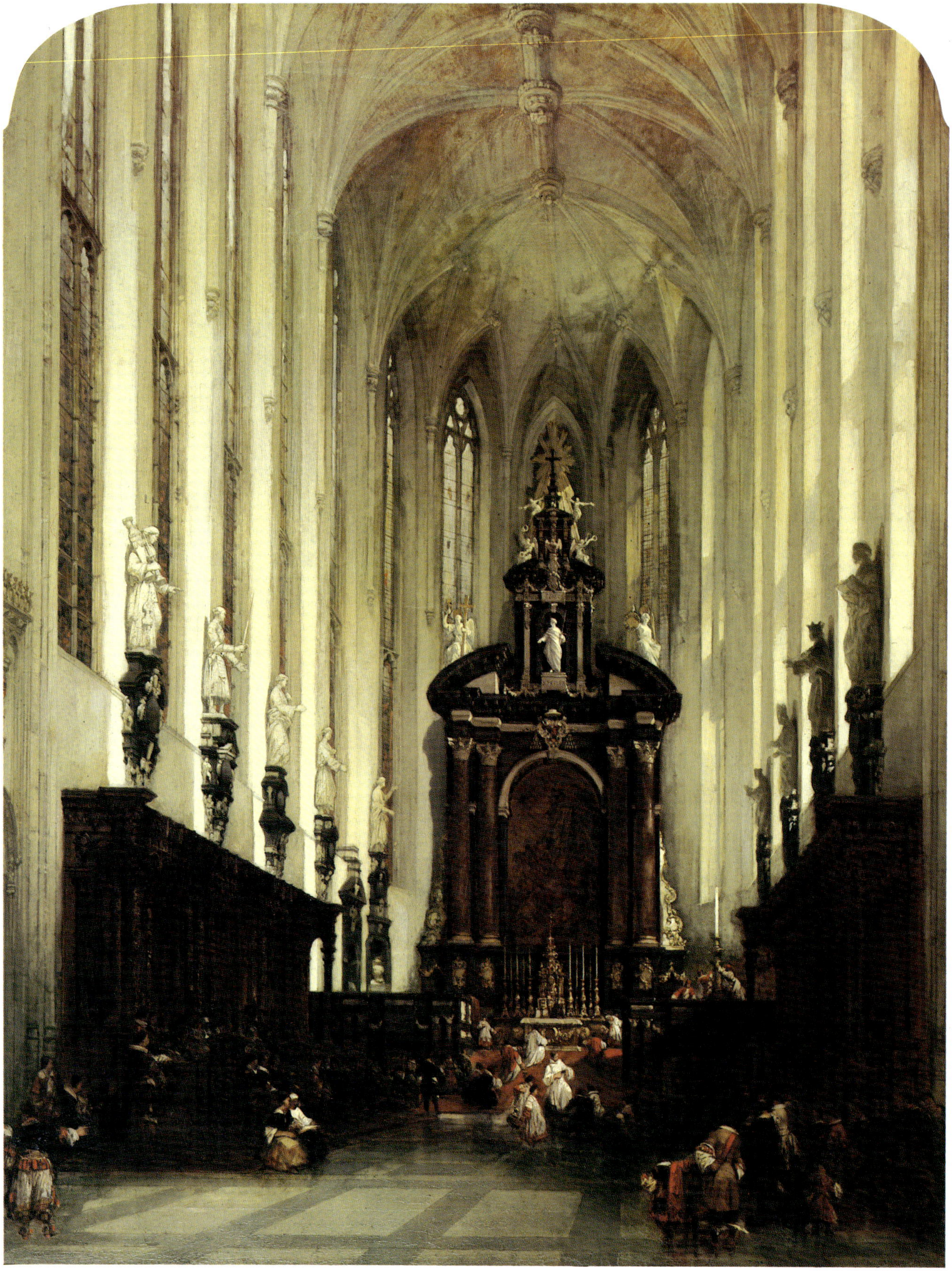

53. *Collegiate Church of St. Paul, Antwerp*, 1848, Tate Gallery, London. Cat.70.

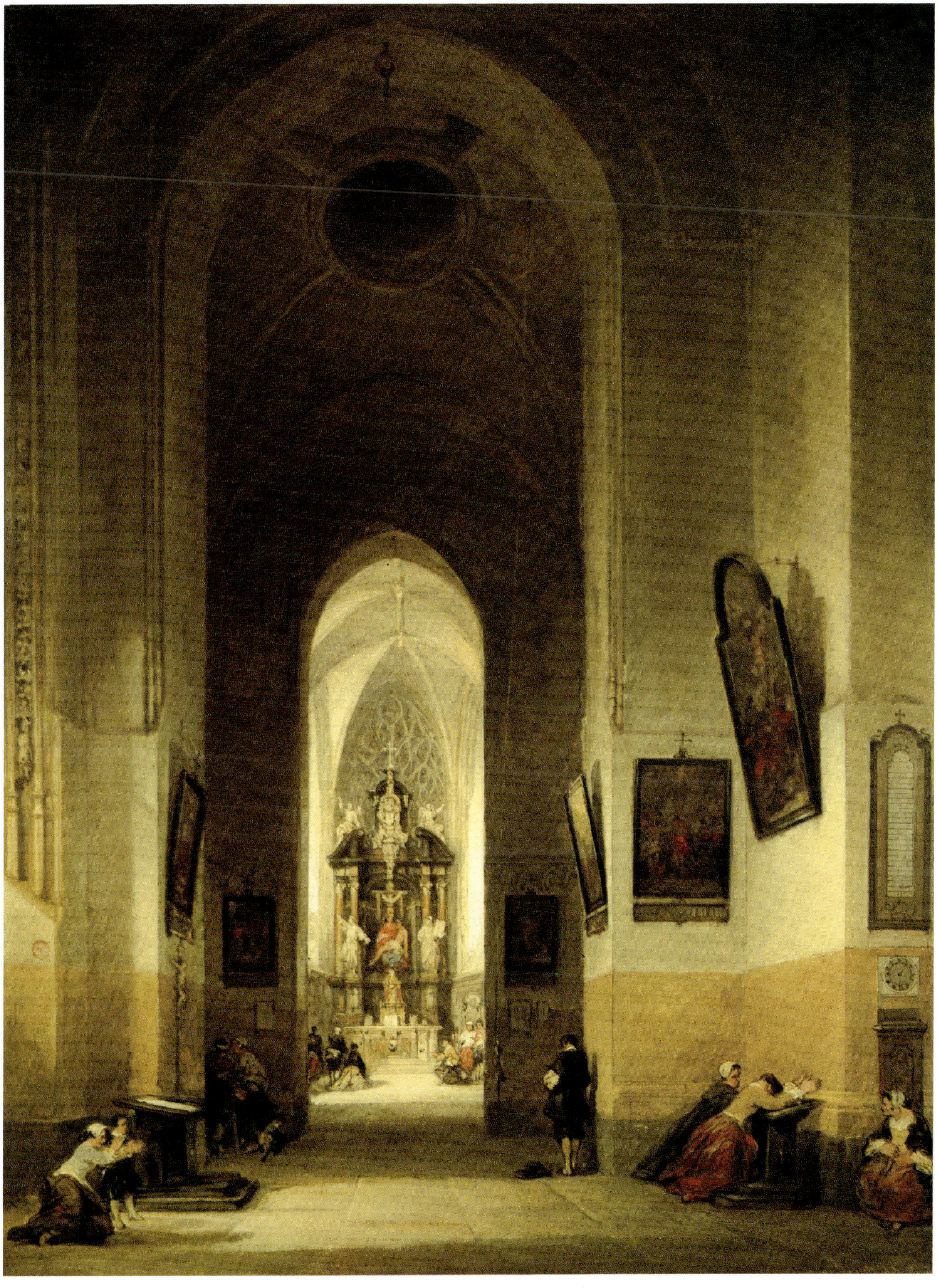

54. *Chapel in the Cathedral of Notre Dame, Bruges*, 1862, The Earl of Shelburne. Cat.71.

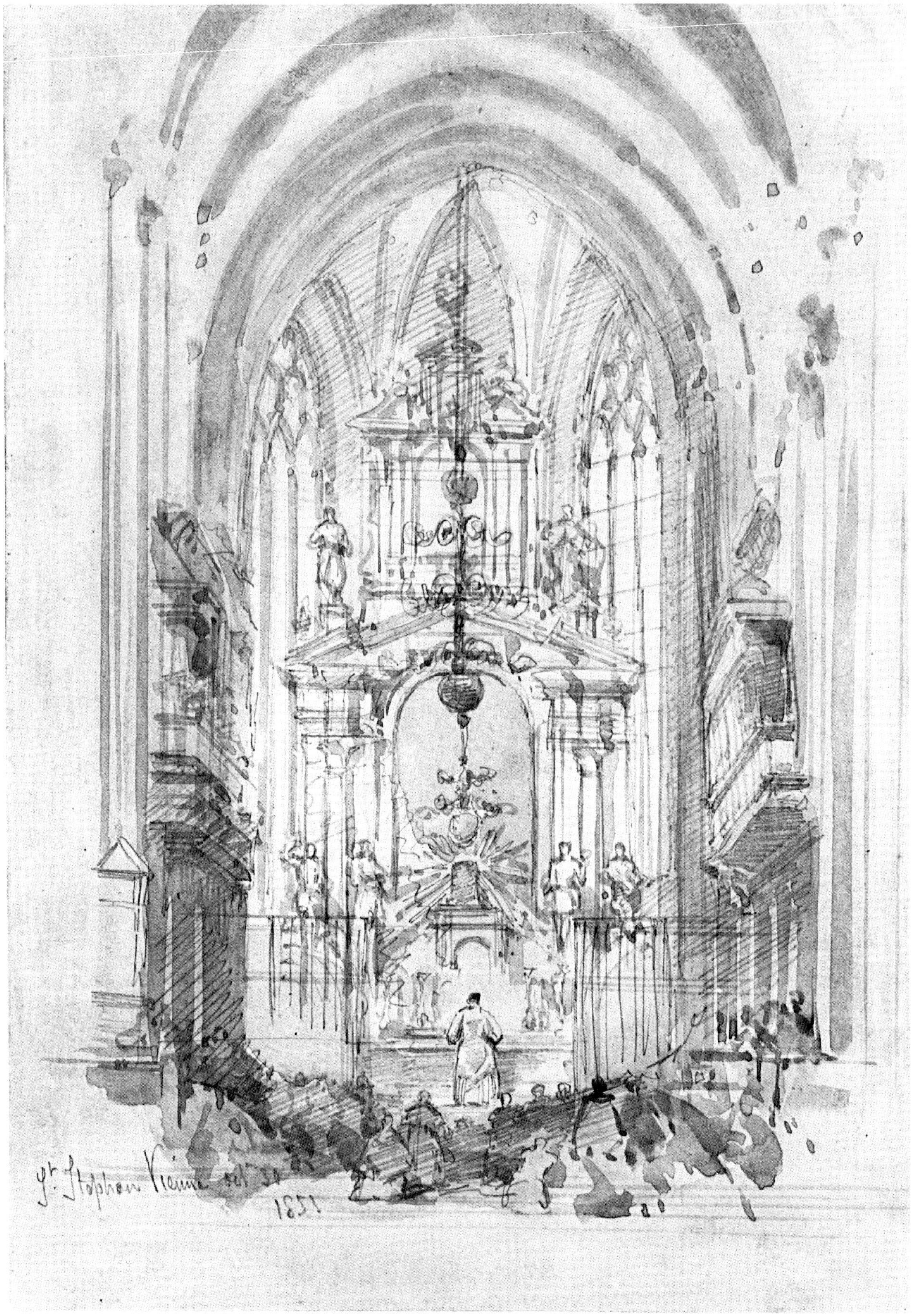

55. *St. Stephen's Cathedral, Vienna*, 1851, Private collection. Cat.203.

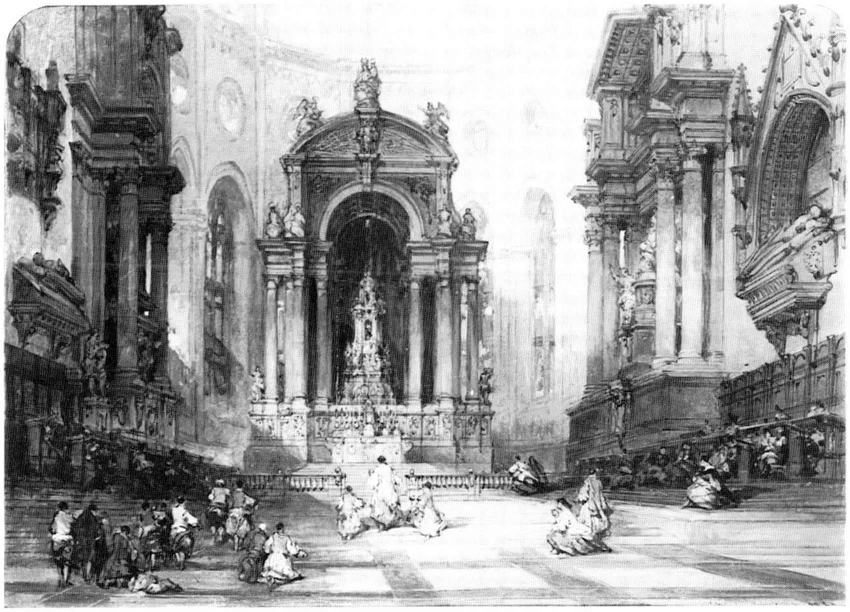

56. *SS Giovanni e Paolo, Venice,* 1861, Guildhall Art Gallery, City of London. Cat.198.

Among the admirers of Roberts's Spanish sketches was John Sell Cotman. He was invited by Roberts to see them in January 1834 when he, Roberts and Lewis were attending one of London's popular artists' conversaziones. Several hundred of Lewis's Spanish sketches were on display, and they together with Roberts's sketches deeply affected Cotman.[26]

Roberts and Lewis were both members of the major conversazione: the Artists' and Amateurs' Conversazione (established in 1828), and the Graphic Society (established in 1833). Their activities were recorded in the press, and works by Roberts which are mentioned as being shown at meetings included a volume of his Normandy watercolours lent by Lord Wharncliffe, a view of the old palace at Heidelberg, and Spanish sketches. Works by Turner and Bonington were special favourites, and other admired loans included Harding's Italian studies for the *Landscape Annual,* and Owen Jones's elaborate drawings of the Alhambra. Publishers such as Hodgson and Graves, Fuller, and Heath found these meetings of artists and collectors good venues for advertising the next season's illustrated volumes.

The success of Roberts's lithographs of Spain greatly surprised the artist himself, twelve hundred sets being sold in a space of only two months. He had spent seven months on their production because he was not satisfied with the way his drawings had been copied on to the lithographic stones by other artists. 'I may say', he wrote in his *Record Book,* 'without anything like egotism that whatever merit the work has it is in great measure owing to my having entirely gone over the drawings again myself and in many of them, the shading excepted, intirely erasing the Old and substituting new.'[27]

The Spanish lithographs were widely admired. A review of books on Spain in 1846 made it clear that even Spanish artists owed a debt to Roberts. 'One of the best modern painters of Madrid', G. Pérez Villa-Amil, was considered 'an imitator, at a respectful distance, of David Roberts, whose charming landscapes and architecture have long been to his continental colleagues at once a model and a stumbling-block'.[28] That same year Baudelaire referred to Roberts in his Salon review, in connection with an exhibit by Villa-Amil 'less fine in tone, but . . . firmer in colour than the pictures of the same type for which M. Roberts has a liking'.[29]

Thus, as the audience for art increased rapidly during the 1830s, artists responded by actively seeking new subjects, styles and methods. Exhibition reviews became more general, and dealers and publishers were quick to see the opportunities in the purchasing power of the growing middle classes. Roberts's work and approach were ideally suited to this new climate of enterprise, enabling him to join the ranks of 'talents of the highest class' in Britain.

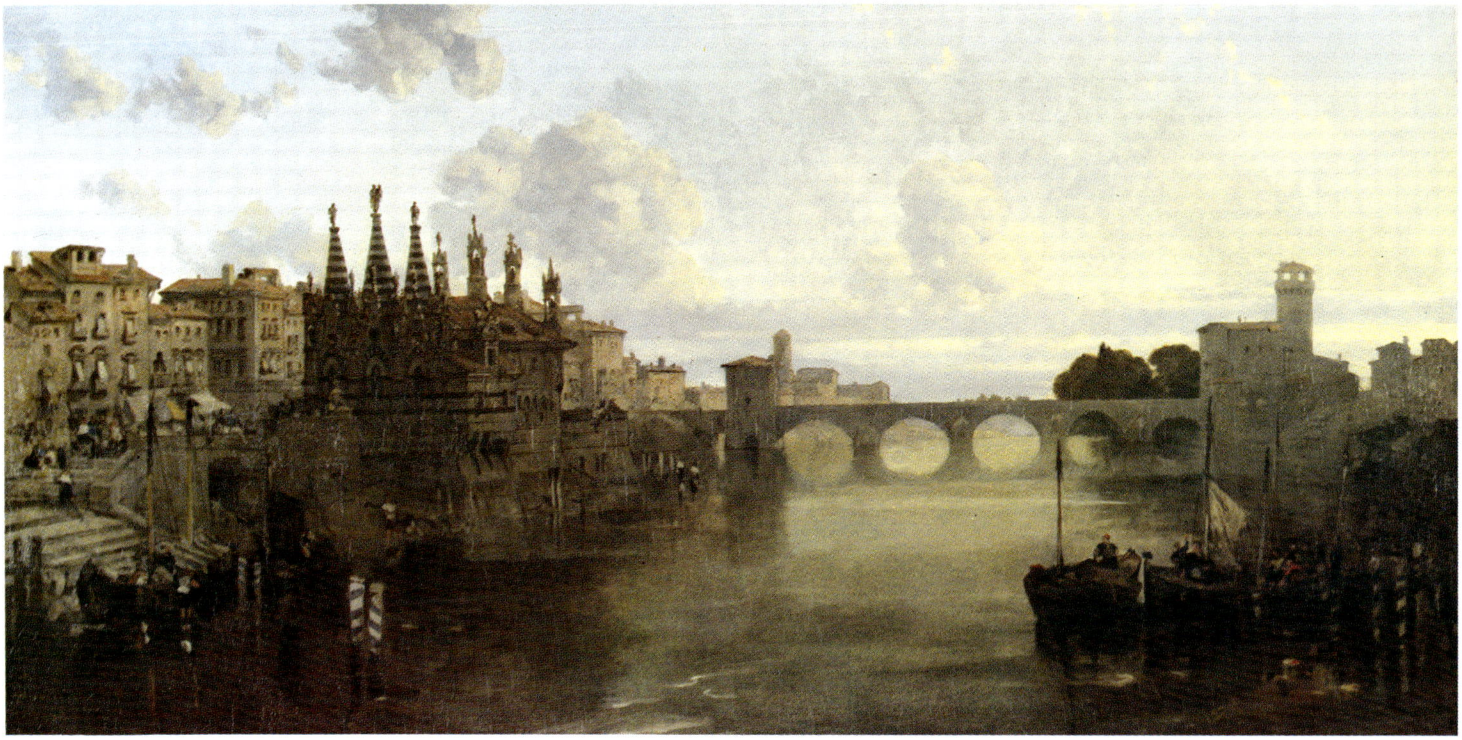

57. *Santa Maria della Spina, Pisa,* 1855–6, Private collection. Cat.185.

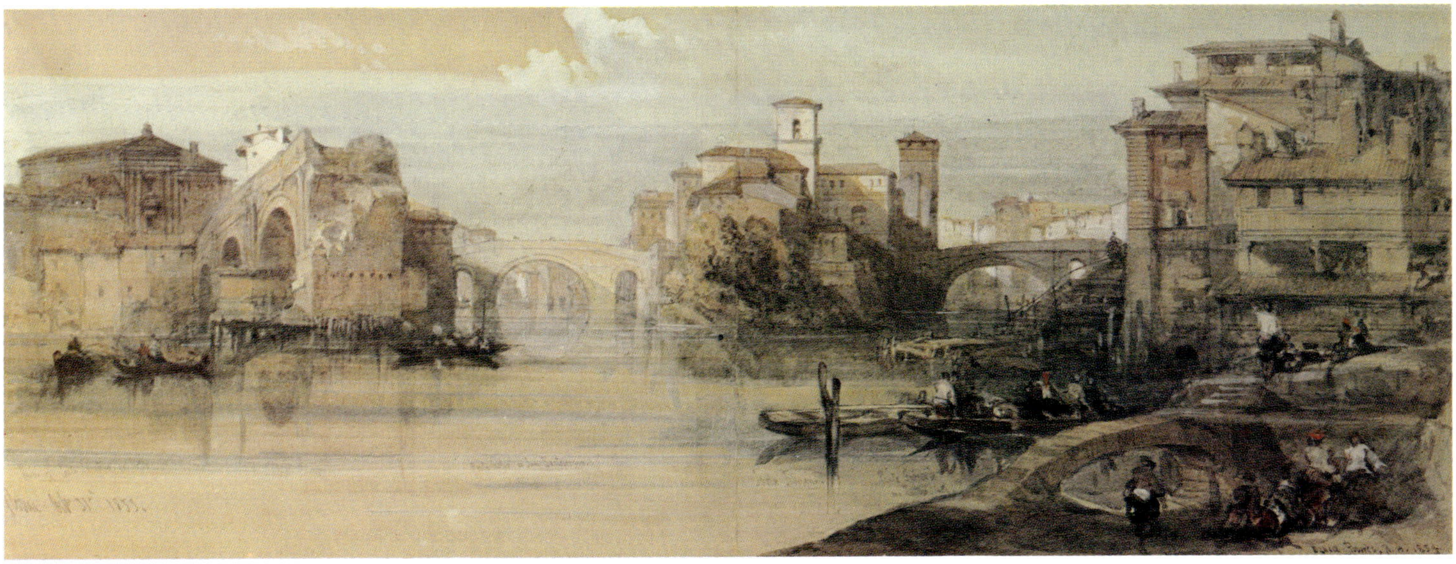

58. *Ruins of the Ponte Rotto, Rome*, 1853, Cecil Higgins Art Gallery, Bedford. Cat.195.

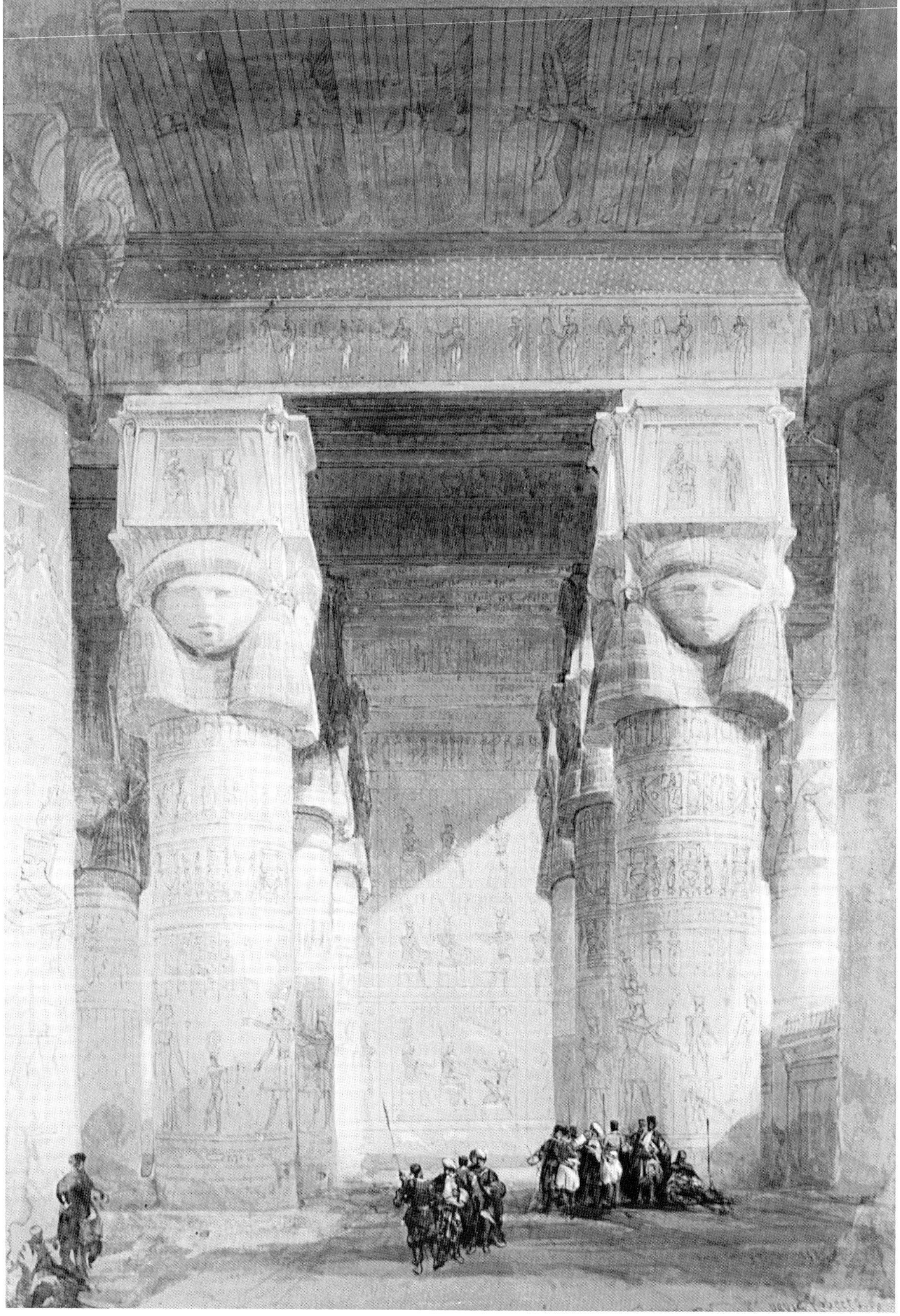

59. *Dendera*, 1848, Aberdeen Art Gallery and Museums. Cat.130.

Roberts's Pictures of the Near East

'One of the richest folios that ever left the East'

BRIONY LLEWELLYN

David Roberts's visit to the Near East in 1838–9 was, as his friend and biographer James Ballantine recognized, the 'great central episode of his artistic life'; it was the fulfilment of 'the dream of his life from boyhood'.[1] According to the 'Notice of Mr. Roberts's Journey in the East' which prefaced the great sequence of lithographs from his views, 'To visit the Holy Land and make drawings of the scenes of sacred history and the antiquities of Egypt, had been, long before this journey was undertaken by Mr. Roberts, the brightest of his anticipations as an artist.'[2]

In 1842, three years after Roberts's return from the East, a dinner was held in his honour in Edinburgh at which Lord Cockburn gave a eulogistic address. Describing the achievements of the artist's Near Eastern journey he said, 'He explored that patriarchal land; he searched its inmost recesses, and returned to his native country laden with the richest treasures, after having completed the finest pilgrimage of art which has ever perhaps been performed by a single man.'[3]

Roberts returned from the East with 272 sketches, a panorama of Cairo and three full sketchbooks, knowing that he had materials that 'will serve me for the rest of my life'.[4] Over the next decade he made 'a serries of intire new drawings',[5] probably for each of the 247 lithographs executed by Louis Haghe for *The Holy Land, Syria, Idumea, Arabia, Egypt & Nubia*, published between 1842 and 1849 (Cat.211). He painted more oils of the East than of any other region he visited. Ballantine records fifty-five, most of which were painted during the 1840s but the last in 1862, only two years before his death.[6] Thirty-one of these were exhibited at the Royal Academy. Further oil paintings, sketches and commissioned watercolours are also known.

During the 1830s Roberts had been acclaimed as a painter of European topographical and architectural views, but in 1841 a critic wrote: 'High as the reputation of this artist has stood, it seems to rise upon the public with every new opportunity, and, indeed, to force the public mind to rise with it. We never had such elevating illustrations of the Holy Land, and its contemporaneous Egypt, as have now been made familiar by his splended talents.'[7] That year Roberts was elected a full Royal Academician. During the 1840s and early 1850s his eastern oil paintings, exhibited at the Royal Academy, British Institution and elsewhere, received accolades from nearly all the art journals and newspapers. Many of these paintings had been commissioned, and he had few difficulties selling others. His work was bought by aristocrats, including Lord Francis Egerton, but mainly by collectors such as Elhanan Bicknell, John Sheepshanks and Joseph Arden (see p. 89). He was able to command high prices for his

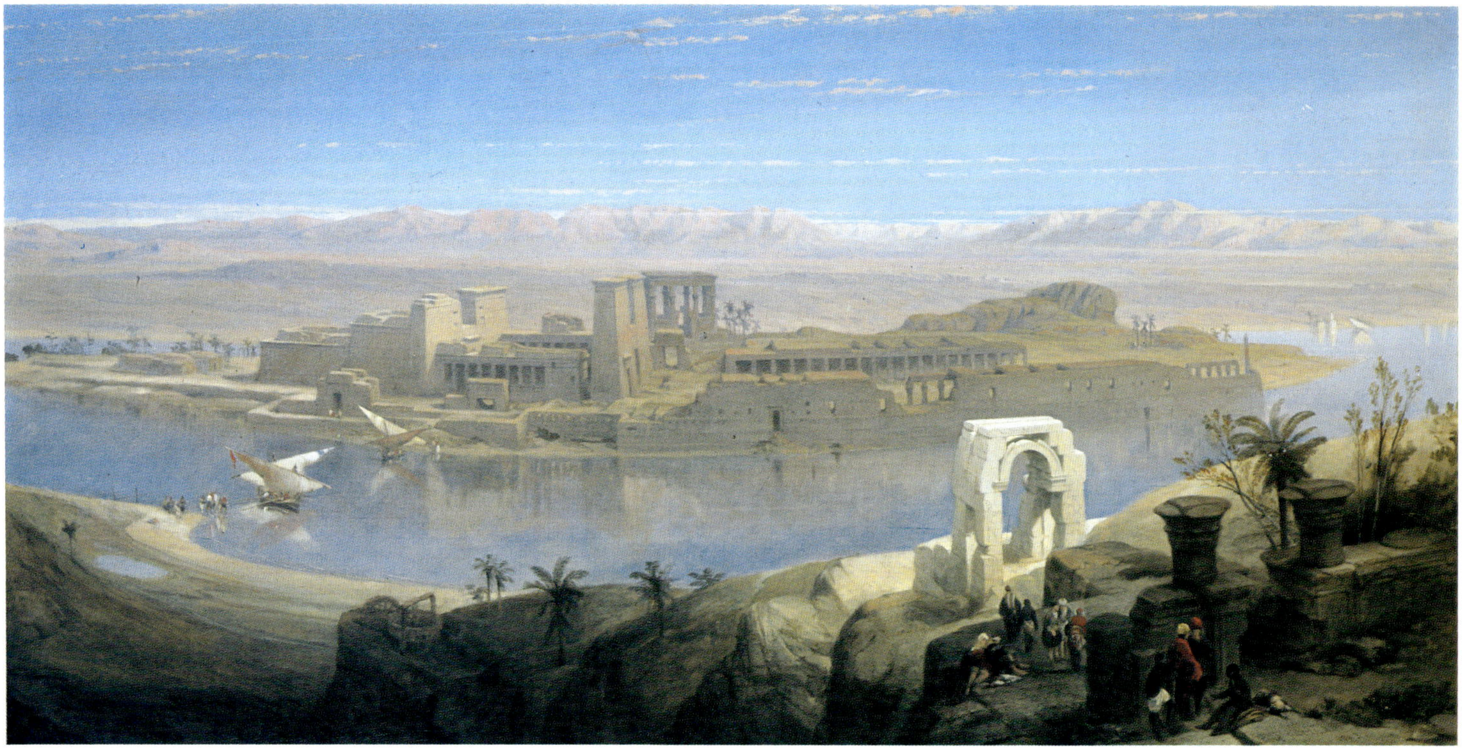

60. *Island of Philae, Nubia,* 1843, Private collection. Cat.121.

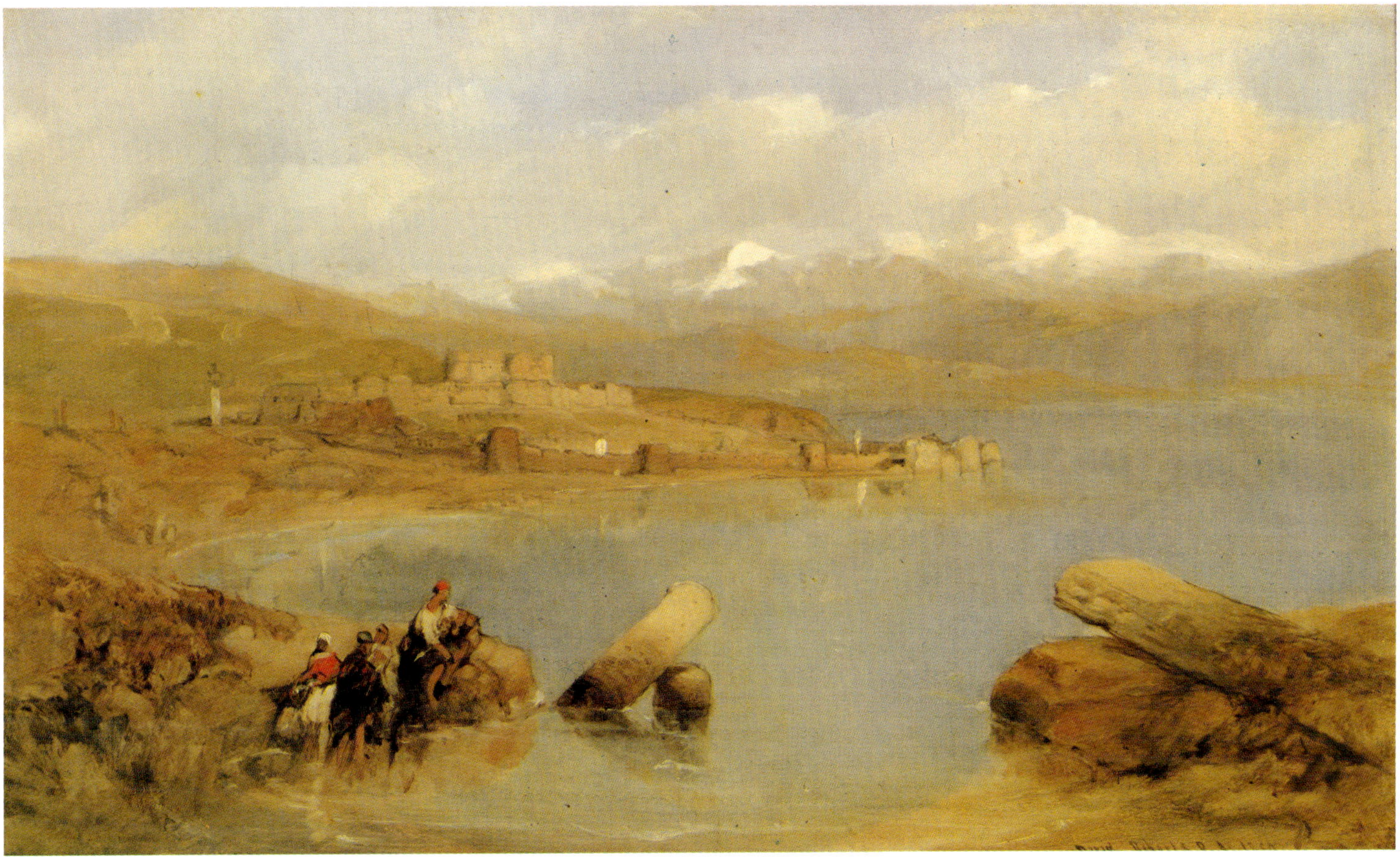

61. *The Sea of Galilee,* 1850, Private collection. Cat.172.

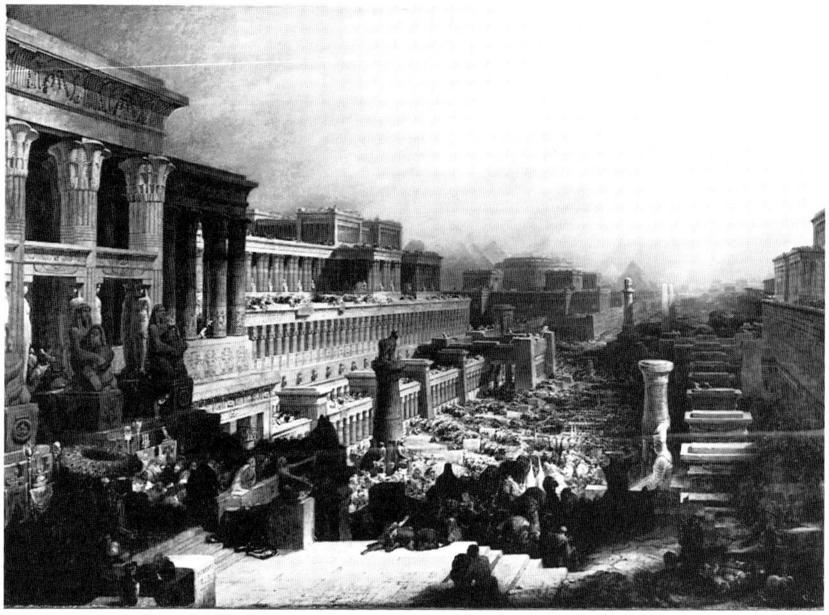

62. *The Israelites Leaving Egypt*, 1829, Birmingham City Museum and Art Gallery. Cat. 114.

paintings, and was among the artists of national repute whose works were bought and sold by leading dealers such as Ernest Gambart.

The success of Roberts's eastern oils was matched by that of the series of lithographs after his drawings, *The Holy Land and Egypt*. This was described as 'a noble and beautiful work . . . foremost of the productions of the age and country', and later as 'one of the most valuable publications of our day—vividly illustrating our readings in history, sacred as well as profane'.[8] One of the reasons for its popularity was this portrayal of places associated with western history, both biblical and classical. The biblical theme is expanded in one of the many reviews pasted into Roberts's *Record Book* (Cat.220): 'It has been the aim of Mr Roberts to portray every object associated with Scripture—to bring vividly before us every architectural remain, and every feature of natural scenery which can give reality to the incidents of sacred writings, or impress us with deeper conviction of their truth, and elevate our reverential feelings.'[9]

Many Victorians regarded the Near East primarily as the setting for the Bible. Its monuments, landscape and people were viewed in relation to biblical events and characters. There, solid, tangible evidence of the roots of Christianity could be found. Thus Roberts, in common with many other travellers at the time, was constantly seeing analogies with Bible stories. Even an event as fundamentally Islamic as the departure of the *Mahmal* from Cairo 'brought vividly before the mind the passage of the Israelites through the wilderness with the Ark borne in the Centre'.[10]

During the 1830s the number of people able to visit these Bible lands for themselves was increasing, as travel became easier through the development of rail and steam communications. In addition, the consolidation and extension of the authority of Muhammad Ali, Pasha of Egypt, and, in this decade, *de facto* overlord of Syria, created safer conditions for tourists. The decade also saw a proliferation of travel books, and those which described and illustrated places in the Holy Land were extremely popular. *Landscape Illustrations of the Bible* (1836) contained etchings by the Finden brothers from travellers' on-the-spot sketches redrawn in London by professional artists, including Turner, Stanfield, Harding and Roberts. Another work, J. Carne's *Syria, The Holy Land, Asia Minor, &c.* (1836–8), was published by Fisher and Sons, who commissioned two well-established topographical draughtsmen, William Bartlett and Thomas Allom, to visit the area and make their own sketches for reproduction. In 1838 the American scholar Dr Edward Robinson undertook a more scientific investigation of biblical sites, and published his *Biblical Researches in Palestine, Mount Sinai and Arabia Petraea* in 1841.

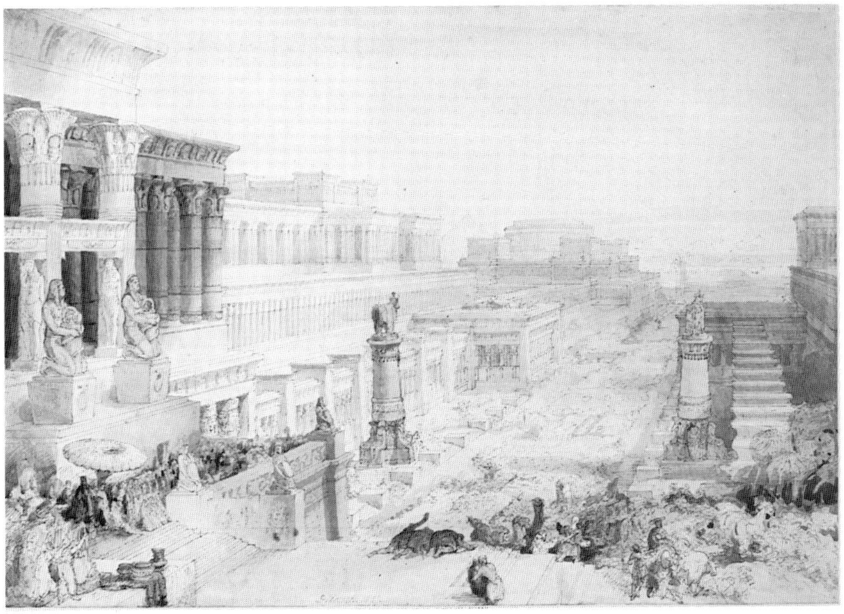

63. *Study for 'The Israelites Leaving Egypt'*, 1827, British Museum, London. Cat.113.

Encouraged by the favourable reception of Roberts's Jerusalem views, his publisher, Francis Graham Moon, brought out the rest of his eastern subjects over the next seven years. Not all of the views had biblical associations, as Roberts had also visited places of antiquarian interest, notably the ancient Egyptian tombs and temples along the Nile. These, too, had been the focus of intense European interest, especially since Napoleon's invasion of Egypt in 1798. The most important result of the French campaign in this context was the work of a group of *savants*, whose study of all aspects of ancient and modern Egyptian culture was eventually published between 1809 and 1829 as the *Description de l'Egypte*. Earlier, the artist and scholar Baron Vivant Denon had published his own observations in *Voyage dans la Basse et la Haute Egypte* (1802); this was translated subsequently into English and was very influential. In the 1810s, twenties and thirties, many other Europeans had excavated and studied the Egyptian ruins, notably Belzoni, Champollion and Wilkinson.[11]

Roberts was familiar with all these publications but he was determined to use his own artistic talents to surpass them. He was also well aware of the potential commercial value of images of Egyptian temples, Islamic mosques, and the ruins and landscape of the Holy Land: together, his sketches of them would make 'one of the richest folios that ever left the East'.[12] However romantic his response to the magnificent sights of the East, it was based on the sound practical knowledge that his journey would bring him fame and fortune, for no artist of his calibre had previously attempted such an ambitious topographical project.

On his Nile voyage Roberts drew every temple then known between Abu Simbel and Dendara, and when he returned to Cairo was convinced that his portfolio was 'the most interesting that has ever left the country', more likely to do justice to the ruins than anything before.[13] Some days earlier he had written in his *Journal*: 'I am the first Artist at least from England that has yet been here and there is much in this. The French work I now find conveys no idea of these splendid remains. We shall see what impression they make in England. Subjects of another class of equal interest remain yet in Cairo.'[14]

Roberts now devoted his attention to Cairo's architecture and people, and obtained permission to sketch inside the mosques provided he wore Turkish dress and did not use hog's-hair brushes. He was not strictly accurate in his claim to be the first English artist in Egypt, but he was the first professional artist of Academic status (he was made an Associate of the Royal Academy in 1839) to visit the country independently of a patron or expedition. He seems also to have been unaware that his visit coincided with that of the young Bristol artist, William James

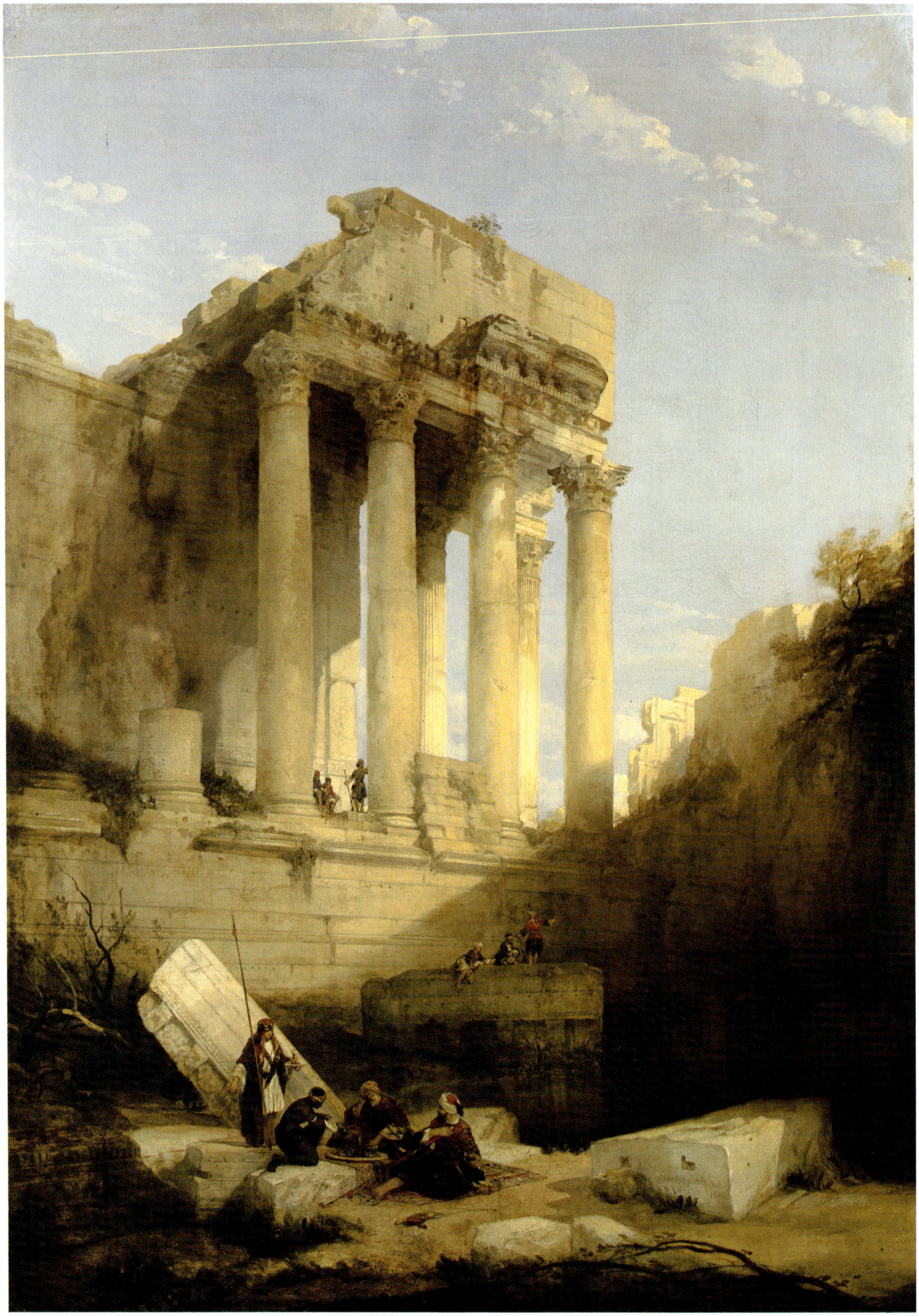

64. *Portico of the Great Temple at Baalbec*, 1840, Walker Art Gallery, Liverpool. Cat.177.

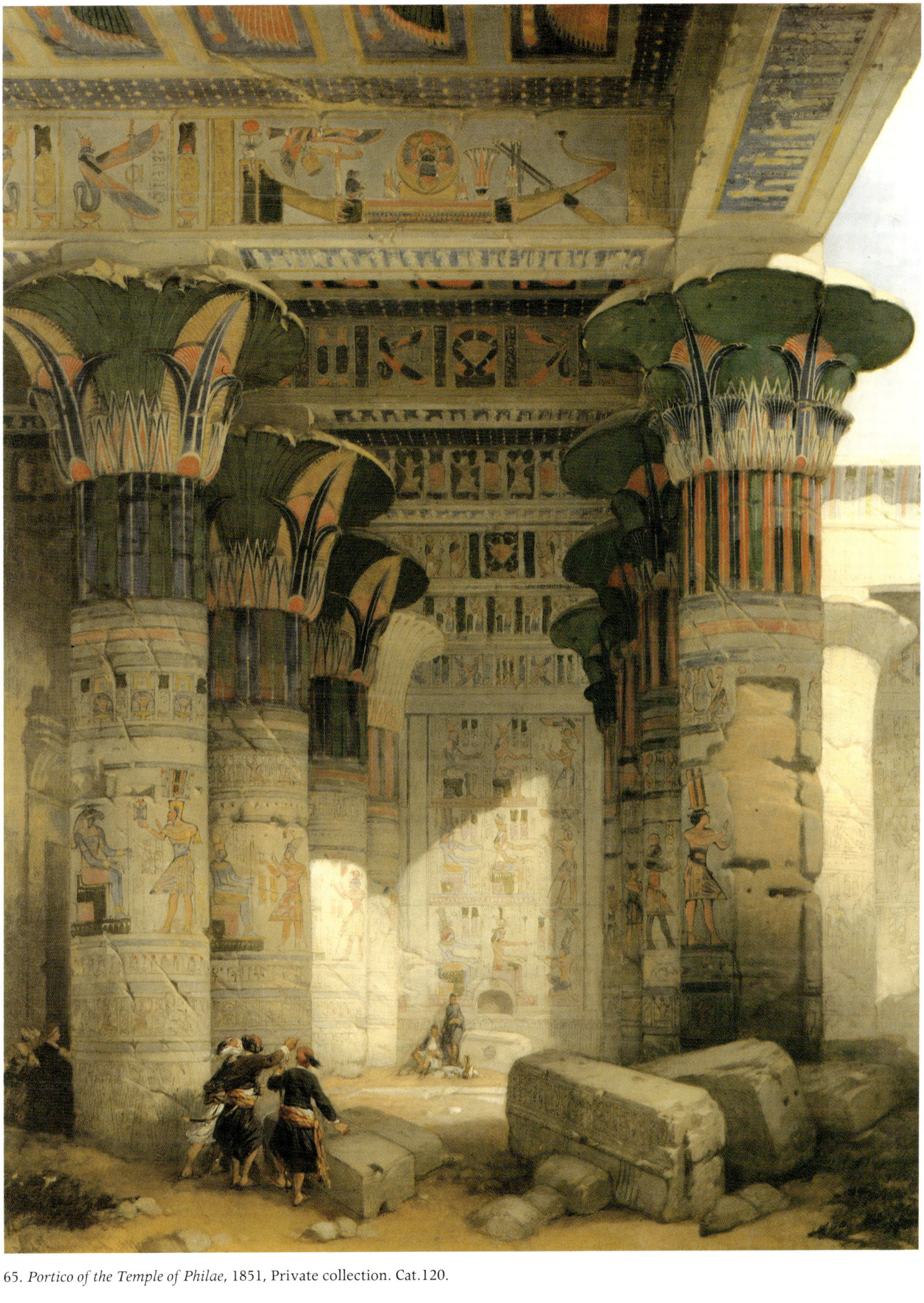

65. *Portico of the Temple of Philae*, 1851, Private collection. Cat.120.

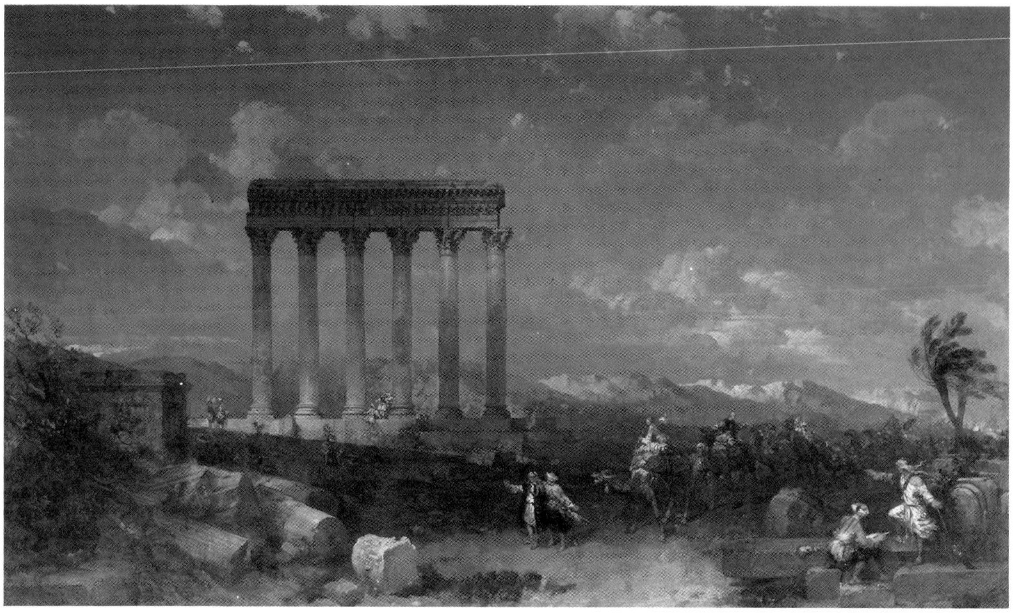

66. *Surprise of the Caravan, Baalbec*, 1847, The Garrick Club, London.

Müller. Müller drew the Nile temples as far as Luxor, and the streets and bazaars of Cairo, but, unlike Roberts, found the mosques 'a closed sanctum'.[15]

The discovery of new places to paint was, as Roberts had found with the success of his Spanish pictures, vital to topographical artists, who could not rely on the resources of their imagination for fresh subject-matter. At the end of his long and strenuous tour of the East, he wrote, 'I leave for England with a series of sketches that at all events carry novelty with them.'[16] Within a decade, all his hopes of success had been justified. Images of the Near East had been seen before but never on such a scale. No publication before *The Holy Land and Egypt* had presented so comprehensive a series of views of the monuments, landscape and people of the Near East. Small black and white etchings or engravings from drawings by Bartlett and others were one thing; large coloured lithographs 'which unite to their correctness a higher sense of the picturesque and the feeling of the painter'[17] were quite another. More recently, the series has been called 'one of the most important and elaborate ventures of nineteenth-century publishing, and . . . the apotheosis of the tinted lithograph'.[18]

The paintings of ancient pagan ruins and early Christian churches in the East, which Roberts exhibited from 1840 onwards, were also 'comparatively new to art'.[19] Never before had these subjects received such skilful treatment by an artist who had observed them at first hand. As the critic of the *Literary Gazette* wrote: 'We had fed our expectations with something extraordinary from the pencil of this truly able and adventurous artist, and we have not been disappointed. Different in form, colour, and effect, from any thing the English eye has been accustomed to contemplate, this version of past ages is calculated at once to excite our admiration and to fix our attention.'[20] In fact, Müller had begun to exhibit and receive critical acclaim for similar subjects at that time, and had it not been for his early death in 1845 might have rivalled Roberts's fame.

The paintings of Roberts and Müller represent a change in attitude from the fantastical treatment of oriental ruins popular in the 1820s and 1830s. This was seen at its most splendid in the work of John Martin but several other artists, including Roberts and Müller, experimented with oriental *capriccios*. In 1827–9 Roberts had painted *The Israelites Leaving Egypt* (Plate 62) in a Martinesque manner, and had selected the subject 'more as a Vehicle, for introducing—That Grand allthough simple style of architecture, the Egyptian' than for its historical or biblical content.[21] His *Rising of the Nile*, engraved for *The Amulet* in 1832, was another opportunity for a fantastic display of Egyptian colonnades, pylons and obelisks. By the end of the 1830s tastes

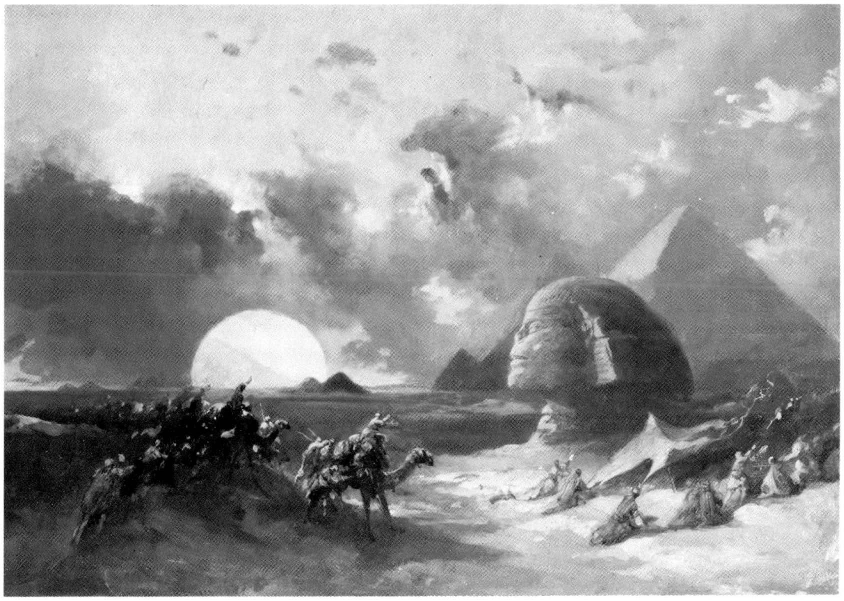

67. *The Simoon*, 1850, Private collection. Cat.134.

were changing, and when they visited Egypt in 1838–9 both Roberts and Müller deliberately rejected such frivolities and attempted a more realistic interpretation of the country's ruins.

Roberts's efforts to record his subjects faithfully were not without difficulties. Sometimes, as with the huge columns at Karnak or the 'stupendous rocks' at Petra, he felt his task to be impossible.[22] However, his experience with handling architectural subjects on a vast scale for stage scenery was invaluable, and in general he succeeded. At Karnak he wrote in his *Journal*, 'you must be under them [the columns] and look up and walk round them' to gain a true impression of their grandeur.[23] His low viewpoint in the watercolour of the Hypostyle Hall illustrates this, achieving an almost overwhelming sensation of huge columns soaring above the heads of the small figures below (Plate 80).

The demands of pictorial effect sometimes conflicted with those of topographical accuracy. Roberts often used artistic licence to achieve greater dramatic impact and to re-create the mood that the subject itself evoked. In doing so, he was able to create a truer impression of its visual and emotional impact on the spectator than even a camera with a wide-angle lens can achieve. The most common example of this is his exaggeration of the height and width of buildings, whether temples, mosques or churches, by altering proportions and reducing the scale of his figures. On occasions he filled in architectural details that had disappeared long before, as in the *Portico of the Temple of Dendera* (1841) where he added faces to the Hathor columns.[24] He also moved stones, and even repositioned the monuments themselves, as in several Baalbek views, or the Sphinx in *The Simoon* (Plate 67). This painting was criticized by William Holman Hunt as being untruthful, but praised by Charles Dickens, for whom it was painted, as 'a poetical conception'.[25]

Clearly Roberts was first and foremost a picture-maker working within the pictorial conventions of his time. The liberal sprinkling of the adjectives 'picturesque' and 'sublime' throughout his *Journal* of his eastern tour reveal how firmly rooted in tradition his pictorial vision was. The Sinai mountains, for example, 'allthough destitute of all vigitation whatever were picturesque in form' and 'nothing can exceed [the desert] in sublimity accompanied with a feeling of utter desolation'.[26] Not all his subjects could easily be moulded to conform to established conventions. At first, he experienced some difficulties in selling paintings of Egyptian temples:

> . . . for allthough treated with strictest attention to detail in the ellaborate sculpture

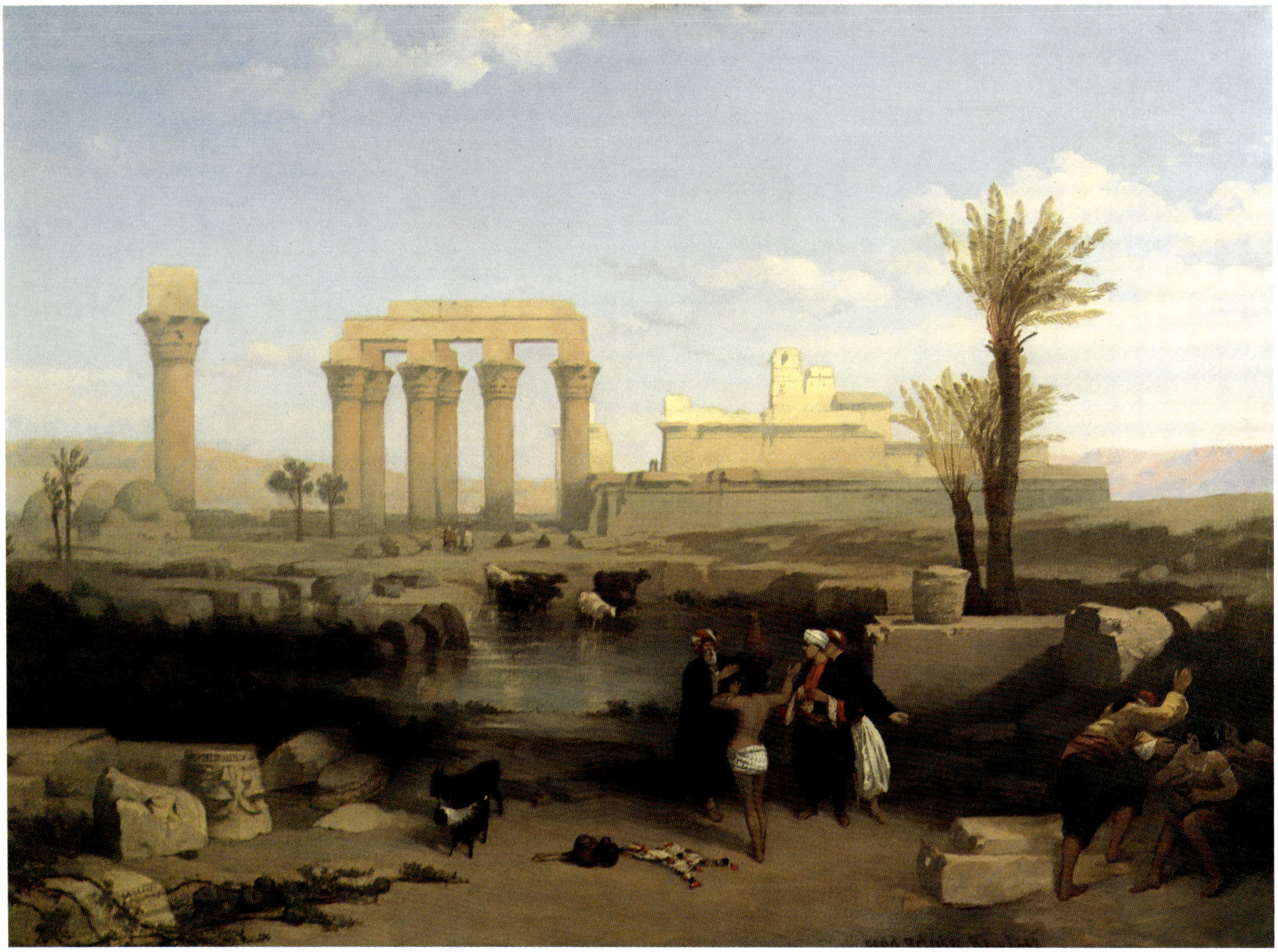

68. *Ruins of the Temple of Hermonthes, Upper Egypt*, 1848, Private collection. Cat.125.

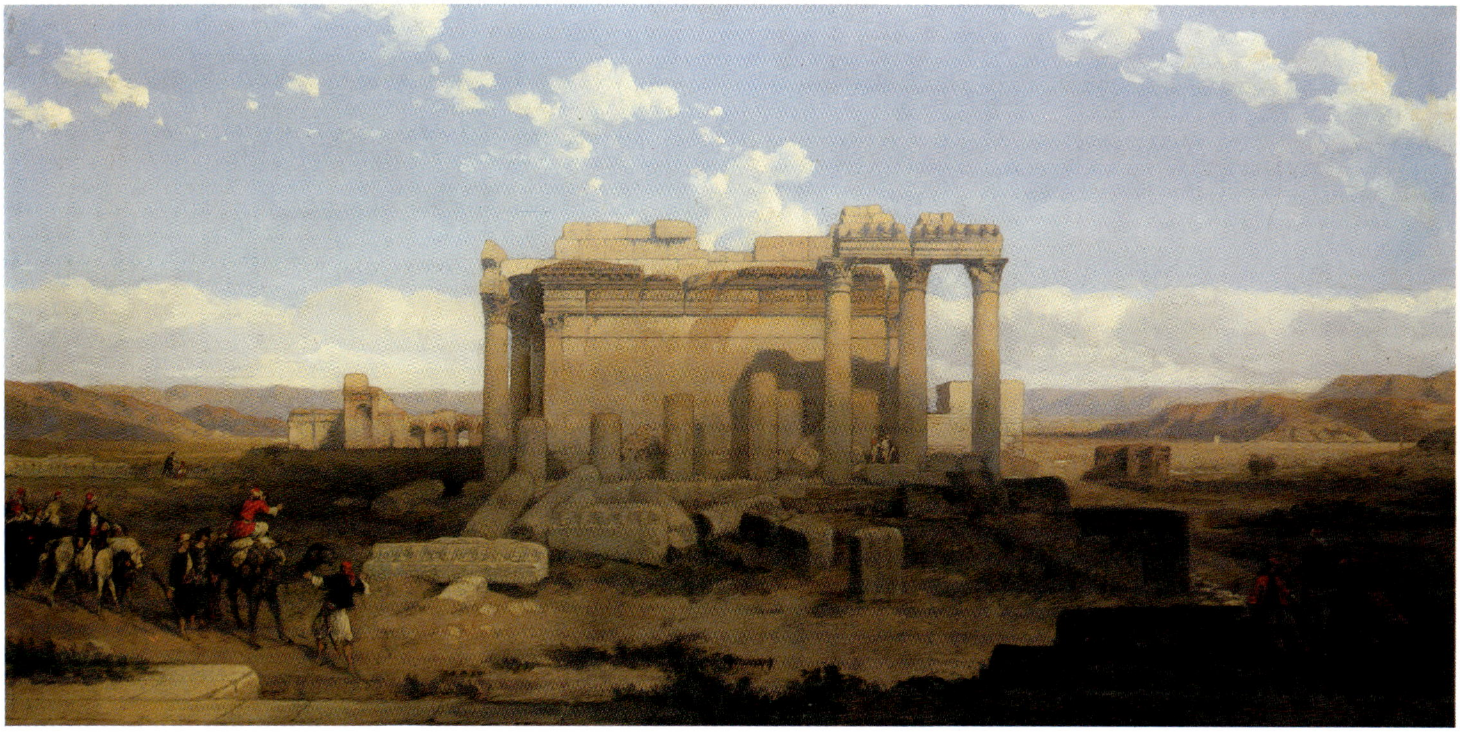

69. *The Ruins of the Smaller Temple at Baalbec*, 1850, Private collection. Cat.179.

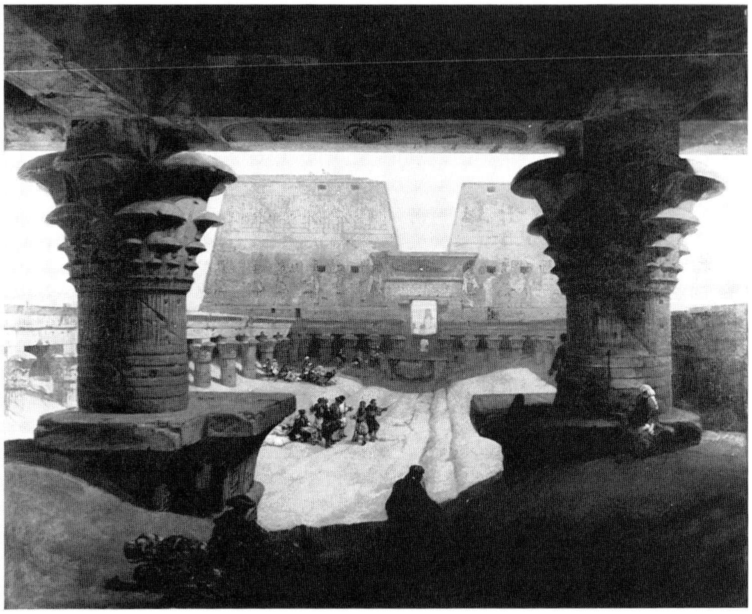

70. *Dromos, or Outer Court of the Great Temple at Edfou in Upper Egypt*, 1840, Family collection. Cat.124.

by which every part of it is overlaid, yet there is a tottal absence of that which constitutes the great charm of all other ruins, vegetation and picturesque foilage. Ponderious as are the dimensions of those glorious remains there wants something beside the deep blue of an Eastern Sky the arid granite rocks, and the white sand of the Desert—they strike the beholder with wonder, but not pleasure, an ivy mantled tower with a brawling burn conveys I rather think more pleasurable sensations than the Land of the Pharaohs with all its wonders.'[27]

He tackled this problem with a variety of pictorial devices, sometimes using unconventional variations of established formats. In his panoramic view of the island of Philae (Plate 60), he supplied foreground interest through the usual ruins and group of figures, but closed the composition by exaggerating a curve in the Nile, as if it were seen through a fish-eye lens. In his *Outer Court of the Great Temple of Edfou* (Plate 70) he used the unusual silhouette of the great columns to frame his view into the sunlit courtyard beyond. In *Ruins of the Great Temple of Karnak* (private collection) he balanced a group of figures in the right foreground against the water of the sacred lake on the left, to soften the starkness of the ruins in the background. Sometimes, as in *The Simoon*, he used colourful weather conditions to create striking effects. His methods were judged successful by at least one contemporary critic: 'We may remark of the pictures painted by this gentleman from scenery in Egypt and adjacent countries that they very often consist of subjects having only historical interest, and which very few other artists could invest with any pictorial beauty.'[28] His most successful compositions seem to be those which combine his sense of drama, derived from his experience as a stage scene-painter, with his considerable powers of observation, perfected when depicting the intricate tracery of Gothic and Moorish architecture. At times his use of conventional pictorial devices nowadays appears obtrusive, as in *Ruins of Hermonthes* (Plate 68), with its stiffly handled foreground ruins and figures, and the artificial introduction of cattle drinking at a pool in front of the central motif of the temple. Paradoxically, this painting was praised for its 'truth': 'Travellers in that country [Egypt] are always astonished with the minute truth of every detail and individuality in these paintings, before which the rest of the world stand admiring the splendour of their conceptions and execution.'[29]

This was precisely the kind of picture-making which drew stringent criticism from the fiery critic, John Ruskin. While applauding the 'fidelity of intention and honesty of system of

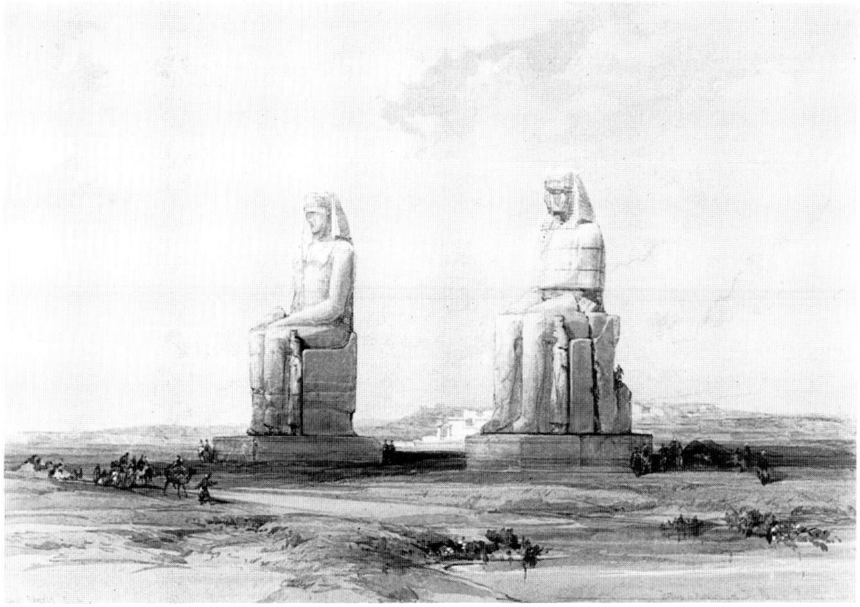

71. *Statues of Memnon in the Plain of Thebes*, Ingram Family Collection. Cat.128.

Roberts' he found too much similarity in the compositions of his Holy Land drawings and bitterly regretted that 'the accuracy and elegance of his work should not be aided by that genuineness of hue and effect which can only be given by the uncompromising effort to paint, not a fine picture, but an impressive and known verity'.[30]

Ruskin disliked Roberts's pictorial device of using figures for foreground colour: 'thus we have been encumbered with caftans, pipes, scimitars, and black hair, when all that we wanted was a lizard, or an ibis'.[31] Sometimes Roberts's figures do fail to harmonize with their surroundings, but Ruskin disregarded totally the reason for their inclusion—to add human interest and scale, and to give a further dimension to an otherwise austere landscape or architectural ruin. This was established topographical practice at the time, and Roberts's skilful employment of it was recognized by several other critics. According to the *Literary Gazette* in 1841, the pilgrims in the foreground of *Jerusalem, from the Mount of Olives* (Plate 75) 'animate the canvass in a singularly effective manner, and impart to it a picturesqueness of infinite variety and beauty'.[32] In 1846, the *Art-Union* noted in the foreground of *Grand Cairo* 'one of those characteristic Oriental groups which are seen nowhere but in the works of this artist'.[33]

Roberts admitted readily that figure painting was not his strong point. Often, while watching groups of Arabs in the Near East, he had regretted the absence of his friend David Wilkie. Only a year after Roberts's return to England, Wilkie embarked on his own tour, purposely to find figural subjects for biblical paintings. Roberts did not study the people of the Near East as thoroughly as did two other contemporaries, John Frederick Lewis and William Holman Hunt. Nevertheless, he showed a genuine interest in them which is often overlooked. It is likely that each of the three sketchbooks (most untraced, but see Cat.181) to which he referred at the end of his tour contained studies for the caravans, encampments, parleys and other figure groups which enliven most of the oriental scenes. A few of the plates in *The Holy Land and Egypt* are almost entirely figure subjects. He was as much astonished by the 'picturesque population' of Cairo as by its streets and mosques, and as enchanted by Bedouins gathered round camp-fires as by the desert and mountains of Sinai.

At the same time, Roberts was sickened and horrified by the squalor and human misery that he witnessed, especially in Cairo and Jerusalem. He believed that the cause of much of this degradation was Islam, which he considered 'a religion of barbarism'.[34] But these were the natural reactions of a compassionate man and a pious Presbyterian, and they do not intrude into his pictures. He may have had little understanding of, or sympathy with the Muslim way of life

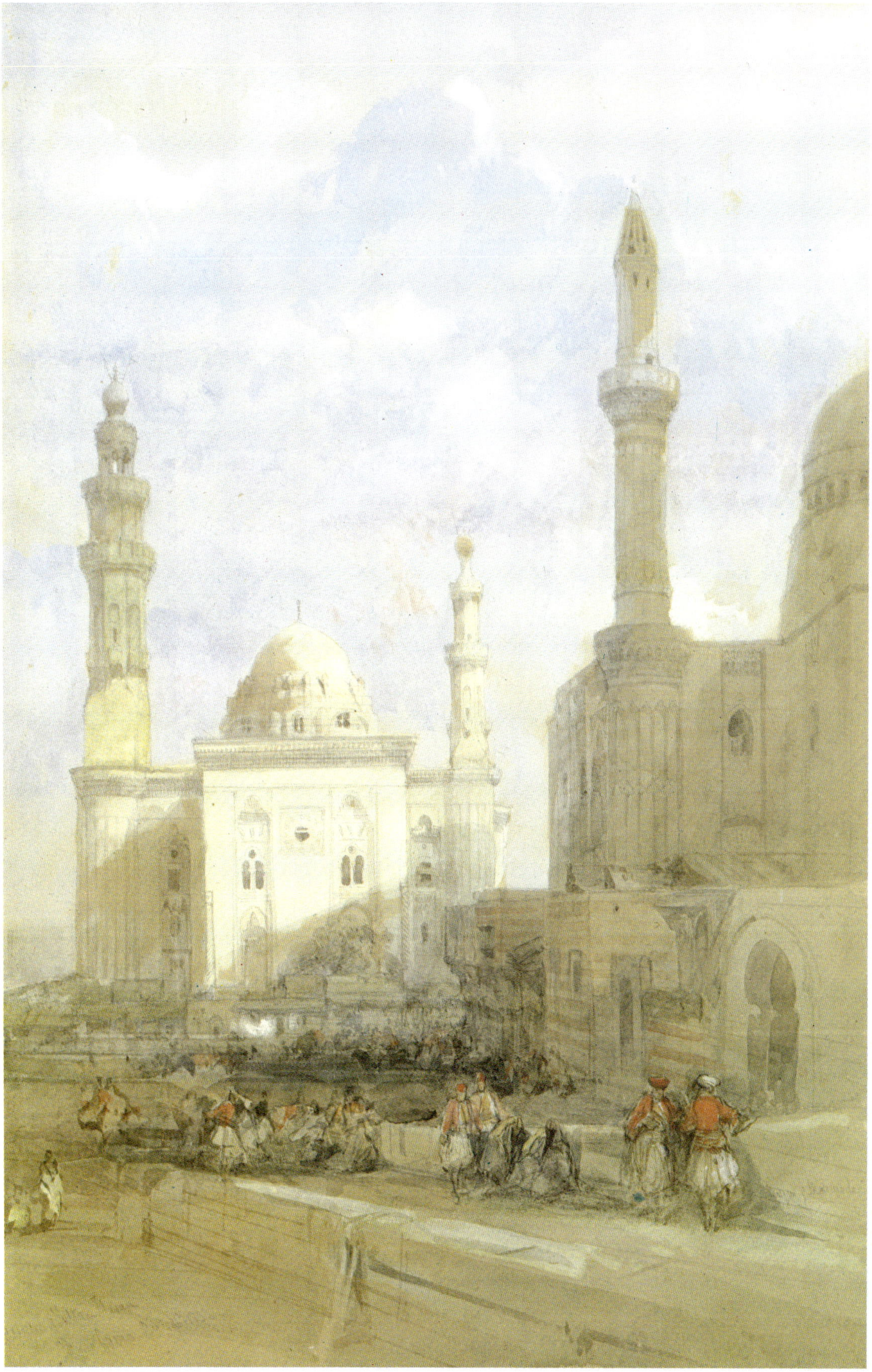

72. *Mosque of Sultan Hassan, Cairo*, 1838, The Provost and Fellows of Eton College. Cat.136.

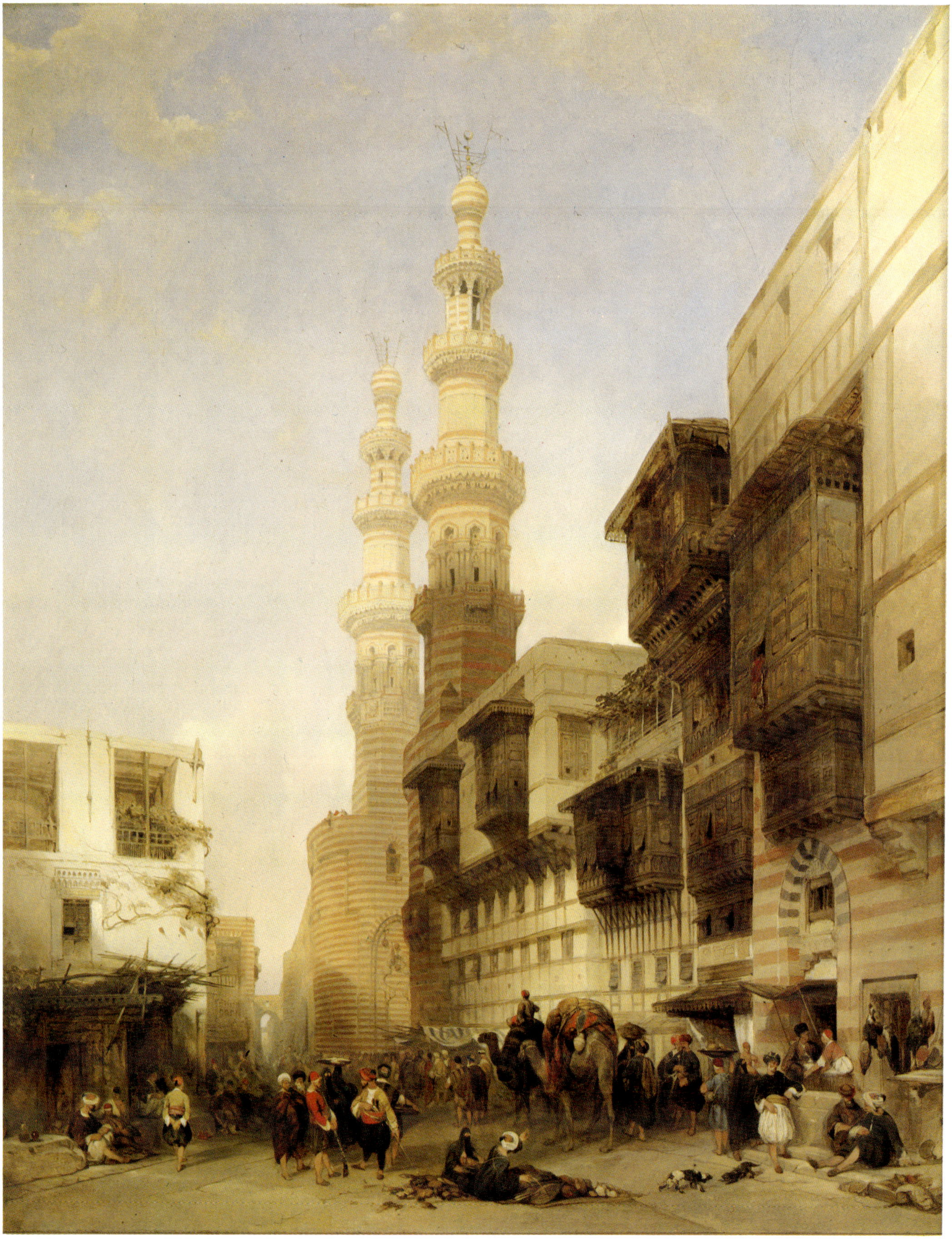

73. *Gate of Metwaley, Cairo*, 1843, Victoria and Albert Museum, London. Cat.146.

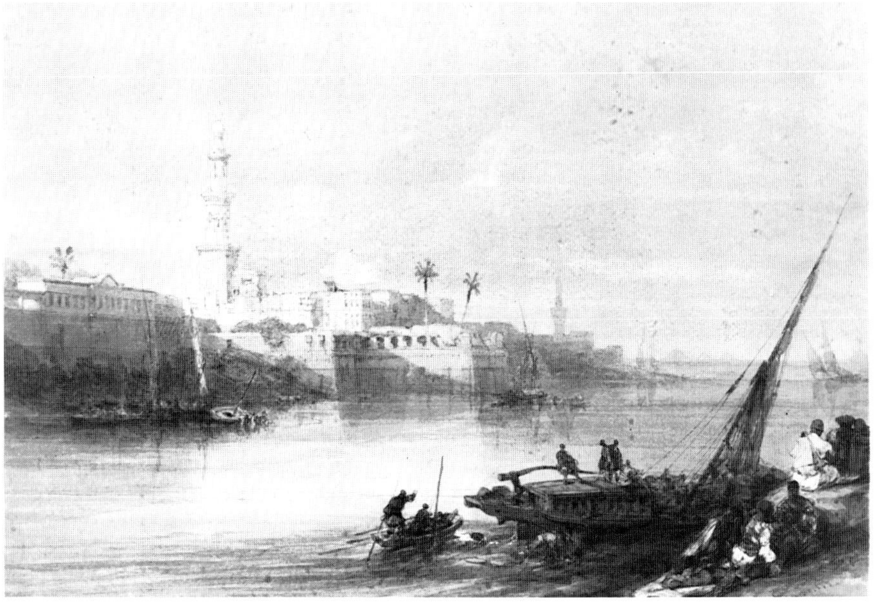

74. *Ferry to Ghizeh*, Private collection. Cat.135.

but, if he did regard the inhabitants of the Near East as secondary to its monuments, he certainly realized also their importance in orientalizing his images. This applies as much to the groups of apparently idle Arabs in his compositions, as to the spirited cavalcades that sweep dramatically through them.

Roberts was also undoubtedly convinced that the Arabs were to blame for much of the decay of the splendid ancient remains. At Baalbek he exclaimed:

> Alas! What a change in all but Nature herself—the fountain the temple, the mosque are a mass of ruins overgrown with lichen & wild flowers through the midst of which the chrystal stream still winds its way; but where are the gay citizens that once frequented its banks where the maids who resorted here to make their offerings to its protecting deity, where the wealth & plenty that once belonged to the proud city? Ask the followers of the great Prophet, the founder and projector of a creed that could bring the most fruitful & civilised portion of the globe into worse than barbarism again accompanied with sufferings & crime that could render life even in this paradise a misery.[35]

This theme was taken up in reviews of Roberts's paintings such as *The Surprise of the Caravan: a Scene in Syria* (untraced, similar to Plate 66), exhibited at the Royal Academy in 1851. One critic commented on the admirable treatment of the figures of 'the marauding Arnouts, on their wild horses, and the frightened travellers', but continued, 'these are subservient to the solemn remains of ancient beauty, the noble columns and sculptured fragments that tell so sad a tale, and give a sentiment to the picture of greatness long passed away.'[36] Roberts's melancholic meditations on the past grandeur and present decay of these great monuments were typical of his time and derived from the romantic attitude to ruins—not only those of the Near East—that had been common since the early nineteenth century.

It seems that Roberts often intended his figures to add a narrative element to his topographical views. But they never form the main subject of his oil paintings, and always act simply as staffage. Whether or not he intended them to be symbolic in any way is open to debate, as Roberts himself seldom discussed his own work. His pictures of oriental ruins are certainly not merely topographical views as Bartlett's are; nor, on the other hand, though impressive, are they the imaginative masterpieces that Turner might have made them. Roberts

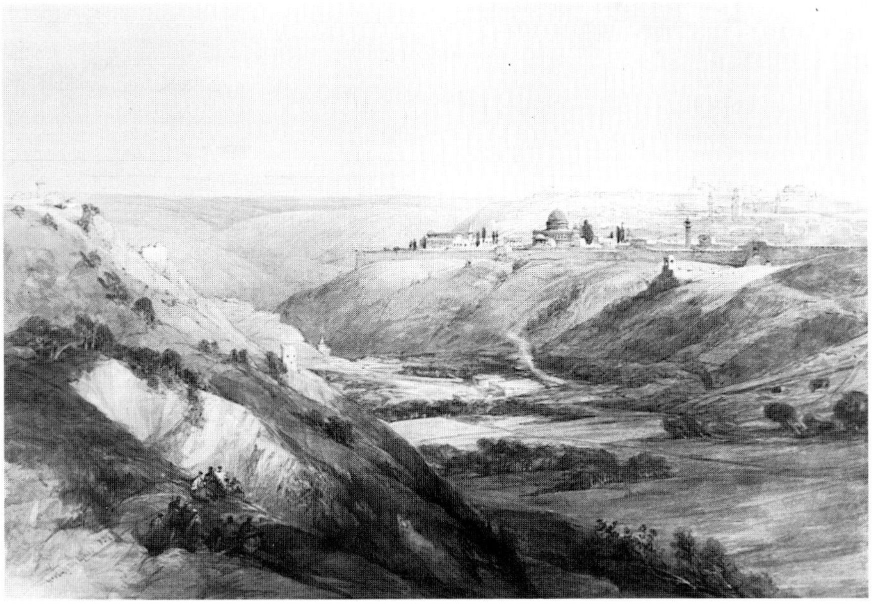

75. *Jerusalem from the Mount of Olives*, 1839, Private collection. Cat.158.

appears not to have felt truly at ease with subject painting, and after his eastern journey attempted only one major historical subject. This was the large *Destruction of Jerusalem*, which took him two years—from 1847 to 1849—and much effort to paint (see Cat.166). He may have realized by this time that straightforward representations of the monuments of the east could not sustain public interest for much longer. Such subjects were no longer novel and within a few years critical enthusiasm for them certainly waned. He continued to paint eastern ruins but, after 1851, they are heavily outweighed by his Italian and British views. Curiously, despite the popularity of Roberts's oriental pictures, not one can be singled out as a great triumph on the scale of, for example, Lewis's *The Hhareem*, exhibited at the Old Water-Colour Society in 1850. Perhaps this was because *The Hhareem* was essentially a narrative painting of a brilliantly handled oriental theme, and therefore, in the Victorian hierarchy of subjects suitable for painting, it deserved a higher place than paintings of static architectural views.

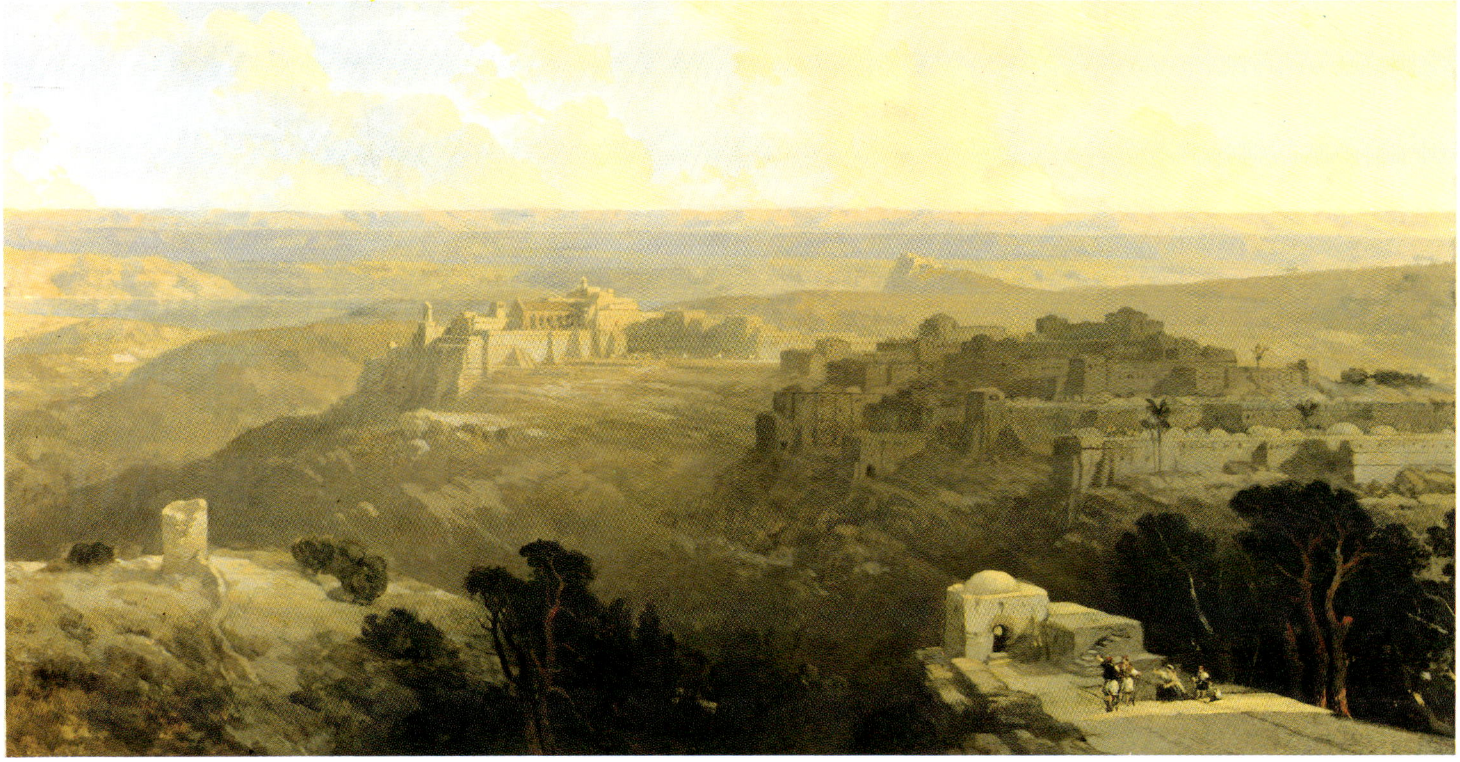

76. *Bethlehem, Looking Towards the Dead Sea*, 1853, Private collection. Cat.157.

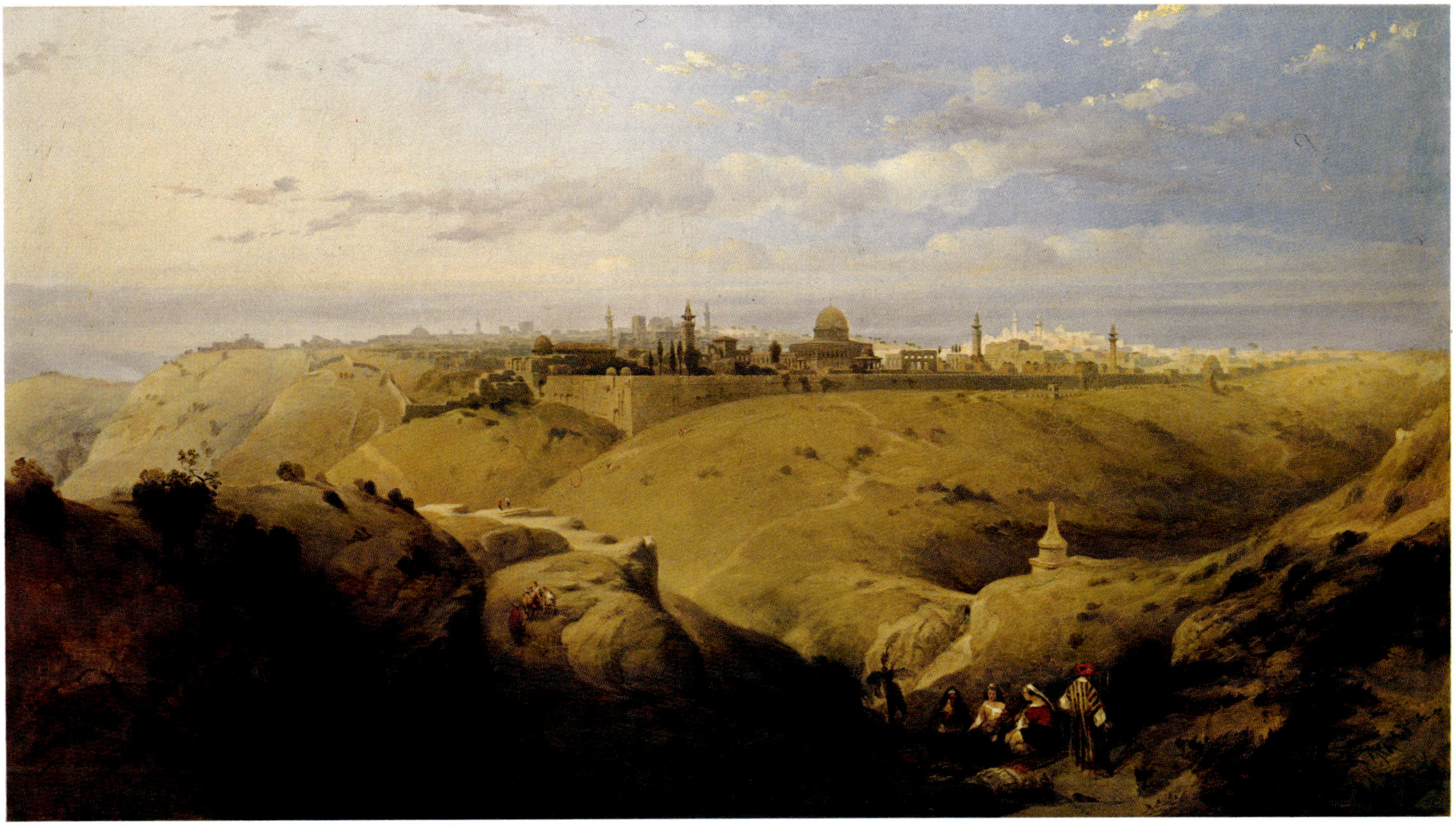

77. *Jerusalem from the Mount of Olives with Pilgrims Entering from the River Jordan*, 1842, Norwich Castle Museum. Cat.164.

Notes

The spelling of quotations follows the original text (except in *Roberts and the Theatre*). Titles of oil paintings are taken from those noted by Roberts in his *Record Book* (Cat.220), and follow Roberts's spelling of place names.

House-painting and Architecture
Ian Gow

1. James Ballantine, *The Life of David Roberts, R.A.*, 1866.
2. Scottish Record Office, SC70/1/28, p. 185.
3. See Ian Gow, 'A Stencilled Room and a Painted Floor', *Bulletin of the Scottish Georgian Society*, n. 8, 1981, for a discussion of Edinburgh house-painting in the first quarter of the nineteenth century.
4. The former for Edinburgh's flamboyant Roman Catholic bishop, James Gillie; the latter for Col. Mure at Caldwell Castle.
5. Ballantine.
6. For Hay's improvements see Ian Gow, 'The First Intellectual House-painter', *The World of Interiors*, May 1984.
7. National Library of Scotland MS 3501–2, David Roberts to D. R. Hay, 24 February 1845.
8. Ibid., David Roberts to D. R. Hay, 12 December 1846.
9. Edward Croft-Murray, *Decorative Painting in England*, Vol. 2, 1970.
10. NLS MS 3501–2, David Roberts to D. R. Hay, 24 January 1838.
11. Kemp was a journeyman carpenter turned self-taught architectural illustrator.
12. See note 10.
13. Ballantine.
14. NLS MS 3501–2.
15. Victoria and Albert Museum MS 86JJ.16.

The author is grateful to Helen Guiterman, Dr Lindsay Errington, Meta Viles, Ierne Grant, Shona McGaw, Dr Iain Brown, Tristram Clarke, David Walker, Joe Rock and Duncan Bull for their kind assistance.

Roberts and the Theatre
Pieter van der Merwe

1. W. A. Donaldson, Sen., *Fifty Years of an Actor's Life*, 1858, p. 31.
2. By the scene-painter Frederick Lloyds, *Practical Guide to Scene-Painting*, 1875.
3. Roberts MS *Record Book* (Guildhall Library photocopy BR 643, catalogued as *Notes*), on which James Ballantine's biography is based. Extracts from the *Record Book* cited in this essay use standardized spelling and the photocopy pagination.
4. *Record Book*, pp. 203–6.
5. Ibid., p. 203.
6. Ibid., pp. 14–15.
7. Peter Cunningham, 'Sketch of the History of Scene-Painting', *The Builder*, 28 May 1859. The 'Scotch-wash' may refer to Grieve's Perth ancestry or, possibly, to the composition of the glaze, Scotch or size glue being the usual scenic binder.
8. *Thirty Years Passed among the Players*, New York, 1845, p. 38.
9. *Record Book*, p. 3.
10. Ibid., p. 20.
11. W. M. Thackeray in L. Marvy, *Sketches after English Landscape Painters*, 1850.
12. *Record Book*, p. 5.
13. Ibid., p. 6.
14. Ibid., p. 13.
15. A. MacGeorge, *William Leighton Leitch, A Memoir*, 1884, p. 30.
16. *Record Book*, p. 200.
17. Ibid., pp. 19–20.
18. Ibid., p. 22.
19. Ibid., p. 24.
20. *European Magazine*, April 1823, pp. 370–1.
21. *Record Book*, pp. 26–7.
22. Laidlaw to Roberts, 24 March 1825 for the request (private collection). Information from the Theatre Museum, Amsterdam; Verner Neite, 'Das Diorama in Köln', *Jahrbuch des Kölnischen Geschichtsvereins*, Vol. 48, 1977, p. 201; *Record Book*, p. 31.
23. Ballantine, p. 30; *Hull Packet* 26 and 29 August 1828. Roberts was repeating the subject he had just done for the Covent Garden pantomime diorama in *Harlequin and Number Nip*, December 1827.
24. *Record Book*, p. 26.
25. Ibid., pp. 48–9. *The Seraglio* opened on 24 November 1827. The playbill only lists fifteen scenes.
26. See Ralph Hyde and Pieter van der Merwe, 'The Queen's Bazaar', *Theatrephile*, Vol. 2, no. 8, 1986.
27. These figures warrant some caution due to the sources available. They are based on the writer's general survey of scenic work at Drury Lane in the 1820s.
28. *New Monthly Magazine*, cited by Ballantine, p. 27.
29. Of *Masaniello*; review in *The Times*, 18 February 1825.
30. Such scenery of his as was used for Shakespeare was taken from 'stock' rather than specially painted.
31. A. Joubin ed., *Eugène Delacroix. Correspondance generale*, Paris 1935, Vol. I, p. 160; cf. C. Murray, 'Elliston's Production of Faust . . .', *Theatre Research*, Vol. 11, nos. 2 and 3, 1971.
32. In *Five Minutes Too Late*; review in *The Times*, 6 July 1825.
33. In *Harlequin Jack of All Trades*; review in *The Times*, 27 December 1825.
34. Cited by Ballantine, p. 16.
35. 'Horace Foote' [pseud.], *Companion to the Theatres . . .*, 1829, p. 120.
36. 2 October 1828.
37. *Literary Gazette*, 3 January 1829 (in *Harlequin and Little Red Riding Hood*).
38. *The Times*, 27 December 1828.
39. cf. *Weekly Review* and other cuttings in *Record Book*, p. 58; R. and S. Redgrave, *A Century of Painters of the British School*, 1866, Vol. 2, pp. 455–9.
40. Lloyds, op. cit., p. 97.
41. For an architectural drop at Her Majesty's, subsequently designed by Stanfield.
42. See note 33.

Travel, Topography and Prints
Michael Pidgley

1. H. Ottley, *A Biographical and Critical Dictionary of Recent and Living Painters and Engravers*, 1866, p. 139.
2. R. Lockett, *Samuel Prout 1985, p. 92.*
3. *Art Journal*, 1855, p. 24.
4. J. H. Fuseli, *Lectures on Painting*, p. 185; cited in *Landscape in Britain c.1750–1850*, Tate Gallery publication, 1973, p. 10.
5. F. T. Palgrave, *Gems of English Art of this Century*, 1869, p. 81.
6. *Quarterly Papers on Architecture*, ed. J. Weale, 1844, p. 7.
7. Palgrave, op. cit., p. 78.
8. Cited by R. Lockett, op. cit., p. 64.
9. *Nature and Art*, Vol. 2, June 1867, p. 193.
10. *The Chromolithograph*, 12 September 1868, p. 338.
11. R. and S. Redgrave, *A Century of Painters of the British School*, 1866; reprinted 1947, p. 406.
12. W. M. Thackeray, 'A Pictorial Rhapsody: Concluded', *Fraser's Magazine*, July 1840; cited in G. Saintsbury ed., *The Paris Sketch Book and Art Criticism*, Vol. 2 of the *Oxford Thackeray*, n.d., p. 526.
13. D. Sutton ed., *Letters of Roger Fry*, 1972, Vol. 1, p. 116.
14. W. M. Thackeray, 'A Word on the Annuals', *Fraser's Magazine*, December 1837; cited in Saintsbury, op. cit., pp. 337, 345.
15. W. M. Thackeray, 'Our Annual Execution', *Fraser's Magazine*, January 1839; cited in Saintsbury, op. cit., p. 370.
16. S. Uwins ed., *A Memoir of Thomas Uwins*, 1858, Vol. 2, p. 187. Lawrence to T. Uwins, 31 October 1828.
17. S. C. Hall, *Retrospect of a Long Life*, 1883, Vol. 1, p. 310.
18. J. Eagles, *The Sketcher*, 1856, p. 32. Originally published in *Blackwood's Magazine*, 3 April 1833. cf. *The Gallery of Modern British Artists*, 1835, p. 17 on Turner: 'There is so much genius and Knowledge of art in his pictures, that his engravings from them have become works of reference to many of his contemporaries.'
19. A. N. W. Pugin, *Contrasts . . . shewing the Present Decay of Taste*, 1836, p. 30.
20. Palgrave, op. cit., p. 81.
21. A. Cunningham, *Life of Sir David Wilkie*, 1843, Vol. 3, p. 107. Wilkie to W. Collins, 12 September 1835.
22. See note 15.
23. See Helen Guiterman *et al.*, *David Roberts, Artist Adventurer*, 1981, p. 51, for a list of other volumes to which Roberts contributed.
24. Cunningham, op. cit., p. 219. Wilkie to W. Collins *c.* February 1837.

25. E. Helps ed., *Recollections of a Royal Academician by John Callcott Horsley, R.A.*, 1903, pp. 240, 244. Also see Thackeray, cited in Saintsbury, op. cit., pp. 528–9, on his dislike of bodycolours.
26. S. D. Kitson, *The Life of John Sell Cotman*, 1937, p. 310.
27. Roberts's *Record Book*, 22 August 1837. Private collection.
28. *Quarterly Review*, LXXVII, 1846, p. 500.
29. J. Mayne trans. and ed., *Art in Paris 1845–1862. Salons and Other Exhibitions Reviewed by Charles Baudelaire*, 1965, p. 77.

Roberts's Pictures of the Near East
Briony Llewellyn

1. Ballantine, pp. 78, 231.
2. *The Holy Land*, 1842, Vol. I.
3. Ballantine, p. 150.
4. *Eastern Journal*, 28 January 1839. Roberts's journal of his eastern tour reveals much about his attitudes to the people and places that he visited (see Cat. 219).
5. Roberts to D. R. Hay, from Fitzroy Street, London, 28 May 1842.
6. Ballantine, pp. 249–53.
7. *The Literary Gazette, and Journal of the Belles Lettres*, 1841, p. 315.
8. *The Art-Union*, 1842, p. 15; *The Athenaeum*, 1847, p. 843.
9. *Record Book*, 1842, [p. 147] (see Cat. 220).
10. *Eastern Journal*, 13 January 1839. The *Mahmal* was the covered litter of state borne by 'sacred camel' to Mecca.
11. See Brighton Museum and Art Gallery, *The Inspiration of Egypt*, 1983.
12. *Eastern Journal*, 29 January 1839.
13. Roberts to D. R. Hay, from Cairo, 4 January 1839.
14. *Eastern Journal*, 20 December 1838.
15. W. J. Müller, 'An Artist's Tour in Egypt', *The Art-Union*, 1839, p. 131.
16. *Eastern Journal*, 23 May 1839.
17. *The Athenaeum*, 1847, p. 843.
18. J. R. Abbey, *Travel in Aquatint and Lithography 1770–1860*, London, 1956–7, Vol. 2, p. 341.
19. *The Art-Union*, 1840, p. 75.
20. *The Literary Gazette*, 1841, p. 315.
21. *Record Book*, 1829, [p. 57].
22. *Eastern Journal*, 7 March 1839.
23. *Eastern Journal*, 23 October 1838.
24. The City of Bristol Museum and Art Gallery.
25. W. Holman Hunt, *Pre-Raphaelitism and the Pre-Raphaelite Brotherhood*, London, 1905, Vol. II, p. 217.
26. *Eastern Journal*, 13 and 15 February 1839.
27. Roberts to D. R. Hay, from Fitzroy Street, London, 28 May 1842.
28. *The Art-Union*, 1844, p. 162.
29. *The Literary Gazette*, 1848, p. 315.
30. E. T. Cook and A. Wedderburn, ed., *The Works of John Ruskin*, London, 1903, Vol. III, pp. 223–6; (*Modern Painters*, Vol. I, 1843). Müller's Egyptian sketches—unacknowledged by Ruskin—had come nearer to achieving the effect he advocated. Another critic had unfavourably compared the smoothness or 'French polish' of Roberts's paintings with Müller's—'vigorous in colour and effect' (*Blackwood's Edinburgh Magazine*, 1841, p. 33).
31. See note 30.
32. *The Literary Gazette*, 1841, p. 315.
33. *The Art-Union*, 1846, p. 180; the painting was 'rubbed out': *Record Book* [p. 163].
34. *Eastern Journal*, 19 January 1839.
35. *Eastern Journal*, 6 May 1839.
36. *The Literary Gazette*, 1851, p. 365.

The Contributors

Ian Gow, of the Royal Commission on the Ancient and Historical Monuments of Scotland, has made a special study of Scottish house-painters and published several articles on the subject.

Helen Guiterman is an acknowledged authority on David Roberts and has devoted many years to researching him.

Briony Llewellyn is a specialist in Oriental artists and has been involved with several recent exhibitions on this theme.

Michael Pidgley, lecturer at Exeter College of Art and Design, is an expert on John Sell Cotman and early nineteenth-century British art.

Pieter van der Merwe, of the National Maritime Museum, researched and co-organized the 1978 exhibition *The Spectacular Career of Clarkson Stanfield* for the Tyne and Wear Museums, and is an expert on theatre and panoramas.

Note on Roberts's Patrons and Friends

James Ballantine (1808–77). Author of biography of Roberts, published 1866. Stained-glass designer and writer of bad verse.
Thomas Baring (1799–1873). Financier. Chancellor of the Exchequer 1852 and 1858.
Elhanan Bicknell (1788–1861). Whale-oil merchant. Had a large collection of works by British artists. Became very good friend of Roberts. One of his sons married Roberts's daughter, Christine.
J. B. Bunning (1802–63). Architect to the City of London.
Thomas Cubitt (1788–1855). Builder. Responsible for a great deal of contemporary development in London.
Ernest Gambart (1814–1902). The most important art-dealer of his day.
Sir John Watson Gordon (1788–1864). Eminent Scottish portraitist. President of the Royal Scottish Academy, 1850. Queen's Limner for Scotland.
D. R. Hay (1798–1866). Interior decorator.
D. O. Hill (1802–70). Painter, pioneer photographer. Secretary to the Scottish Academy for thirty-nine years.
S. Jones Loyd (1796–1883), first Baron Overstone.
Sir Francis Graham Moon (1796–1871). Started business as a print-seller. Became publisher, and published *The Holy Land, Syria, Idumea, Arabia, Egypt & Nubia*.
Robert Napier (1791–1876). Marine engineer and shipbuilder.
Lord Northwick (1770–1859), second baron. Had a large collection of works by British artists and old masters.
John Pender (1815–96). Pioneer of sub-marine telegraphy. MP for Totnes.
John Sheepshanks (1787–1863). Leeds clothier. Collected mainly British artists; presented his collection to the nation in 1857.
F. Hall Standish (1799–1840). Connoisseur and author. Bequeathed his collection to King Louis-Philippe.
Robert Vernon (1774–1849). Contractor for army horses. Bought mainly from British artists; presented his collection to the nation in 1847.
James White (1803–62). Clergyman and author of plays and other writings.

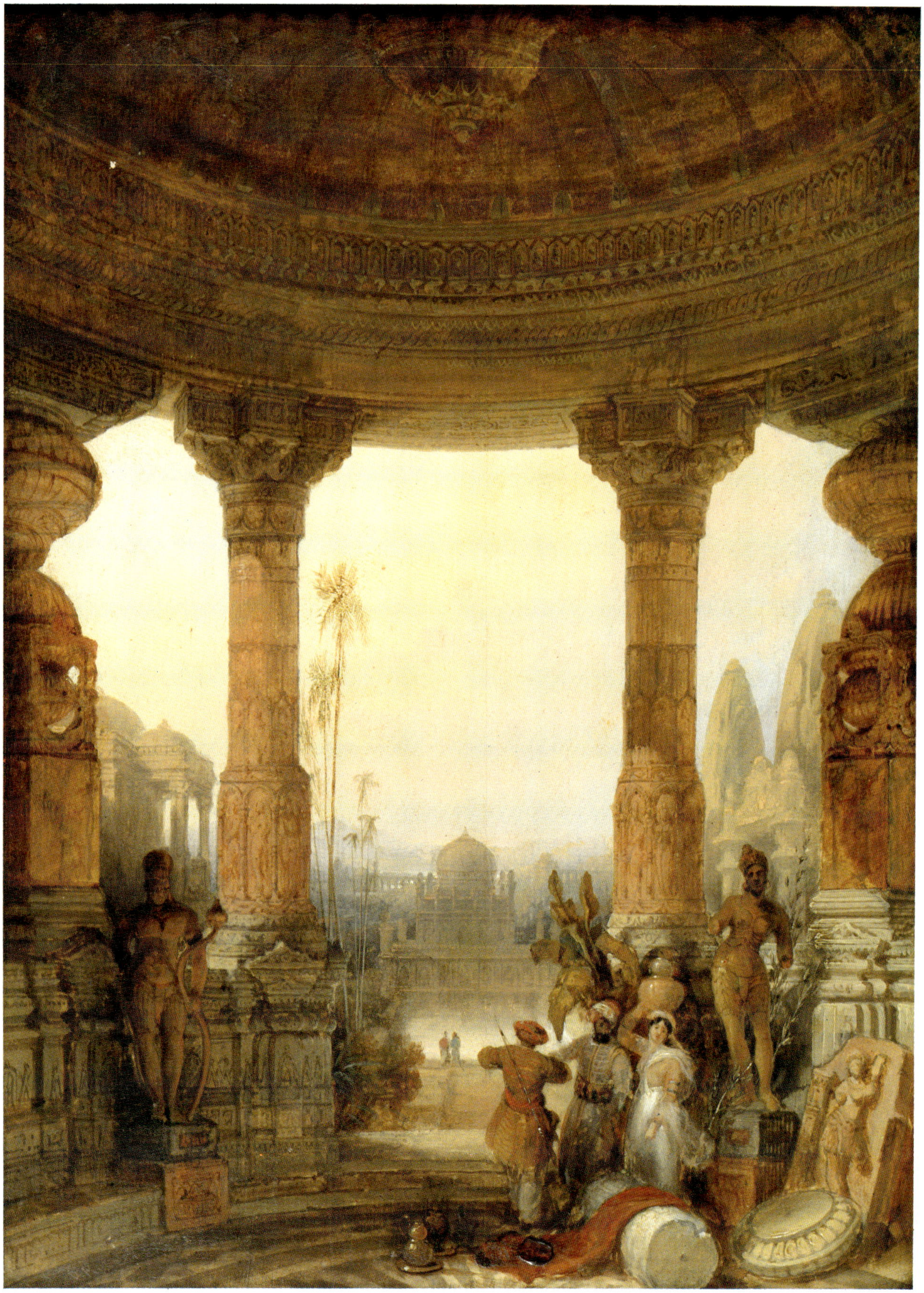

78. *Hindoo Architecture: A Composition*, 1829, Private collection. Cat.111.

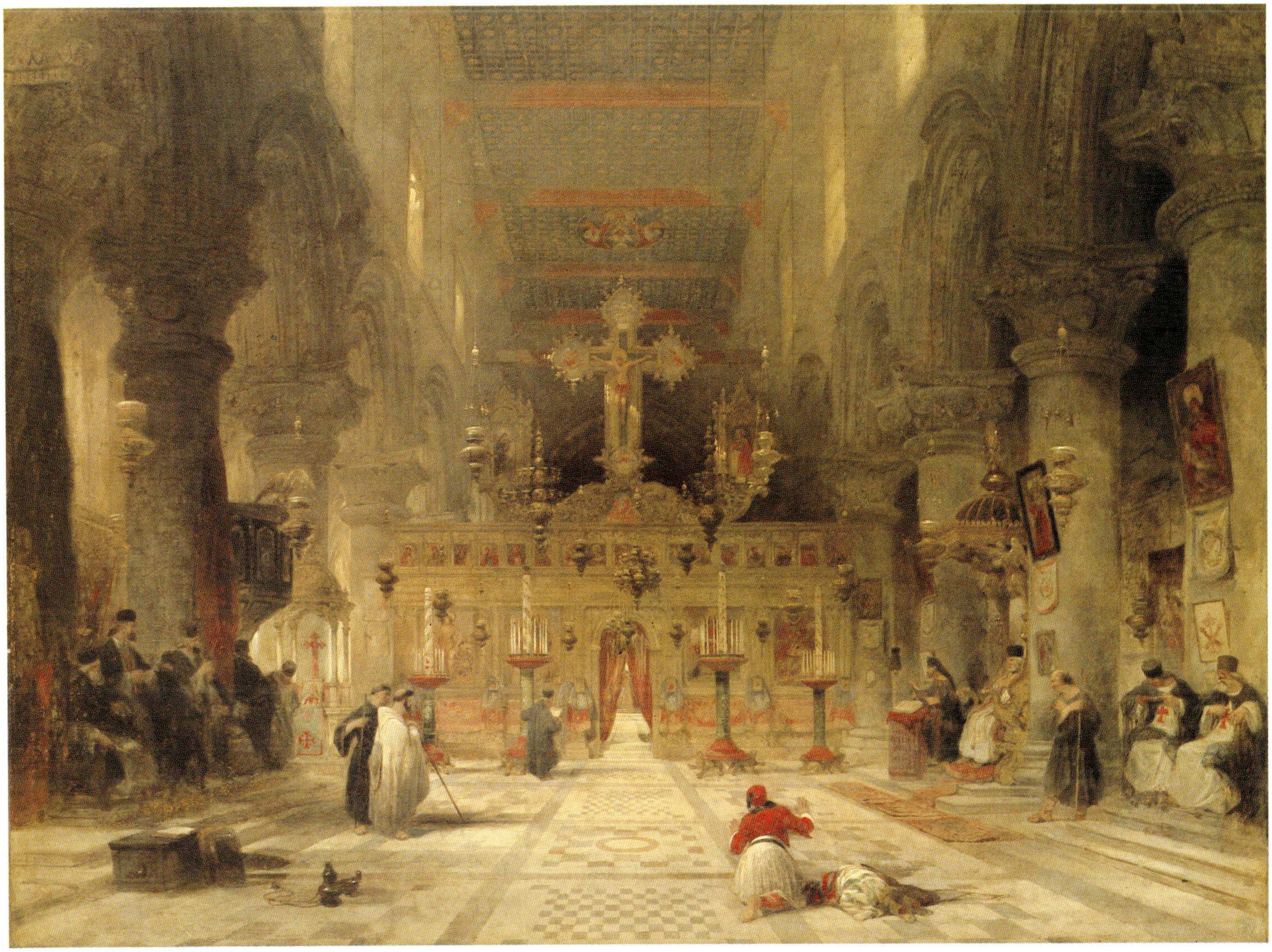

79. *The Chapel of the Convent of St. Catherine, on Mount Sinai*, 1842, Private collection. Cat.150.

David Roberts – A Chronology of his Life and Related Events

Helen Guiterman

1796 24 October: David Roberts born at Stockbridge, Edinburgh, the first of five children, of whom only David and one sister survived. His father was a shoemaker.

1802 J. M. W. Turner elected R.A.

1805 Battle of Trafalgar.

1807 Abolition of British Slave Trade.

*c.*1808–15 Roberts apprenticed to Gavin Beugo, house-painter, for seven years at two shillings weekly.

1808–14 Peninsular War.

*c.*1815 Began easel painting with fellow apprentices. First recorded painting was of the Battle of Trafalgar.

1815 Completion of apprenticeship; employed as a house-painter at Scone Palace, Perthshire. ● Became a Freemason.
Battle of Waterloo.

1816 Employed as a scene-painter with a strolling company for £1 10s. weekly, visiting Carlisle, Newcastle, Hull and York; drew in and around York.

1817 Returned to house-painting in Edinburgh, at Abercairney Abbey and Dunbar House. ● Made many drawings.

1818 Spring: painted Gothic Library at Castle of Craigcrook. ● Ceased house-painting for employment at Edinburgh Pantheon, at £1 5s. weekly.

1819 Employed at Theatre Royal, Glasgow, at £1 10s. weekly. Invited to paint two scenes for *The Heart of Midlothian* at Theatre Royal, Edinburgh.

1820 3 July: married Margret, possibly an actress. ● Went to Ayr and Dumfries to scene-paint, and made many drawings. ● October: began work as a scene-painter at Theatre Royal, Edinburgh, at £2 weekly. ● Introduced to Clarkson Stanfield, who was employed with a London company visiting the Edinburgh Pantheon.
Death of George III. Accession of George IV.

1821 4 June: Roberts's only child, Christine, born. ● Roberts sent an oil painting of *New Abbey, Dumfriesshire* (untraced) to the Fine Arts Institution of Edinburgh; it was rejected. ● Visited Melrose and Dryburgh to draw.

1822 August: dismissed from Theatre Royal, Edinburgh. Went to London by sea. Engaged at Coburg Theatre to work with Stanfield. Following a trial for Theatre Royal, Drury Lane, in September, returned to work for Theatre Royal, Edinburgh, until Christmas. Subsequently engaged at Drury Lane for five guineas weekly. ● Sent three paintings to the Fine Arts Institution, Edinburgh; all were accepted and two were sold.

1823 Society of British Artists founded; Roberts an early member. ● Brought his wife and daughter to London. ● Returned to Edinburgh Theatre Royal to paint scenery for a pantomime; spent two weeks after Christmas painting at Dublin Theatre.
Death of Sir Henry Raeburn.

1824 Living at 24 Elliotts Row, Newington. ● Panorama of *Bombardment of Algiers* painted with Stanfield, to be exhibited on the Continent, including Amsterdam and Cologne (1825–7). ● Roberts exhibited at the Society of British Artists for the first time: *Dryburgh Abbey, East Front of Melrose Abbey* and *South Transept of Melrose Abbey* (all untraced); the two latter sold. ● Painted scenes for *The Merry Wives of Windsor, Kenilworth, Zoroaster, Der Freischutz, Revolt of the Greeks* and *The Enchanted Courser*, working with Stanfield and Marinari. ● Went to Dieppe, Rouen and Le Havre; made drawings of Rouen.
Foundation of National Gallery, London.

1825 Living at 18 Mount Street, Lambeth. ● First work shown at British Institution: *New Abbey, Dumfriesshire* (untraced). Four paintings exhibited at the S.B.A.; *The West Front of Notre Dame, Rouen* (private collection) bought by Sir Felix Booth, and a replica of it commissioned by Lord Northwick (untraced). ● Probably went to Paris, Abbeville, Caen and Amiens.

1826 Scenery for three productions, including a panorama. In April left Drury Lane and in August began work at Covent Garden for £10 a week. ● Scenery for *The White Maid* with Madame Vestris. Painted single-handed all fifteen scenes for first London production of *The Seraglio*, which took him nearly eighteen months. ● Three paintings at the S.B.A., including *Interior of the Church of St. Geneviève at Paris* (Cat.64); one at B.I. First exhibit at R.A.: Lord Northwick's *Rouen Cathedral*. ● Probably went to Belgium, to Antwerp, Malines (Mechelin), Louvain, Brussels and Tirlemont.

1827 In October, began painting two transparency pictures to accompany two by Stanfield, each measuring 40 × 30 feet, for the 'British Diorama' at the Queen's Bazaar. Later painted grand panoramic Naumachia of the Battle of Navarino (Oct. 1827), in collaboration with other artists including Stanfield. ● 24 November: first night of *The Seraglio*. Much praised but scenery obliterated at end of run. ● Eight paintings at S.B.A., B.I. and R.A., including subjects from Amiens, Antwerp and Abbeville.

1828 Undertook interior decoration of Covent Garden theatre and painted a new act-drop, of statue of Shakespeare with the Muses and St. Paul's in the background. ● Panorama of Russian Army's march to Turkey and diorama of polar expedition, all for Covent Garden. ● Exhibited five paintings: four at S.B.A. and one at B.I.

1829 Living at 8 Abingdon Street, Westminster. ● Became treasurer of S.B.A. ● Completed second diorama for the Queen's Bazaar, with Stanfield; destroyed by fire along with the previous diorama and the Bazaar. ● Painted *The Israelites Leaving Egypt* (Cat.114) for Lord Northwick; engraved by Moon, Boys & Co., and exhibited at S.B.A. with an Indian subject, and at the B.I. with two more paintings. Also sent a painting to the opening exhibition of the Scottish Academy, beginning a long association. ● June: went to Paris for a month. July/August: went to Scotland for a long tour, including Staffa, Iona and Mull.
Death of George IV. Accession of William IV.

1830 Vice-President of the S.B.A. ● Painted an act-drop for the Theatre Royal, Edinburgh, and three scenes for a pantomime at Covent Garden. Left Covent Garden and scene-painting for good at end of year. ● Sent *The Israelites Leaving Egypt* to the S.A., and exhibited nine paintings in London. Began *Staircase at Stafford House* (Cat.47) for the Marquis of Stafford, which was not completed until 1832. ● Stayed with Lord Northwick. ● Summer: went to Rotterdam, Mannheim, Frankfurt, Cologne, Koblenz and Heidelberg.
Liverpool and Manchester Railway opened.

1831 President of the S.B.A. ● Exhibited six works at the S.B.A., one at B.I. and two at the S.A., including *Grand Entrance to Rouen Cathedral* (Cat.65). ● Foundation of Garrick Club. Roberts became a member and remained one until his death. ● Went to Coronation of William IV. ● Autumn: went to Dunfermline, Abbotsford, Melrose, Jedburgh and Kelso to complete the drawings for a set of etchings of monastic antiquities. ● Sent his wife back to live in Scotland.

1832 Exhibited four paintings at the S.B.A., one at B.I. Made a series of drawings for *Pilgrims of the Rhine*. Worked on illustrations to *Waverley Novels* (Cat.205).
Reform Bill passed. Death of Sir Walter Scott.

1832–3 August 1832: went to Calais for a week. 18 October: left for Spain via Paris, Orléans, Angoulême, Bordeaux and Bayonne, where he was quarantined for three weeks; again quarantined at Irun for two weeks. Went to Vitoria and Burgos, and reached Madrid 16 December; stayed there three weeks. Left for Cordoba *c*. 9 January 1833; stayed there for three weeks and then in Granada for three weeks. Thence to Malaga, Ronda, Gibraltar and Morocco; and on to Cadiz, Jerez and Seville, where he spent five months. Driven away by cholera, reached England on 22 October. ● Living at 22 Howland Street, Fitzroy Square, towards end of year.

1834 Living at 24 Mornington Place. ● First fruits of Spanish tour. Exhibited *The Moorish Tower at Seville, called the Giralda* (Cat.104) and a Cordoba subject at S.B.A., and *Interior of the Cathedral of Seville* . . . (Cat.102) at B.I. Also sent other works to both exhibitions and two to Scottish Academy. Made 21 drawings and nine vignettes for the 1835 *Landscape Annual* (Cat.207), for which he was paid £420. ● Went to Edinburgh; helped D. R. Hay to decorate pavilion for banquet to Earl Grey. ● Submitted two designs for the Scott Monument competition (Cat.13). ● His wife returned to London for about a year but was sent back to Scotland; he never saw her again.
Palace of Westminster destroyed by fire.

1835 Exhibited *The Cathedral at Burgos* at R.A., and *Old Buildings on the Darro, Granada* (both untraced) at B.I. Painted *Fortress of the Alhambra, Granada* (Fogg Art Museum, Harvard University) for Lord Northwick. Made 21 drawings and ten vignettes for the 1836 *Landscape Annual*; vignettes engraved on wood by Roberts (Cat.207). Publication of 1835 *Annual, Granada*. ● Resigned from S.B.A. ● Autumn: stayed with Lord Northwick; went to Blenheim.

1836 Reached agreement with publishers Hodgson and Graves to make 37 drawings for lithographs for *Picturesque Sketches of Spain* (Cat.210), for which he was paid £350. Exhibited *Chapel of Ferdinand and Isabella, Granada* (untraced) at R.A.; bought by William Beckford (Cat.92 for drawing). One other painting exhibited at R.A., five at B.I. and two at S.B.A., the last time he exhibited there. *Interior of the Cathedral of Seville* . . . (Cat.102) sent to S.A. Commissioned to paint *The Alhambra* (untraced) for the Marquis of Lansdowne, to hang at Bowood, his largest work to date (96 × 87 in. [243.8 × 220.9 cm.]). ● Publication of 1836 *Annual, Andalusia* (Cat.207). Made drawings for 1837 *Landscape Annual*. ● Went to Beverley, York, Kirkstall, Ripon, Richmond and on to Edinburgh.
Charles Barry won competition to design new Palace of Westminster.

1837 August: *Picturesque Sketches in Spain* published. ● Roberts took his daughter to Calais, St. Omer and Dunkirk. ● Made 20 drawings for *Landscape Annual* 1838. Publication of 1837 *Annual, Biscay and the Castiles*. ● One painting exhibited at R.A., none elsewhere.
Death of William IV. Accession of Victoria. ● Death of Constable.

1838 Elected A.R.A. ● Went to Edinburgh to see his parents. ● *St. Paul's with the Lord Mayor's Procession* (Walker Art Gallery, Liverpool) was engraved by Edward Goodall. ● Three exhibits at the B.I. and one at the R.A.

1838–9 On 21 August 1838 left London for his Eastern journey. Arrived Alexandria 24 September, and proceeded to Cairo (30). Visited the Pyramids at Giza, then (6 October) began voyage up the Nile as far as the Second Cataract, visiting the temples of Dendara (19–20), Luxor and Karnak (23), Esna (24), Edfu (26), Kom Ombo (28), Philae (30 October–1 November) and Abu Simbel (8–9 November). Began the return journey to Cairo 11 November, stopping to draw temples on the way, visiting Philae (17–19), Kom Ombo (21), Edfu (23), Esna (24), Karnak (27–30), Luxor (1 December), Plain of Thebes (3–4), Dendara (6–8). Reached Cairo 21 December and spent over a month working there before leaving for Syria 7 February. Travelled to Jerusalem via Suez (10–11), the Monastery of St. Catherine (18–23), Akaba (27 February–3 March), Petra (6–12), Hebron (16–18), Gaza (20–3) and Jaffa [Tel Aviv] (25–7). Arrived Jerusalem 28 March, leaving for Jericho (1 April), the Jordan and the Dead Sea, returning via the Monastery of St. Saba (3–5) and Bethlehem (5–8). Spent a week in Jerusalem (8–15), before making his way north to Nablus (16), Sabastiya (17), Nazareth (19), Cana and the Sea of Galilee (21), Tiberias (21–2), Acre (23), Haifa (24–5), Tyre [Sour] (26–7), Sidon [Saïda] (28–9), Baalbec (2–8 May) and Beirut [Beyrouth] (10). Sailed for England 13 May, spending a week in Alexandria (15–23), and a month's quarantine in Malta (28 May–27 June) on the return journey. 21 July: returned to London. October: went to Edinburgh to see his parents. ● Tried to get publisher for his Eastern subjects. ● December: moved to 7 (now 38) Fitzroy Street, where he lived until his death.
Penny postage introduced. ● Beginnings of photography by Daguerre and others.

1840 February: sat for Robert Scott Lauder portrait, *Roberts in Eastern Dress* (Scottish National Portrait Gallery). F. G. Moon agreed to publish *The Holy Land, Syria, Idumea, Arabia, Egypt & Nubia* (hereafter referred to as *The Holy Land and Egypt*), which appeared in monthly parts between 1842 and 1849, to be bound up into volumes (see Cat.211). Roberts's original on-the-spot drawings were exhibited in London, Edinburgh and provincial towns to obtain subscribers. ● May: death of Roberts's father; went to Edinburgh for the funeral. ● First Eastern paintings, *Greek Church of the Nativity at Bethlehem* (Paisley Art Gallery) and *Dromos, or Outer Court of the Great Temple at Edfu* . . . (Cat.124), both painted for Frank Hall Standish, exhibited at R.A. together with three others, including *Portico of the Great Temple at Baalbec* (Cat.177), painted for Elhanan Bicknell.
Marriage of Queen Victoria and Prince Albert. ● Death of Alexander Nasmyth.

1841 Elected R.A. ● First commission for Queen Victoria: *Bridge of Toledo* (Royal Collection). *Jerusalem from the Mount of Olives* . . . (Royal Holloway College), painted for Lord Monson, exhibited at R.A.; two Eastern subjects at B.I. ● June: Roberts's daughter, Christine, married Henry Bicknell, second son of Elhanan Bicknell. Roberts went to Tunbridge Wells with elder Bicknells while young ones on honeymoon. ● September: went to Scotland with Robert Dadd, Richard Dadd's father; visited Edinburgh, Roslin, Hawthornden, Stirling, Callander, Ellen's Isle, Loch Katrine, Loch Lomond, Dumbarton, and Glasgow. ● Working on *Holy Land* drawings.
Death of Sir David Wilkie.

1842 April: first part of *The Holy Land* appeared. Diploma painting of *Gateway of the Temple of Baalbec* presented to R.A. Four Eastern subjects showing Thebes, Chapel of Convent of St. Catherine, Kom Ombo and Petra exhibited at R.A. Queen Victoria commissioned *Fountain at Madrid* (Royal Collection) for Prince Albert. ● Roberts on Hanging Committee of R.A. ● Completing new drawings of first ten parts of *The Holy Land*. ● October: to Edinburgh and Roslin, Glasgow and Liverpool. 19th: official dinner in Roberts's honour at Barry's Hotel, Edinburgh, organized by D. R. Hay with Lord Cockburn in the chair. ● Arranged for Wilkie's palette to be given to R.S.A. ● First grandchild, Henry David, born.
Income tax introduced.

1843 August: went to St. Malo, Dinan, Dol and Mont St. Michel, where he stayed. Then to Grandville, Coutances, Bayeux and Caen. ● On return to England learnt of his friend Dadd's murder by his son. ● October: stayed with Lord Northwick, went to Birmingham and on to Edinburgh. ● Three Eastern subjects, including Diploma painting, exhibited at R.A., and two sent to R.S.A. ● Christine and Henry moved from Fitzroy Street to Brixton.

1843–7 D. O. Hill and Robert Adamson in photographic partnership, Edinburgh.

1843–60 Ruskin's *Modern Painters* published.

1844 Roberts ill. ● Four subjects at R.A., two French and two Eastern. ● Completed 122 drawings of the Holy Land for his lithographer, Louis Haghe, and sold 72 of them to Lord Francis Egerton for £1,400 (sold at Christie's 2 April 1870). ● September: to Paris for two weeks. November: to Edinburgh.

1845 Arranged for paintings by Scottish artists living in England to go to R.S.A. exhibition and continued to do this regularly. ● Exhibited two eastern subjects at R.A., of Karnak and Jerusalem; and a Scottish one at R.S.A. ● May: stayed with Jens Pell (a friend from Syria) and Lord Northwick. ● June: joined his family at Sidmouth. ● July: Roberts's mother died; went to Edinburgh for the funeral. ● August: his sister came to live with him. ● September: visited Brussels from 21 September, and Antwerp for about four weeks until 21 October (see Cat.211).

1846 January: working on drawings for *Egypt* (see Cat.211). ● March: commissioned by a publisher and print-seller, Mr Hogarth, to provide 40 drawings for *Scotland Delineated*, for £1,000. ● June–July: joined family in Isle of Wight for three weeks. ● September–October: went to Scotland to draw for *Scotland Delineated*, visiting Bamborough Castle, Holy Island, Berwick, Kelso, Jedburgh, Melrose, Linlithgow and Edinburgh. ● Five works exhibited at R.A., none at B.I. and two at R.S.A. Repeal of Corn Laws.

1847–52 Publication of *Scotland Delineated* in monthly parts. Only 15 drawings by Roberts used.

1847 March: *Panorama of Cairo* (private collection), taken from drawings by Roberts, shown by Robert Burford, Leicester Square. ● August: his sister returned to Scotland. ● September: he joined his family at Scarborough for two weeks. ● November: Part I of *Egypt and Nubia*, a continuation of *The Holy Land and Egypt* published. Completed drawings for Volume I of *Egypt and Nubia*. ● Elected to Committee of Garrick Club; presented *Surprise of the Caravan, Baalbec* to the Club. Stanfield and Haghe also presented paintings. ● Began *Destruction of Jerusalem by Titus* (Cat.166 and 167 for study and lithograph). Exhibited three paintings at R.A. including *West Front of Antwerp Cathedral* (Cat.69) and one at B.I.

1848 May: to Ramsgate to stay with Mr and Mrs Bicknell, senior. June–July: to Sidmouth with Henry and Christine. ● August: to Worcester for meeting of Archaeological Institute; visited Sedley Castle. ● September–October: went to Aberdeen by sea, thence to Elgin, Pluscarden Abbey, Dunottar Castle, Arbroath, Brechin, Dundee, Perth, Dunkeld, Dunblane, Stirling, Linlithgow and Edinburgh. ● Exhibited three works at R.A., including *Collegiate Church of St. Paul, Antwerp* (Cat.70).
Third French Revolution; Louis-Philippe fled to England. ● Formation of Pre-Raphaelite Brotherhood.

1849 January: Roberts ill. ● Completion of publication of *The Holy Land and Egypt*. ● June: invited by the Fine Arts Commission to submit designs for frescos for the new Palace of Westminster, but declined. ● Arranged memorial exhibition of works by William Etty at the request of the Royal Society of Arts. ● Autumn: wrote a letter of protest to *The Scotsman* about the threatened destruction of John Knox's house, Edinburgh. ● *The Destruction of Jerusalem by Titus* (untraced) exhibited at R.A., and two Eastern subjects at R.S.A. ● August–September: to Belgium and Holland with Louis and Charles Haghe, visiting Paris, Versailles, St. Cloud, Brussels, Antwerp, Rotterdam, The Hague, Haarlem, Amsterdam, Utrecht, returning via Antwerp, Lierre, Brussels, Hal, and Tournay. ● Two paintings by Roberts, one Edinburgh and one Spanish subject, shown at an exhibition in Antwerp; very well received.
Death of William Etty.

1850 June/July: *Destruction of Jerusalem* exhibited Edinburgh, Glasgow and London to obtain subscriptions for the lithograph by Louis Haghe (Cat.167). ● August: went to Scotland with the Haghes, visiting Edinburgh, Stirling, Perth, Dunkeld, Killiecrankie, Aberfeldy, Taymouth, Callander, Glasgow and Greenock. September: went to Bruges and Ghent. ● Commissioned to paint *The Donaldson Hospital, Edinburgh* (Cat.21) by its architect. ● Attempted to persuade the R.A. to open in the evening, as the R.S.A. already did (was not successful until 1862). ● Gave *The Simoon* (Cat.134) to Charles Dickens. ● Seven paintings exhibited at R.A.: Belgian, Spanish and Eastern subjects.

1851 On Council of R.A. (Sir Charles Eastlake was then President). ● 1 May: Roberts present at opening of Great Exhibition, Crystal Palace. ● *Donaldson Hospital* finished; sent to Edinburgh. ● May: together with Stanfield, Hague and others made scenery for Dickens's production of *Not so Bad as We Seem*, performed 16 May, Devonshire House. ● Four paintings exhibited at R.A., two Belgian subjects, one French, one Eastern; and one Eastern subject at B.I. ● September–November: to Italy, via Brussels, Cologne, Bonn, Mannheim, Frankfurt, Heidelberg, Basle, Lucerne, Altdoorf; visited Como, Milan, Brescia, Verona, and stayed in Venice for five weeks. Returned via Vienna, Prague, Dresden, Berlin, Cologne, Leipzig, Hanover and Brussels. ● On his return to London in November, wrote to *The Times* decrying the Austrian erection of a battery in front of San Giorgio Maggiore to keep Venice in subjection. ● While in Venice he was commissioned by Queen Victoria to paint a record of the Great Exhibition.
Death of J. M. W. Turner.

1852 September: went to Manchester, Preston, Dumfries, Caerlaverock, New Abbey, Lincluden, Edinburgh. ● November: still working on Queen's commission of Crystal Palace. ● Three paintings of Venice, Antwerp and Vienna, at R.A.; *Donaldson Hospital* at R.S.A.
Death of Duke of Wellington. ● Death of Samuel Prout.

1853 Gave evidence to Select Committee on affairs of the National Gallery on how best to manage the preservation, exhibition of, and addition to the works in its collection. ● May: to Isle of Wight with one of his granddaughters. ● Exhibited at R.A. one painting each of Venice, Verona, and Bethlehem (Cat.157). Also exhibited there his painting of Crystal Palace, but in April 1854 worked on it again at Windsor at request of Queen Victoria and Prince Albert.
Start of Crimean War.

1853–4 September 1854: met Haghes in Paris; went to Chalons, Lyons, Avignon, Arles, Genoa, Livorno, Pisa and Florence. Spent the winter in Rome, and visited nearby Tivoli and Frascati. Went to Naples in February 1854; from Naples to Pompeii, Paestum and Pozzuoli.

1854 June: Roberts present at reopening of Crystal Palace at Sydenham. ● August–September: sat to Sir John Watson Gordon for his portrait (R.S.A.). ● Went via York to Scotland with Joseph Arden, visiting Berwick, Coldingham, St. Abb's Head (Fast Castle), Norham, Edinburgh, Linlithgow, Hopetoun House, Stirling, Dunkeld, Killiecrankie, Callander, Loch Lomond, Glasgow, Lanark, and Bothwell Castle. ● October: returned to London unwell. ● Designed four stained-glass windows for Scott Monument executed by Ballantine. ● Exhibited three works at R.A., two of Venice and *A Proposed Restoration of the Temple of the Sibyl . . .* (Cat.15); and a Venice subject at R.S.A.
The Charge of the Light Brigade. ● Death of John Martin.

1855 July: Roberts seriously ill. ● September: possibly visited Exposition Universelle, Paris, where he was exhibiting *Interior of the Church of St. Gomar, Lierre* (Wallace Collection), *Interior*

of the Cathedral of St. Stephen's, Vienna (untraced), *Portico of the Great Temple at Baalbec* (Cat.177) and *View on the Grand Canal, Venice* (private collection). ● Awarded a second-class gold medal, which infuriated him; Stanfield received a first-class one. ● *Rome, from the Convent of St. Onofrio . . .* (Cat.187) at R.A. ● Reduced-size edition of *The Holy Land and Egypt* published.
Fall of Sebastopol; end of Crimean War.

1856 Bought house in Fitzroy Street, formerly rented. ● July: at Winterbourne, Isle of Wight, with family. ● Prepared designs for new National Gallery, London (Cat.16). ● July–August: went to Edinburgh, Linlithgow, Glasgow. Visited his patrons James Tennant Caird and Robert Napier. ● September: eldest grandson to Boulogne to stay with Dickens and family. ● Exhibited two Roman, two Venetian, and one unidentified subject at R.A. ● Member of the *ad hoc* committee (with Stanfield and H. A. J. Munro) appointed to consider what should be done with Turner's bequest to the nation of his watercolours.

1857 Was unwell for most of the year. ● Appointed by Royal Commission for Fine Arts as one of judges for competition to design new War and Foreign Offices in Whitehall. ● Presented *Rome, from the Convent of St. Onofrio* to R.S.A. Elected Honorary Member of R.S.A. ● September: Roberts's eldest grandson went again to Boulogne to stay with Dickens family. ● Roberts went to Winterbourne, Isle of Wight, with family. ● October: went to see Manchester Art Treasures Exhibition, in which he was exhibiting *Interior of the Cathedral of Seville, The Giralda, The Cathedral of St. Stephen, Vienna* (Cat.204) and *Rome, from the Convent of St. Onofrio*, as well as many watercolours. ● Exhibited one Roman, one Milanese and one Belgian subject at R.A., and one French subject at R.S.A. ● Became member of Athenaeum Club.

1857–8 Indian Mutiny.

1858 June: still unwell. ● July: to Winterbourne to look after grandchildren. ● September: visited Edinburgh with Stanfield, who was to receive diploma and bronze medal as Honorary R.S.A., while Roberts was to receive Freedom of the City. ● Went to Linlithgow, Glasgow and Burnfoot by Ayr, Brig o'Doon, Greenock, and St. Andrews. ● Exhibited three Venetian and one Roman subject at R.A.; two Eastern paintings at B.I.; and *Milan Cathedral* (Government Art Collection) and *Rome, from the Convent of St. Onofrio* at R.S.A.

1859 On Council and Hanging Committee of R.A. ● January: made designs for orchestra and screen for the Crystal Palace. ● July: last of his nine grandchildren born. ● August: with Elhanan Bicknell to stay with mutual friend; went on to Edinburgh, Linlithgow, Dundee, Glamis Castle, Aberdeen, Inverness, and Greenock. Went to Roslin Chapel to see restoration work. ● October: reworking Spanish drawings, 75 of which were sold to Gambart, who exhibited them at German Gallery, Bond Street (with catalogue notes by Roberts). ● Gaslight installed in his studio. ● Exhibited two Venetian subjects at R.A., and one of Venice and one of Rome at B.I.
Death of Lord Northwick.

1860 July: death of Roberts's wife. ● August: began drawings for series *London from the Thames*. ● September: went to Edinburgh, Linlithgow, Glasgow, Bothwell Castle and Greenock. ● September–October: to Winterbourne, Isle of Wight, with family. ● October: to Rickmansworth, to stay with Joseph Arden. ● November: with Stanfield, contributed to one of the houses for 'decayed actors' established by Dickens and others. ● Four Italian and one Belgian subject at R.A.
Death of Sir Charles Barry.

1861 On Council of R.A. ● January: sent his photograph to all his friends. ● March: death of Roberts's sister; he was not well enough to attend funeral. ● Portrait painted by J. J. Napier (whereabouts unknown). 17 August: went to Belgium with the Haghes, visiting Brussels, Antwerp to attend Art Congress, Dixmunde, Bruges; was back in London by 27 August. ● September: to Scotland for about four weeks; returned via Blackburn. ● November: death of Elhanan Bicknell. ● December: Gave £1,000 towards rebuilding of Garrick Club. ● Roberts unwell again. ● Completed first four pictures of London series. ● One Eastern and one Italian subject exhibited at R.A., one Italian and one Belgian subject at R.S.A.
Death of Prince Albert.

1861–5 American Civil War.

1862 January: made designs for Captain Fowke for the decoration of South Kensington Museum. ● May: International Exhibition, South Kensington, at which he exhibited *Milan Cathedral* (Government Art Collection), *Interior of San Lorenzo at Rome* (untraced), *Interior of Church of St. Gomar, Lierre* (untraced) and *The Surprise of the Caravan; A Scene in Syria* (untraced). ● June: with Stanfield to Gadshill to stay with Charles Dickens for three days. ● July: official dinner to Louis Gallait, Belgian artist, at Willis's rooms. ● September–October: to Dollar, Kinross, Linleven, Stirling, Linlithgow, Edinburgh, Greenock, Glasgow; returned south via Manchester and Matlock, visiting Chatsworth and Haddon Hall. ● October: sent a snuff-box once owned by Robert Burns to Ballantine for the Burns Museum, Edinburgh. ● Autumn: Christine and Henry on tour in Italy with two of their daughters. ● Exhibited two Belgian and four London subjects, including *The New Palace at Westminster . . .* (Cat.40) and *St. Paul's from Blackfriars* (Cat.42), at R.A.

1863 February: had a severe cold. ● April: sale of Elhanan Bicknell collection at Christie's. ● June: stayed with James Nasmyth, son of Alexander. ● Continued painting his London series. ● August–September: last visit to Scotland; went to Edinburgh, Linlithgow, Glasgow; became unwell while he was there. ● Sat for portrait by Daniel Macnee (R.S.A.). ● September–October: to Paris with his family. ● Exhibited two Thames subjects, one of Milan, and one of Vienna at R.A.
Death of J. D. Harding. Death of W. M. Thackeray.

1864 Continued to paint his London subjects. ● May: sat to Macnee for another portrait (Cat.214). ● June: death of Sir John Watson Gordon. ● August–September: at Winterbourne with family for six weeks. ● October: gave copies of theatrical drawings after Nasmyth (private collection, and untraced) to the latter's son James. ● Last exhibits at R.A., one Belgian and one Roman subject. ● 25 November: Roberts died and was buried in Norwood Cemetery next to Elhanan Bicknell.

1866 James Ballantine's biography was published, dedicated to Clarkson Stanfield.
Death of D. R. Hay. Publication of R. and S. Redgrave: *A Century of Painters of the British School*.

1867 Death of Clarkson Stanfield.

1872 Death of Christine Bicknell.

1880 Death of Henry Bicknell.

1881 Henry Bicknell sale at Christie's.

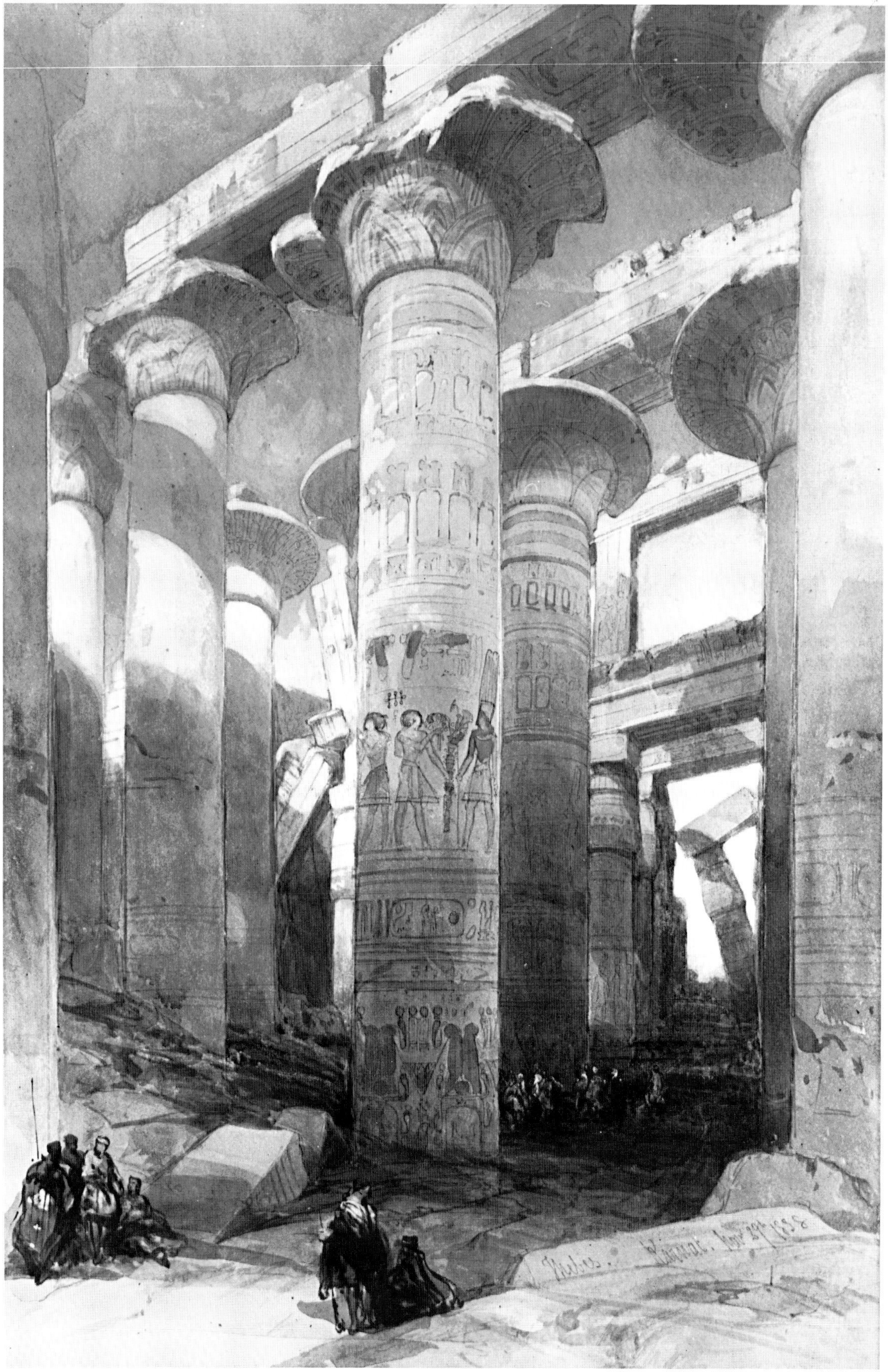

80. *Thebes, Karnac*, 1838, Manchester City Art Galleries. Cat.126.

Catalogue

Catalogue entries by Helen Guiterman, Briony Llewellyn and Kathy McLaughlan, with contributions by Pieter van der Merwe and Michael Pidgley. Entries are arranged by subject group, and alphabetically within groups of countries by place names, except the Near East section where places are arranged in the order that Roberts visited them.

Titles of the oils are as noted by Roberts in his *Record Book*, except a few whose settings were noted incorrectly, in which case the RA title is given. Works described as 'oil' are oil on canvas. Dimensions are given in inches followed by centimetres. Signature, date and inscription are abbreviated to s., d., and insc.; only inscriptions are given in full. Provenance is only referred to for works commissioned or purchased by Roberts's patrons, or to distinguish between numerous versions of a subject; for full provenances, see forthcoming *catalogue raisonné* by Helen Guiterman and Briony Llewellyn, to be published by Phaidon Press. All manuscripts quoted use original spelling; sources are abbreviated to EJ (Roberts's *Eastern Journal*, see Cat. 219), RB (Roberts's *Record Book*, see Cat. 220), and locations of sources to EUL (Edinburgh University Library), NLS (National Library of Scotland), and PC (private collection). For other abbreviations, see Bibliography. Exhibition locations are abbreviated to: BI (British Institution), RA (Royal Academy), RSA (Royal Scottish Academy), SBA (Society of British Artists). In Near East section, numbers given for lithographs in *The Holy Land* and *Egypt* are the authors', and follow two separate sequences beginning with the first lithograph after a Roberts drawing.

Roberts's studio exhibition was held at the Architectural Rooms, Conduit Street, London, spring 1865. His studio sale was held at Christie's, May 1865. Henry Sanford Bicknell's sale (HBS 1881) was held at Christie's, April 1881.

Scenery and Panoramas

Roberts began scene-painting in 1816, working at the Theatre Royal, Drury Lane, 1822–6, and at Covent Garden, 1826–30. Very little visual record of his stage-design work survives; all is included here, with examples of work by Clarkson Stanfield and the Grieves, his principal colleagues and rivals, 1822–30. (See pp. 27–44.)

1 *Heads of Drury Lane Scene-painters*, c.1825.
Photograph of an unlocated sketch, pencil & wash, with annotations by Roberts, 6 × $9\frac{1}{4}$ (15.2 × 23.5). Reproduced from Hesketh Hubbard, *Some Victorian Draughtsmen*, C.U.P., 1944, pl. 27.

Annotated top, left to right: Stanfield, Roberts, Thomas Andrews (faint), Roy, Adams; bottom: Roberts, (Thomas?) Drury 'the Grinder', T. Andrews.

Andrews was the son of 'Old' Robert Andrews (d. 1822). Drury, the colour grinder, may have been an ex-seaman who later became Stanfield's servant.

2 *Design for a Cut Scene*. Pl. 25.
Watercolour & bodycolour, $10\frac{3}{4}$ × $14\frac{1}{2}$ (27.3 × 36.8).
London, Trustees of the British Museum.

'The exquisite drawing . . . of Roberts's [scenic] architecture charmed me beyond measure and the masses of shadows gave his work great grandeur and breadth . . .' (A. McGeorge, *William Leighton Leitch, A Memoir*, 1884, p. 30).

The only design by Roberts so far known to survive; probably for a cloth rather than a flat, the cut suggesting use in some sort of transformation. The scale, apparently $\frac{1}{2}$in : 1ft, suggests that it was for a Drury Lane or Covent Garden back scene. It may relate to *Faustus* (see Cat. 8) or a piece of similar scenic content.

3 *'Gothic Act Drop' for the Theatre Royal, Edinburgh*, 1830.
Photograph of a sketch in Roberts's *Record Book*.

Roberts recorded that in 1830 he painted 'an Act drop together with a rich drapery to match, bearing the Scotish Arms etc. etc. The Architecture was Gothic. Recd. for the same £75.15.8.' This was followed by three Irish views for the Covent Garden Christmas pantomime, which were the last scenes he painted for the professional theatre.

Although very slight, even this sketch shows Roberts's dramatically shadowy technique.

4 *Lithographic Key to Roberts's 'Grand Panoramic Naumachia' in 'Harlequin and Number Nip'*, Covent Garden, 1827. Pl. 32.
Photograph of an original in Family collection.

Moving panoramas or dioramas (the latter term being more current at Drury Lane) were scenic spectacles derived from the stationary circular 'Panorama' of Robert Barker in Leicester Square, and 'The Diorama' or transparency exhibition of Louis Daguerre in Regent's Park. On stage, they comprised a moving cloth about 20 ft. high and 400 ft. long unreeled before the audience with complex effects of light, mechanics and a musical accompaniment. Typically, they were the highlights of Christmas pantomimes of the 1820s and 1830s, took about 20 minutes to display, and combined topographical views and current events as their subject matter. This one culminated in the Battle of Navarino, fought off the coast of Greece by a British and Russian fleet against the Turks on 20 October 1827. The key omits the final scene, 'a splendid allegory in compliment to the valour of the allied forces and the naval prowess of England. We have never seen a stronger effect produced upon an audience by mere painting.' (*The Age*, RB.)

5 *Lithographic Key to Roberts's 'Moving Panorama of the Grand Russian Army's March to Turkey' in 'Harlequin and Little Red Riding Hood'*, Covent Garden, 1828. Pl. 33.
Photograph of an original in Family collection.

A panorama based on the opening moves of the Russo-Turkish War of 1828–9. Roberts's least successful moving panorama, it was criticized for 'vicious colouring' and the poor drawing of figures too palpably copied from other artists.

This key and Cat. 4 were Roberts's own, and he annotated here the ten separate views. His last Covent Garden panorama, Christmas 1829, was a successful rendering of Parry's Arctic expedition of 1824–5, but no key was issued in the audience souvenir 'book of songs', from which this and Cat. 4 are taken.

6 Attributed to William Grieve (1800–44). *'The Grotto of the Dolphins . . .' in 'Harlequin and Number Nip'*, Covent Garden, 26 Dec. 1827.
Watercolour on cut pieces of card, $5\frac{3}{4}$ × $9\frac{1}{4}$ (14.6 × 23.5).
University of London Library.

The design for the grand finale of the 1827 Christmas pantomime. Roberts and others realized that the strength of the Grieve family lay in their close working relationship and the homogeneity of their romantic style. Over 700 of their designs survive, but it is difficult to distinguish between those by Thomas and those by his younger brother, William. The playbill (see Cat. 10) attributes this design to the latter, who was celebrated for his moonlight scenes.

7 Clarkson Stanfield (1793–1867). *Back-drop Design for Handel's 'Acis and Galatea'*, Drury Lane, 1842.
Watercolour on paper laid on card, 17 × $20\frac{3}{8}$ (43.1 × 51.8).
Private collection.

By provenance and elimination this appears to be the back-drop for 'The Temple of Neptune on the Shores of the Bay', scene 4 in W. C. Macready's celebrated production of Feb. 1842. Although Stanfield had retired from stage work in 1834, he executed the scenery in aid of his friend Macready's efforts to raise production standards. The setting is Sicilian, the mountain representing Etna. 'Stanfield and the assistants painting to the last minute', wrote Macready. 'Saw the performance . . . have never seen anything in my life so perfectly beautiful.'

Stanfield painted over 550 scenes in more than 176 shows, but only ten designs by him are currently known, most being slight monochrome sketches.

8 *Playbill for 'Faustus'*, Drury Lane, 1825.
Photograph of an original in the collection of the Garrick Club.

A melodramatic and operatic version of Goethe's *Faust* which opened on 16 May 1825. It was by George Soane, based on his own more serious translation attempt, of which Goethe approved. *The Times* disliked the piece but said the scenery was 'beyond praise . . . Roberts . . . has several scenes of the highest merit'. The French romantic painter, Eugène Delacroix, was greatly impressed by the staging.

9 *Playbill for 'The Seraglio'*, Covent Garden, 1827.
City of London, Guildhall Library.

This play opened on 24 Nov. 1827. All 15 settings were painted by Roberts without assistants, a task which took him from Aug. 1826 to the opening. Although an adaptation, this was the first production of Mozart's opera in England and in English. The celebrated singer and comedienne, Eliza Vestris, played Blonda.

10 *Playbill for 'Harlequin and Number Nip'*, Covent Garden, 1827.
Enlarged photograph from an original in Guildhall Library, City of London.

The Patent house Christmas pantomimes always opened on 26 Dec., Boxing Day (or 27 if 26 fell on a Sunday), and a successful pantomime would keep the theatre solvent for less profitable fare up to Easter, when another spectacle would be produced. If successful, a pantomime might run for over 40 performances and close in mid-Feb.

See Cat. 6 for the Grieve design for scene 21, and Cat. 4 for the 'book of songs' key to Roberts's panorama mentioned at the bottom of this playbill.

11 *Playbill for 'Harlequin and Little Red Riding Hood'*, Covent Garden, 1828.
City of London, Guildhall Library.

Double-page bills were introduced in the 1820s as a result of the rise of scenic spectacle at Drury Lane and Covent Garden—specifically the scenic efforts of Roberts, Stanfield and the Grieves. The format was generally only used for pantomimes and Easter spectacles, and gave space for headline billing of the 'star' painters and the scenery.

See Cat. 5 for the panorama key.

Architecture

Roberts's interest in architecture, generated by his close study of buildings, extended to colouring perspectives for architects, and even to designing buildings himself (none of which were executed); see pp. 17–25.

12 Drawn by Thomas Hamilton (1784–1858), coloured by David Roberts. *Perspective of John Knox Church, Edinburgh*, *c.*1830–1. Pl. 17.
Pen, ink & watercolour, $33\frac{1}{2} \times 25\frac{1}{4}$ (85.1 × 64.1).
Private collection.

Roberts wrote to Hay about this drawing in 1831 (see p. 25), when it was exhibited at the Scottish Academy. The church was Hamilton's first ecclesiastical commission, but was never built. Roberts had sent Hamilton some drawings of the spire of Antwerp Cathedral, and these were probably used for the design of the spire, which is very similar.

13 *Design for the Scott Monument*, (?)1834. Pl. 13.
Pen, ink & watercolour, 25 × 17 (63.5 × 43.2).
Edinburgh, National Galleries of Scotland.

The committee formed to arrange a suitable memorial to Sir Walter Scott (1771–1832) asked Roberts in 1834 to submit a design. He sent two, one an obelisk, the other a Gothic cross; the latter was preferred, but thought too expensive to build. An open competition was organized, for which Roberts submitted two elevations and a ground plan of a monument surmounted by a large statue. Cat. 13 is almost certainly the 1834 Gothic cross; the other drawings are untraced. The competition was won by George Meikle Kemp, whose work had 'leading features of Roberts's design' (Ballantine, p. 71).

In 1854 Ballantine asked Roberts to design stained glass windows for the Monument, which were carried out by Ballantine.

14 Drawn by William Playfair (1790–1857), coloured by David Roberts. *Perspective of the Donaldson Hospital, Edinburgh*, 1838.
Pen, ink & watercolour, $73\frac{1}{4} \times 50$ (186 × 127).
Edinburgh, the Donaldson Trust, Donaldson's School for the Deaf.

After Playfair had submitted drawings and a model, an open competition was arranged, which Playfair was anxious to win; he therefore asked Roberts, via D. R. Hay, to colour his perspectives so as to make the best possible impression (see p. 25). This is one of two coloured for Playfair; the other (Pl. 18) is untraced.

15 *A Proposed Restoration of the Temple of the Sybil at Tivoli on a Rock called Drumsapie, on Arthur's Seat, with a Distant View of the Bay of Aberlady*, 1853. Pl. 19 (colour).
Oil, 19 × 48 (48.3 × 121.9) with an arched mount; s. & d.
New York, the Forbes Magazine Collection.

Samuel Christy, an Edinburgh man and an M.P., wrote to Roberts, 16 Oct. 1851: 'I wish to inspire you with the romance of a project for erecting a building with a view to embelish the neighbourhood of Edinburgh in order to obtain the assistance of your taste and also of your pencil by which we may convey to others some definate idea of what is intended . . .' (NLS). In December, Christy asked David Laing, the Scottish antiquary, to provide Roberts with the dimensions of the loch and the height of the rock. Another letter from Christy had Christy's sketch of the proposal. By Feb. 1852 Roberts had made 'a beautiful drawing in oil of the Drumsapie rock and the loch . . .' (EUL). Christy planned to put his proposal to Parliament early in 1852, but by March 1854 he informed Roberts that the project had been abandoned.

Cat. 15 may be the oil sketch referred to, which was the same size, or it may be the finished work, exhibited RA 1854 (581) and bought by Christy.

The Temple of the Sybil at Tivoli stands on a rock above a waterfall, which may have given Christy his idea for this folly.

16 *Designs for a New National Gallery*, *c.*1856.
a. *Front Elevation.*
Pencil & wash, $21\frac{1}{4} \times 38\frac{1}{4}$ (54 × 97.2).
b. *Interior View.* Pl. 16.
Pencil & brown ink, $23 \times 38\frac{1}{4}$ (58.4 × 97.2).
Family collection.

A Royal Commission was set up in 1856 to determine the possible site of a new National Gallery in London, as well as to decide if the nation's paintings should be combined with the British Museum's collection of fine arts and archaeology. These designs by Roberts were probably for a new building, should the commission have decided upon one. His son-in-law, Henry Bicknell, disapproved of what he thought was a waste of time, but Roberts replied: 'who so fit as a Painter to design such an Edifice? . . . I have Vanity enough to fancy I am the man that can show *what it ought to be* . . .' (18 July 1856, PC).

Scotland

Roberts often returned to his 'ain country' to see friends and to work. He kept in touch with former fellow apprentices and often helped them with gifts of money. He also tried to help Scottish artists to get into the RA, and when he was on the Hanging Committee was accused of favouritism towards them. He was made an Honorary member of the Royal Scottish Academy in 1857 and a Freeman of the City of Edinburgh in 1858.

17 *Abbotsford, the Hall*, 1834. Pl. 5.
Watercolour, $8\frac{3}{8} \times 12\frac{3}{8}$ (21.3 × 31.4); s. & d.
Private collection.

Engraved: T. Jeavons, *Illustrations . . . to the Poetical Works of Sir Walter Scott, Bart.*, 1834, frontispiece.

Roberts visited Abbotsford, the house built by Scott near Melrose, several times. Another version, dated 1831, is in Glasgow Art Gallery and Museum.

18 *The Brig o'Doon*, 1858. Pl. 14.
Pencil & wash heightened with white, $4\frac{1}{2} \times 6\frac{1}{2}$ (11.4 × 16.5); insc. as title & *Sep 13 1858*.
Private collection.

The Brig o'Doon is in Ayrshire, near Burns Cottage; the circular building is the Burns Monument designed by Thomas Hamilton. An oil of 1862 presented to his biographer, James Ballantine, is in Burns Cottage Museum, Alloway.

19 *Dunfermline*. Pl. 6.
Watercolour heightened with white, 10 × 13 (25.4 × 33).
University of Manchester, Whitworth Art Gallery.

Dunfermline, the seat of government and residence of early Scottish kings, is only 15 miles from Edinburgh across the Firth of Forth, so Roberts might have gone there on any of his Scottish visits; it is not therefore possible to date this watercolour.

20 *The Donaldson Hospital*, 1845.
Watercolour, $9\frac{3}{4} \times 13\frac{5}{8}$ (24.8 × 34.6); s. & d., insc. *Edinburgh Oct 3 1845*.
Edinburgh, National Galleries of Scotland.

21 *The Donaldson Hospital, Edinburgh*, 1851. Pl. 15 (colour).
Oil, $46\frac{3}{4} \times 72$ (118.7 × 182.9); signed.
Edinburgh, the Donaldson Trust, Donaldson's School for the Deaf.

Commissioned by its architect, W. H. Playfair, this painting gave Roberts some trouble. He had already coloured perspectives for Playfair (see Cat. 14). Having enlisted the help of Hay's apprentices to check details of the building, he wrote: 'The Picture . . . will be forwarded to Playfair at the end of this week. I have a notion it may not be satisfactory . . . If he expects a dry architectural portrait of the Edifice I fear he will be disappointed . . . I have treated it artistically, so that leaving out of the question The Hospital as a View of Auld Reekie from the Water of Leith it will have a Value . . . the time I have bestowed upon it, no price will pay me.' (28 July 1851, NLS.) Later, he wrote 'The Great Architect has settled for the Picture like a Prince, paying the Frame in addition to the £200.' (Roberts to Hay, 15 Aug. 1851, NLS.)

22 *Edinburgh from the Calton Hill, Looking West*, 1840.
Pencil & watercolour heightened with white, $13\frac{1}{2} \times 19\frac{1}{2}$ (34.3 × 49.5); insc. *Edinburgh from Calton Hill 1840*.
Family collection.

A study for Cat. 23. Lithographed: Robert Carrick, *Scotland Delineated*, 1847–52, facing p. 119, perhaps from another drawing.

23 *Edinburgh from the Calton Hill, Looking West*, 1863. Pl. 4 (colour).
Oil, 20 × 30 (50.8 × 76.2); s. & d.
City of London, Guildhall Art Gallery.

Roberts wrote from London to a Scottish friend in 1862: 'I am at present on two smaller works one of Holyrood from the Calton Hill and the companion from the same hill looking west . . . so that if "my heart [is not] in the Highlands a' chasing the Deer" it is in the town of my boyhood—which is better!' (19 Nov., NLS). The circular building is the monument to Dugald Stewart, designed by Playfair in 1832; the Gothic structure is the Scott Monument (see Cat. 13).

Another version, dated 1858, is in the Art Gallery of New South Wales, Sydney; the companion to Cat. 23, looking east, 1863, is untraced.

24 *Edinburgh Castle from the Grassmarket*, 1828. Pl. 12 (colour).
Watercolour heightened with white, $13\frac{1}{4} \times 10$ (33.7 × 25.4); s. & d., insc. *Edinburgh*.
Family collection.

A study for Cat. 25.

25 *Edinburgh Castle from the Grassmarket*, 1837.
Oil on panel, $19\frac{1}{2} \times 18\frac{1}{2}$ (49.5 × 47); s. & d.
Newcastle-upon-Tyne, Laing Art Gallery.

Roberts gave this work to his friend, Joseph MacGregor. It was exhibited RSA 1846 (384) as *Edinburgh from the King's Stables*, and was a prize in an Art Union lottery the same year. Another version, dated 1831, is in Dundee Art Gallery; Cat. 24 is a study for both oils.

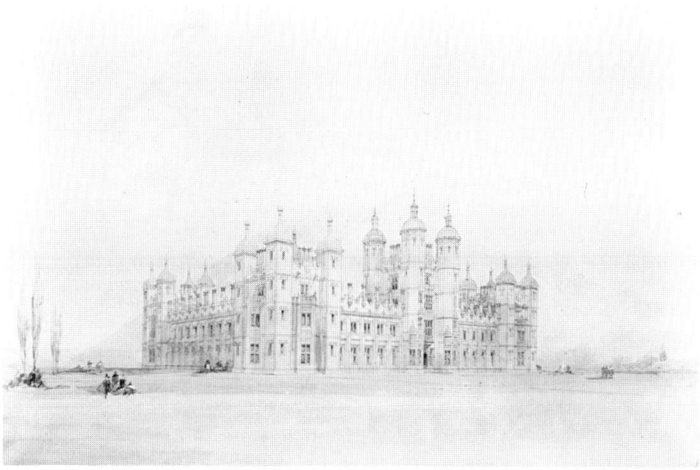

14

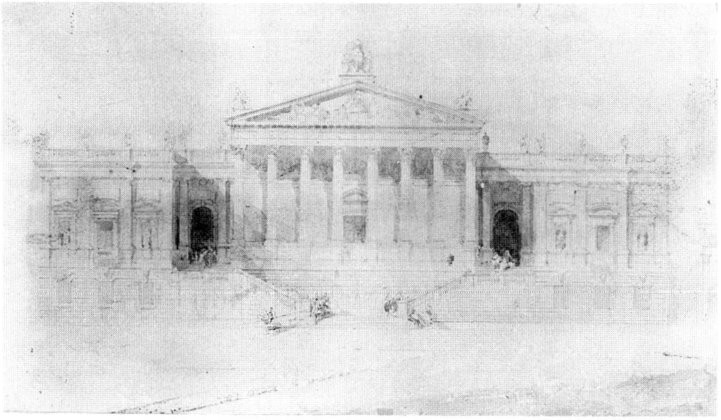

16a

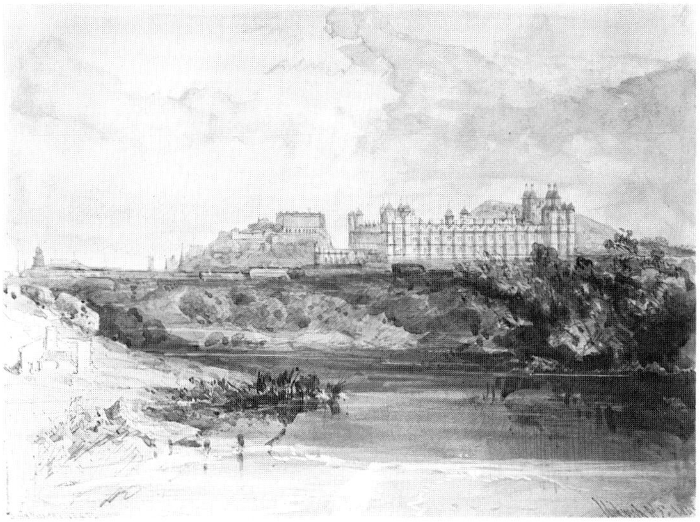

20

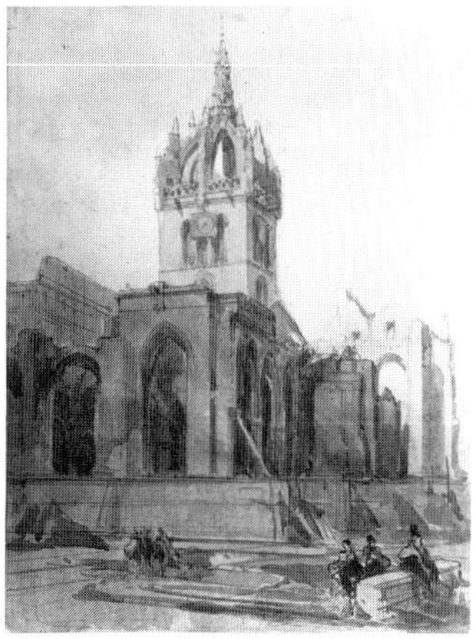

29

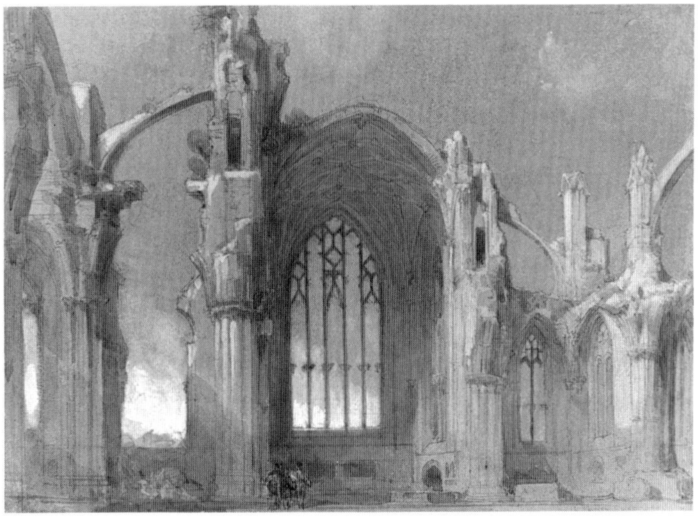

31

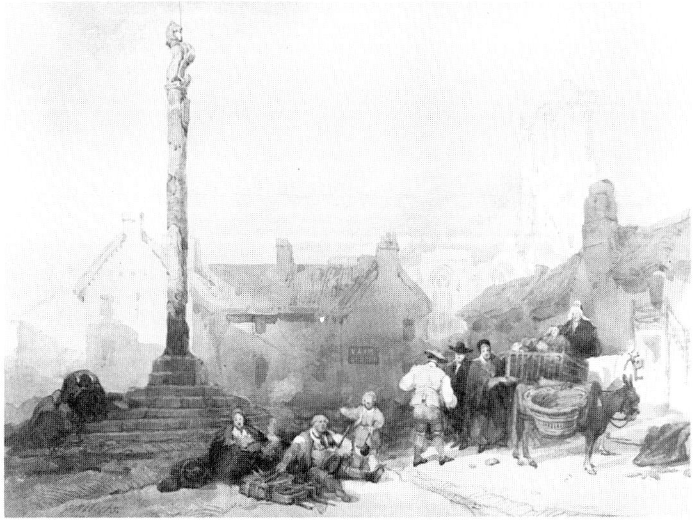

32

26 *Edinburgh Castle from Greyfriars Churchyard*. Pl. 10.
Watercolour heightened with white, 12 × 19 (30.5 × 48.3); s., & insc. *Edinburgh Castle from The Greyfriars.*
Bedford, Cecil Higgins Art Gallery.
Greyfriars Churchyard 'is of awesome monumental grandeur. It includes the burial place of the Adam family of architects.' (Edin. illus. guide.) In 1638, the National Covenant binding the signatories to resist the introduction of Popery and Episcopacy by Charles I was signed here.

27 *Edinburgh Castle from the New Gaol*, 1821. Pl. 9.
Watercolour, 9 × $12\frac{5}{8}$ (22.9 × 32.1); s. & d., insc. *Edinburgh.*
London, Thomas Agnew and Sons Ltd.
This very accomplished early drawing shows the north bridge of 1772, since rebuilt; the tower on the right was the watchtower of the prison.

28 *Street in Edinburgh* (St. Patrick's Church, Cowgate), *c.*1819. Pl. 11 (colour).
Oil over pencil on panel, $15\frac{1}{2}$ × 11 (39.4 × 27.9).
Private collection.
St. Patrick's Church is the building in the background with a circular steeple.

29 *St. Giles, Edinburgh, during Reconstruction*, *c.*1829.
Watercolour, $12\frac{1}{8}$ × 10 (30.8 × 25.4).
University of Glasgow, Hunterian Art Gallery, J. A. McCallum Collection.
In 1829 'only the crowned tower . . . dating from 1500 . . . escaped the necessary refacing by William Burn' (Edin. illus. guide); this gives a possible date for the watercolour.

30 *Ruins of Elgin Cathedral*, 1853. Pl. 23 (colour).
Oil, $19\frac{5}{8}$ × $29\frac{1}{2}$ (49.8 × 74.9); s. & d.
London, Victoria and Albert Museum.
On one of his lengthy tours of Scotland, Roberts wrote to his son-in-law from Elgin: 'I found it better than I had anticipated, *although it is much the worse for wear* and although great pains are taken in its preservation this also has its drawback, as the Ruins are Very naked, but after all a painter ought to make a subject out of any thing. It is not so often the subject is at fault as the Artist . . .' (12 Sep. 1848, NLS). Elgin is *c.*90 miles north-west of Aberdeen.

31 *Melrose Abbey*, 1831.
Pencil & watercolour heightened with white on grey paper, 10 × 14 (25.4 × 35.6); s. & d., insc. as title.
Bill Thomson, Albany Gallery.
Roberts frequently painted subjects of Melrose, but none have been found corresponding to this watercolour.

32 *The Cross of Melrose*, 1831.
Watercolour heightened with white, $8\frac{1}{4}$ × $11\frac{1}{4}$ (20.9 × 28.6); s. & d.
Private collection.
Engraved: W. Finden, *Illustrations to The Waverley Novels*, 1832, between pp. 43 and 44; Sigourney, *Pleasant Memories of Pleasant Lands*, 1843, frontispiece, *Melrose and its Abbey.*

33 *Priory of Pluscardine, Morayshire*, 1848.
Watercolour, 10 × $13\frac{1}{2}$ (25.4 × 34.3); s. & d., insc. as title & *Sep 19th 1848.*
Ingram Family Collection.
Roberts was visiting Scotland to make drawings for *Scotland Delineated*, 1847–52.

34 *Roslin Chapel*, 1842.
Watercolour heightened with white, 10 × 14 (25.4 × 35.6); s. & d., insc. *Roslin Oct 11th 1842.*
Edinburgh, National Galleries of Scotland.
Roberts was in Edinburgh in 1842 for a public dinner given in his honour. Roslin, near Edinburgh, was a favourite haunt; he complained of the cold while working at the chapel on this occasion.
Part of this study was used for *Entrance to the Crypt, Roslin Chapel*, 1843 (Victoria and Albert Museum); one of the dogs reappears in Cat. 35.

35 *Porch of Roslin Chapel*, 1845. Pl. 22 (colour).
Oil, $23\frac{1}{2} \times 17\frac{1}{2}$ (59.7 × 44.5); insc. *Roslyn Chapel 1859* and *To Thomas G Mackinlay from his friend David Roberts.*
Blackburn Art Gallery and Museum.

Roberts often painted both the interior and exterior of Roslin Chapel. This work was clearly re-dated by Roberts, for MacKinley wrote on 28 Aug. 1845: 'Your most welcome gift of the view of the Porch of Roslyn Chapel, a subject most beautifully treated, and exactly suited to the taste of Mrs MacKinley and myself . . . shall be treasured . . . and will have the advantage of increasing every year in value.'

A similar drawing, dated 1845, is in the Victoria and Albert Museum.

36 *Roslin Castle*, 1856. Pl. 3 (colour).
Oil, $28\frac{1}{4} \times 37$ (71.8 × 94); s., & insc. *For my Friend The Revd. James White Bonchurch 1856.*
Private collection.

Roberts gave a number of paintings to his friends, and several to James White, a retired clergyman; it was probably through Mr and Mrs White that Roberts's son-in-law rented a house in Bonchurch, Isle of Wight, for summer holidays. Roberts often went there to stay with his family.

He wrote that he had presented *Roslin Castle* to White 'to replace a miserable daub in his Dining Room which anoyed me' (RB). The painting is more romantic than is usual for Roberts; the castle, near Edinburgh, was familiar to him from boyhood.

37a. *Melrose Abbey.*
b. *Sweetheart Abbey.*
Two etchings, each $10 \times 7\frac{7}{8}$ (25.4 × 20), plate size.
Edinburgh, National Galleries of Scotland.

Two of a set of nine etchings given to J. T. Gibson Craig by Roberts, 29 April 1864. The other subjects include St. Andrews, Icolmkill, and Caerlaverock. Ballantine reproduced all nine in his biography. They are the only etchings known to have been made by Roberts.

'As to the Etchings they are the first of a series I have some thoughts of publishing on the Antiquitys of Scotland but I do not know that they will come to any thing . . . it will be in Monthly Parts, each part to contain 4 or 5 Etchings . . . to consist of say Twenty Parts . . . their will only be a hundred empressions of each.' (Roberts to Hay, 15 July 1831, NLS.) Many years later he wrote to David Laing that 'Circumstances over which I had little control made me leave England and abandon this pet scheme. Spain Morrocco and Syria broke new ground, and so the Ruined Abbeys and Old Castles were left.' (14 Dec. 1859, EUL.)

England

Roberts first came to London in 1822, and lived there for the rest of his life. Although he made drawings and paintings of London subjects in the early years, often for publication, he did not begin his great London series until the 1860s. English subjects were begun when he went 'abroad' for the first time, on his theatrical tour of 1816. Not many paintings or drawings are extant, though he drew on all his holiday visits to Sidmouth, Scarborough, the Isle of Wight, and so on (see *Chronology*).

38 *Fleet Street Looking towards Temple Bar*, 1832.
Watercolour, $5\frac{1}{2} \times 7\frac{1}{2}$ (13.9 × 19.1).
Michael Appleby.

Engraved: George Cooke, *Views in London and its Vicinity*, 1826–32, pl. 22, after a sketch by E. W. Cooke. The church on the right is St. Dunstan in the West; the engraving caption is *St. Dunstan's Church, Fleet Street.*

39 *Greenwich Hospital*, c.1861.
Oil, 11 × 24 (27.9 × 61).
London, National Maritime Museum.

Probably a study for the Worshipful Company of Goldsmiths' painting. A similar study, from a slightly different viewpoint, is in a private collection.

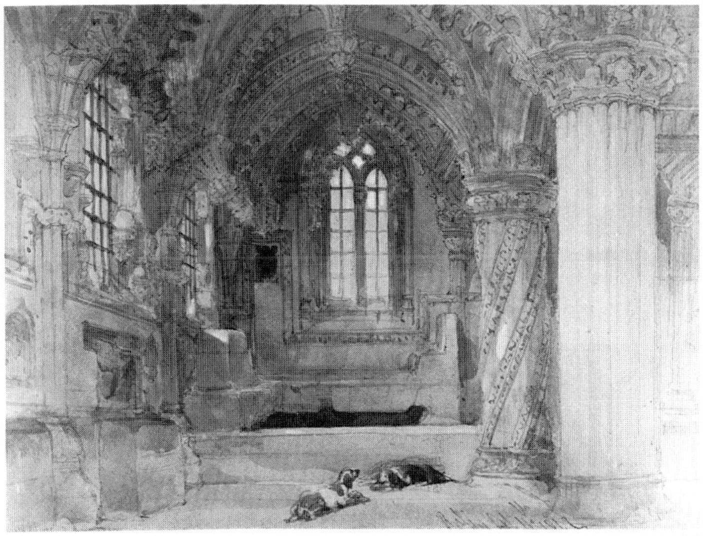
34

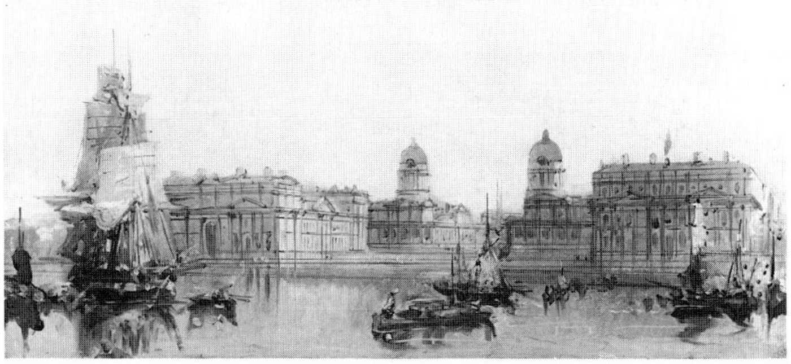
39

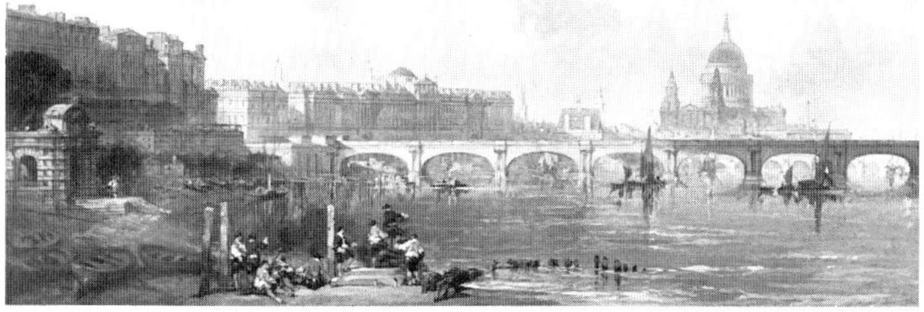

45

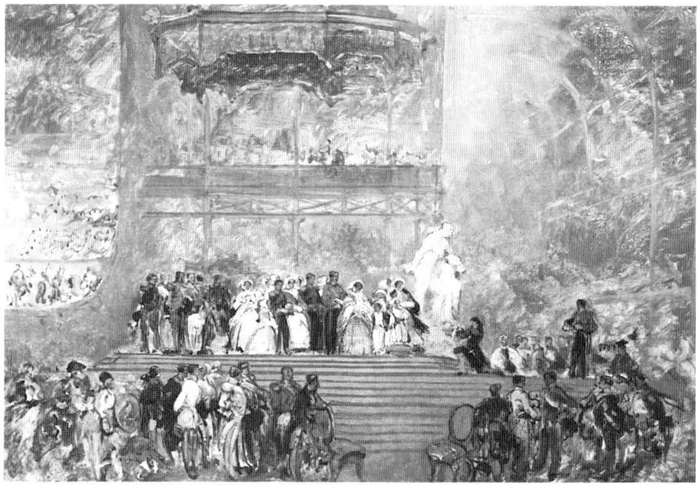

48

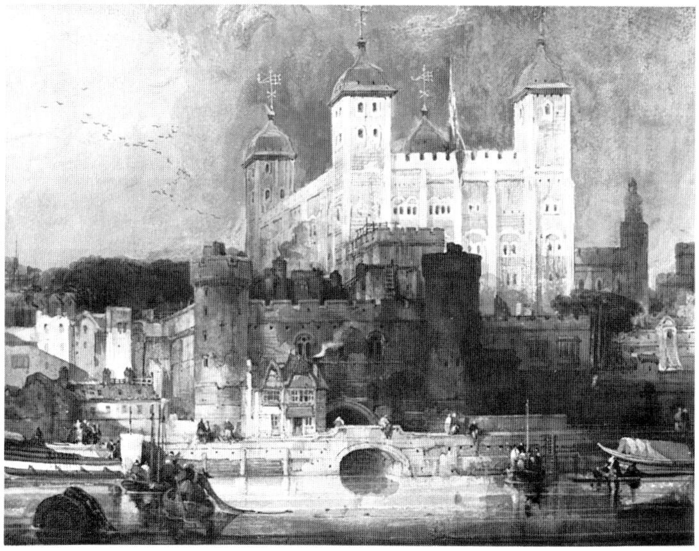

50

40 *The New Palace at Westminster from the River*, 1861. Pl. 26 (colour).
Oil, 34 × 60 (86.4 × 152.4).
London, the Worshipful Company of Goldsmiths.

According to his biographer, James Ballantine, Roberts's series of London paintings had been suggested to him by Turner. Roberts was anxious to get the series completed before the 'great sewrage, which is now going on, to purify it and change it from its present State, and which will tottaly alter its present appearance' (to Hay, 10 June 1861, NLS). He was referring to the building of the Victoria Embankment by Joseph Bazalgette. The Embankment would consist of a new highway, and would also accommodate the Metropolitan District underground railway and the lower level artery of London's new system of sewers.

Exhibited RA 1862 (628), and bought by Charles Lucas, it was presented to the Worshipful Company of Goldsmiths by his grandsons, along with Cat. 42.

41 *St. Paul's and Blackfriars Bridge from the Thames*, 1861.
Pencil & watercolour heightened with white on tinted paper, $9\frac{1}{2} \times 13\frac{1}{2}$ (24.1 × 34.3); s., & insc. *Blackfriars August 28th 1861*.
Bill Thomson, Albany Gallery.

A study from a different viewpoint for Cat. 42. The verso has a watercolour sketch of the Lord Mayor's state barge.

42 *St. Paul's from Blackfriars*, 1862. Pl. 27 (colour).
Oil, 52 × 42 (132 × 106.7).
London, the Worshipful Company of Goldsmiths.

Showing the Embarkation of the Lord Mayor at Blackfriars, a ceremony abolished in 1856. Blackfriars Bridge was built in 1760–9 and rebuilt in 1865–9.

Exhibited RA 1862 (489) as *A Relic of the Past*, it was bought by Charles Lucas (see Cat. 40). It was the favourite painting among those shown at Roberts's 'Private View' in his studio before the RA opening (letter to his son-in-law, 8 April 1862, PC).

43 *St. Paul's, Sunset*, c.1863. Pl. 34 (colour).
Oil, 10 × 23 (25.4 × 58.4).
Private collection.

This unusually free painting was sold at Roberts's studio sale in 1865; later bought by his son-in-law, it passed by descent to the artist's great-grandson. It is probably a study for *St. Paul's from the River Looking West, Sunset*, 1863 (untraced).

44 *St. Paul's Cathedral*, 1863.
Watercolour heightened with white on two joined sheets of paper, 5 × 14 (12.7 × 35.6); insc. *Copice Row Clerkenwell. July 31st 1863*.
Edinburgh, National Galleries of Scotland.

45 *Somerset House and the Adelphi from Hungerford Bridge*, 1861.
Oil, 24 × 42 (61 × 106.7); s. & d.
Private collection.

The bridge in the foreground is Waterloo Bridge.

46 *Somerset House and Waterloo Bridge*, 1862. Pl. 31.
Watercolour heightened with white, $9\frac{3}{8} \times 13\frac{3}{8}$ (23.8 × 34); s. & d.
London, Baring Brothers & Co., Ltd.

47 *The Staircase at Stafford House*, 1832. Pl. 30 (colour).
Oil, $52\frac{1}{2} \times 40\frac{1}{2}$ (133.4 × 102.9).
Government Art Collection.

Roberts wrote to Hay on 10 July 1830: 'I have been honoured with a commission to paint a Picture for the Marquis of Staford, not only one of the richest Noblemen in England, but one of the most refined taste, as regards the Arts . . .' (NLS).

Commissioned to hang at Stafford House (now Lancaster House), the painting was sold at Christie's in 1958 by the Duke of Sutherland (a descendant of the Marquis of Stafford) and, on being bought by the Government Art Collection, was returned to Lancaster House, where it now hangs.

48 *Sketch for Opening of the Crystal Palace at Sydenham,* 1854.
Oil, 22 × $35\frac{1}{2}$ (55.9 × 90.1); insc. recto, with a key to those present, *This sketch of the opening of the Crystal Palace at Sydenham in 1854 by HMGM Queen Victoria* [given] *to Sir Joseph Paxton by his friend David Roberts*; insc. verso *Painted by order of Her Majesty – a sketch for a large picture 1854 and given to Sir Joseph Paxton by his friends.*
The Earl of Shelburne.

Sir Joseph Paxton (1801–65) was the designer of the Crystal Palace. There are two Roberts paintings of the Crystal Palace in the Royal Collection, one of the 1851 opening, and the other of the 1853 one, following its rebuilding at Sydenham.

49 *The Thames at Hungerford Bridge,* c.1861. Pl. 35 (colour).
Watercolour with touches of white, $11\frac{1}{2}$ × $16\frac{1}{2}$ (29.2 × 41.9).
Ingram Family Collection.

Looking across the Thames to the south side where the Shot Tower and the Lion Brewery can be seen; the suspension bridge, designed by Isambard Kingdom Brunel, was built 1841–5.

50 *The Tower of London,* 1830.
Watercolour with touches of white, $8\frac{3}{4}$ × $11\frac{3}{4}$ (22.2 × 29.8); s. & d.
Newport Museum and Art Gallery.

Engraved: E. Finden, *Illustrations to The Waverley Novels,* 1832. Another watercolour of the Tower, dated 1864, was sold at Christie's in 1965.

51 *The Bridge at Blenheim,* (?)1835.
Pencil & wash, $6\frac{3}{4}$ × 10 (17.1 × 25.4); insc. *BLENHEIM.*
Family collection.

Blenheim 'is the finest specimen of an old English park and grounds to say nothing of the Mansion' (Roberts to Hay, 30 Oct. 1835, NLS). It is possible that Roberts revisited Blenheim, therefore the dating is uncertain.

52 *Durham,* 1836.
Pencil & wash, 7 × 10 (17.8 × 25.4); insc. *Durham Sep 14th 1836.*
Leeds City Art Galleries.

Roberts wrote to his daughter the same day that he made this drawing: 'here I am at Durham, which allthough I had seen it many years since is I think independant of rain! rain! rain! most glorious . . . I am so delighted with this place that independant of the weather I shall stop for a day or two.' (NLS.)

53 *East Window, Netley Abbey, Hampshire,* 1824.
Watercolour heightened with white, 12 × 9 (30.5 × 22.9); s. & d.
Richard Walker.

54 *Norham Castle, Northumberland,* 1859.
Watercolour heightened with white, $4\frac{1}{2}$ × $6\frac{1}{2}$ (11.4 × 16.5); insc. *Norham Castle August 30 1859.*
Private collection.

55 *Sidmouth.*
a. *Western View.*
b. *From Verandah of Beacon Place, Peak Hill.*
Lithographs, each $10\frac{1}{2}$ × 14 (26.7 × 35.6); lithographed by R. Carrick, published by Day and Haghe.
Monica Bicknell Lightwood.

Roberts went to Sidmouth with his family twice, in 1845 and 1848. The drawings for these lithographs could have been made on either visit. There is a third view recorded by J. R. Abbey (*Scenery of Great Britain and Ireland,* 1952) of Sidmouth from Salcombe Hill (untraced); the size of the lithographs is given as 15 × $22\frac{1}{2}$ (38.1 × 57.2), so possibly there were two editions.

France

The dates of Roberts's early trips to France are uncertain; his first recorded visit was in 1824 to Dieppe, Rouen and Le Havre (RB). In 1829 he was in Paris for a month, but to judge from paintings of 1826 (Cat. 64) and 1827 (Abbeville, untraced; see Cat. 56), he crossed the Channel at least once between 1824 and 1829, also visiting Caen and Amiens at some stage. Frequent trips followed between 1832 and 1863 (see *Chronology,* pp. 92–5).

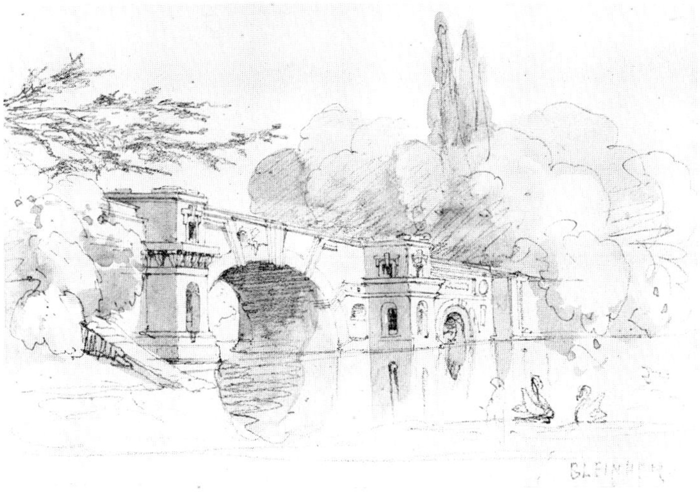
51

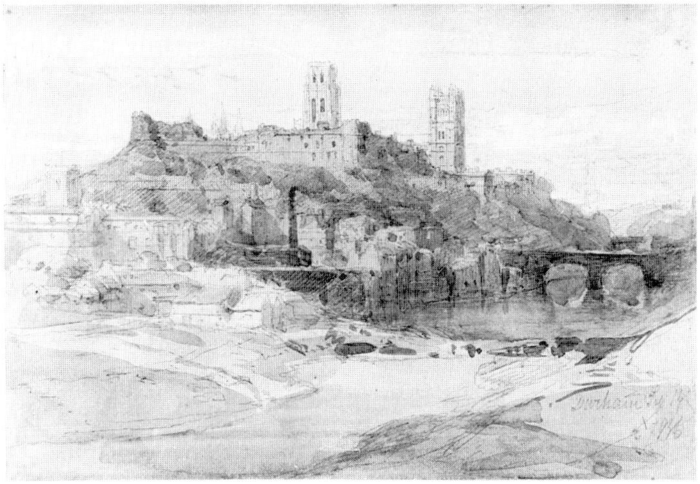
52

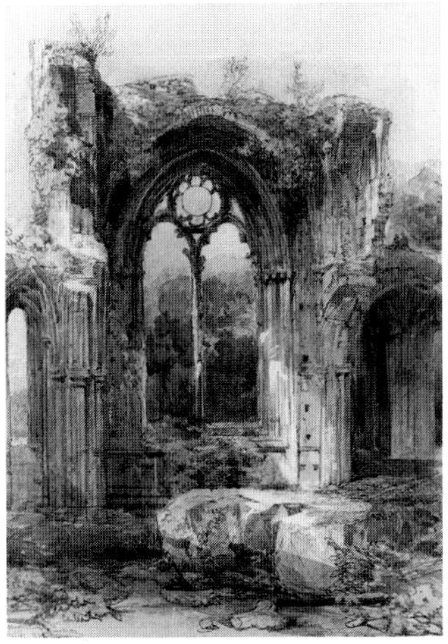
53

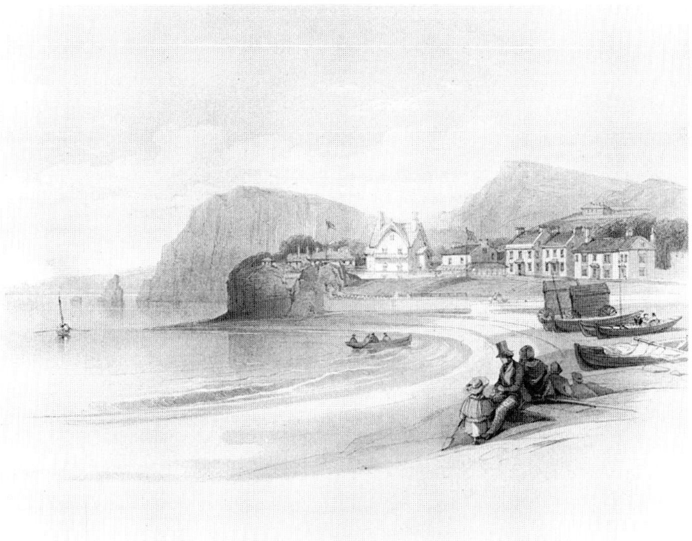

55a

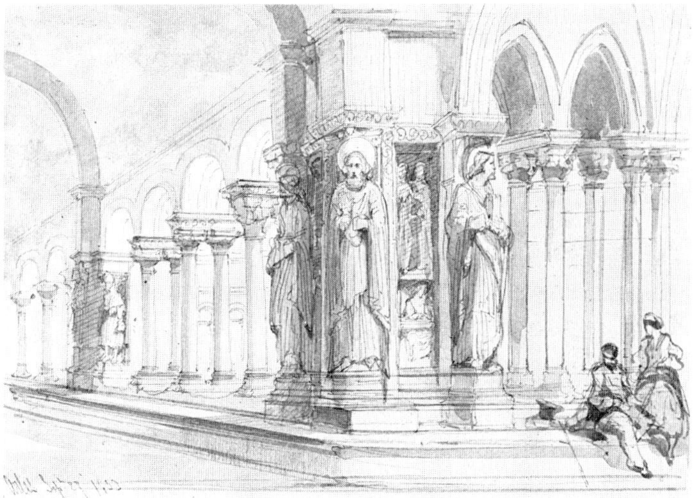

59

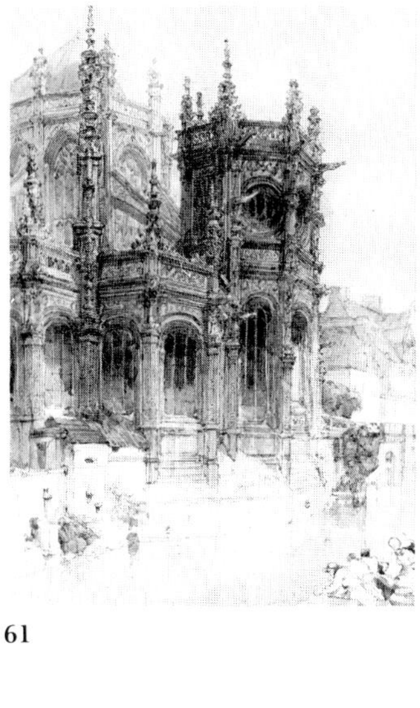

61

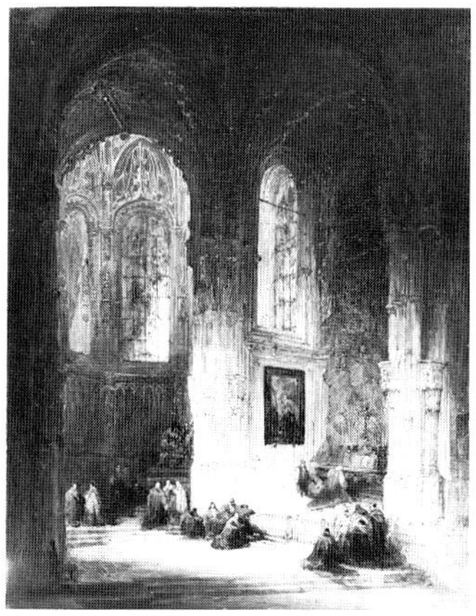

62

56 *Marché au Blé, Abbeville,* *c.*1824–5. Pl. 44.
Pencil, brown ink & wash, $15\frac{1}{2} \times 20\frac{3}{4}$ (39.4 × 52.7); insc. as title.
London, Victoria and Albert Museum.

The church in the background is St. Wulfran, also seen in Cat. 57. Probably used for an oil exhibited BI 1827 (31), bought by Robert Vernon and sold by him at Christie's, 1842 (whereabouts unknown).

57 *Abbeville,* 1830.
Watercolour, $12 \times 8\frac{3}{4}$ (30.5 × 22.2); s. & d.
The Provost and Fellows of Eton College.

Engraved: A. R. Freebairn, *Winter's Wreath,* 1832, facing p. 217. The church is St. Wulfran, the viewpoint similar to that of Cat. 58.

58 *Abbeville,* *c.*1830. Pl. 43.
Oil on panel, 26 × 22 (66 × 55.9).
London, the Merchant Taylors' Company.

Another, apparently similar version was exhibited SBA 1828 (346) and bought by the Marquis of Lansdowne. A third picture of St. Wulfran, also exhibited SBA 1828 (22) was bought by a dealer. Both works are untraced.

59 *Cloisters of St. Trophîme, Arles,* 1853.
Pencil & wash, $7\frac{1}{2} \times 10\frac{1}{2}$ (19 × 26.7); insc. *Arles Sept 27 1853.*
Birmingham City Museum and Art Gallery.

Roberts visited Arles in 1838 on his way to the East, and again in 1853 en route to Rome. Ballantine wrote: 'At Arles Roberts made two drawings of a church which he describes as a curious specimen of the earliest Christian period, and very interesting to the archaeologist as showing the connecting link between the Roman [Romanesque] and the pointed [Gothic] styles of architecture.' (p. 176.)

60 *St. Pierre, Caen,* 1830.
Pen, coloured inks & watercolour heightened with white, $16\frac{3}{4} \times 12\frac{1}{4}$ (42.5 × 31.1); s. & d.
Manchester City Art Galleries.

The church of St. Pierre 'formerly rose abruptly from the waters of the river Orne, painted by a thousand artists' (Augustus Hare, *North-Western France,* 1895, p. 110); by 1895, however, the river had been diverted and a market built on its site.

A slightly different version engraved: J. Tingis, *Gallery of Modern British Artists,* 1835, Pl. 5, as *Caen Cathedral.*

61 *The Lady Chapel, Church of St. Pierre, at Caen,* 1828.
Watercolour, $13\frac{1}{4} \times 9\frac{3}{4}$ (33.7 × 24.8); insc. *Caen 1828.*
Sheffield City Art Galleries.

A similar watercolour from a different viewpoint, dated 1831, is in the Victoria and Albert Museum.

62 *The Lady Chapel, Church of St. Pierre at Caen,* 1832.
Oil on panel, 19 × 15 (48.3 × 38.1).
Manchester City Art Galleries.

Belonged to James Stewart of Dunearn, who bought several of Roberts's early works, including his first recorded painting. Another version, dated 1829, was in Lord Northwick's collection; a third, dated 1830, was bought by William Wells of Redleaf; both are untraced.

An engraving with variations was made from the painting, or a very similar one, but engraver and publication are unknown.

63 *St. Sauveur, Caen.*
a. Pencil & wash on three joined sheets of paper, 13 × 7 (33 × 17.8); s. & d. 1828.
Private collection.
Bought 1983 from Cyril Fry.
b. Watercolour heightened with white, $13\frac{1}{2} \times 9$ (34.3 × 22.9); s. & insc. *S'SAUVEUR . . .* and *Much the Fl . . .*
Private collection.

Bought *c.*1966 from Manning Gallery. Signature probably added later (contains *RA*: Roberts not elected RA until 1841).
c. Watercolour heightened with white, $10\frac{3}{4} \times 8$ (27.3 × 20.3).
Birmingham City Museum and Art Gallery.
Bequeathed by J. Leslie Wright, 1953.

d. Watercolour heightened with white, 9 × 6½ (22.9 × 16.5); s. & d. 1830.
London, Baring Brothers & Co., Ltd.

Bought from the Mrs Cecil Keith collection, 1984.

Four of eight watercolours that have been traced of the interior of this church, taken from two viewpoints. *a* was probably the first and used as a study. There are variations in the three others, e.g. in the ornamental balustrading and the position of the broken window. *b* and one version exhibited Spink, 1981, show the strong shaft of light. *c*, from the other side of the church, is less dramatic. Two other versions are similar, but one (Spink, 1985) is taken from further back and has more people in the foreground. The watercolours would be hard to distinguish were it not for the variations in figures and furnishings. No evidence has been found that any were engraved.

There are three oils of the subject, two undated (Bristol City Art Gallery, and one sold New York, 1983), and a third dated 1831 (untraced). Roberts also used *The Interior of St. Sauveur* as a subject for his 1829 Diorama at the Queens Bazaar. In Roberts's time the church was used as a grain store: see *b*, where men are flailing.

64 *Interior of the Church of St. Geneviève at Paris*, 1826.
Oil, 30¾ × 24½ (78.1 × 62.2); signed.
University of Liverpool.

Exhibited SBA 1826 (105); bought by the Duke of Sutherland and sold at Christie's by the Duke's descendants, 4 March 1949 (71).

St. Geneviève, built between 1764 and 1790, was converted in 1791 to be a national memorial temple to be called The Pantheon.

65 *Grand Entrance to Rouen Cathedral*, 1831. Frontispiece (colour).
Oil, 72 × 54 (182.9 × 137.1); s. & d.
Blackpool, Grundy Art Gallery.

On its exhibition at the SBA, 1831 (161) the *Literary Gazette* wrote: 'Painted to the very letter of the description quoted in the catalogue from *Cotman's Antiquities of Normandy*: "The western front forms a *tout ensemble* of the most imposing character. The very discrepancy in the different parts, by increasing the variety, adds to the effect of the whole." Every body knows Mr Roberts's talents; and they were never more finely exemplified.' After being shown in London, it went to the Scottish Academy, 1834, and to Glasgow, 1835; bought by D. R. Hay, who wrote on 17 Dec. 1835 that he would return it to Roberts for repair as 'some of the Glasgonian artists gave it a touch before hanging it up, but of course inefficiently' (NLS).

This is the West Front so often and so differently painted by Claude Monet. Other versions of the subject by Roberts include two of the West Front, 1825 (private collection) and 1826 (painted for Lord Northwick, untraced), and South Transept, 1825 (Smithsonian Institute, Washington D.C.).

66 *Church of St. Maclou at Rouen*, 1829. Pl. 46 (colour).
Oil on panel, 21 × 15¾ (53.3 × 40); s. & d.
London, Trustees of the Tate Gallery.

Roberts's 1824 visit to Rouen resulted in a number of paintings of its marvellous churches (e.g. Cat. 65). The West Porch of St. Maclou depicted here is very elaborately carved; the painting shows some of the clumsiness apparent in several of Roberts's early oils, especially in the figures. An undated pen, ink & wash drawing from the same viewpoint is in a private collection; an oil, exhibited SBA 1825 (114) is untraced. A lithograph of St. Maclou by Samuel Prout (published by Rowney and Foster, London 1823) has much the same viewpoint, but noticeable variations in the architecture of the entrance porch, especially the foreground.

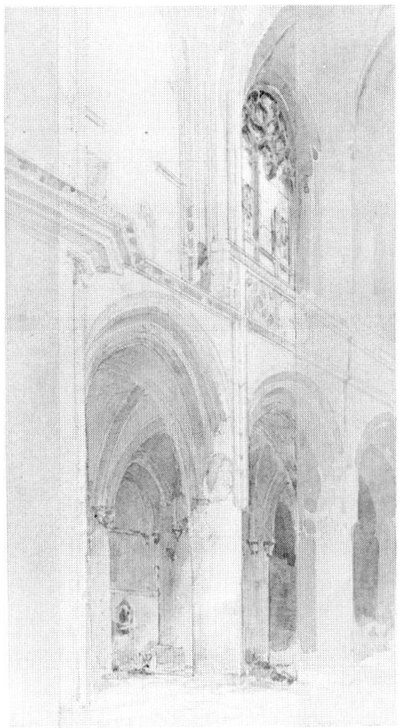
63a

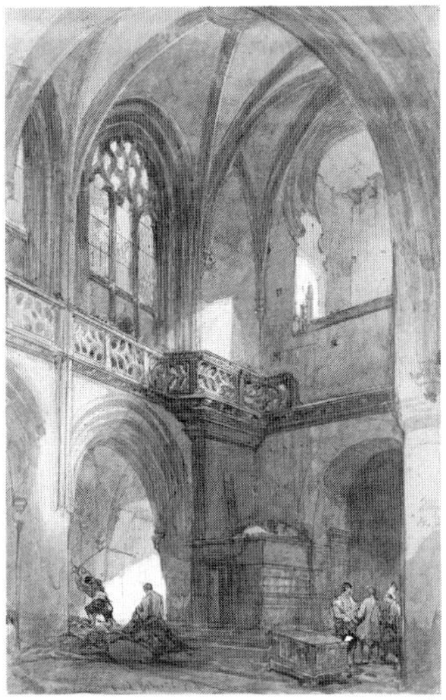
63b

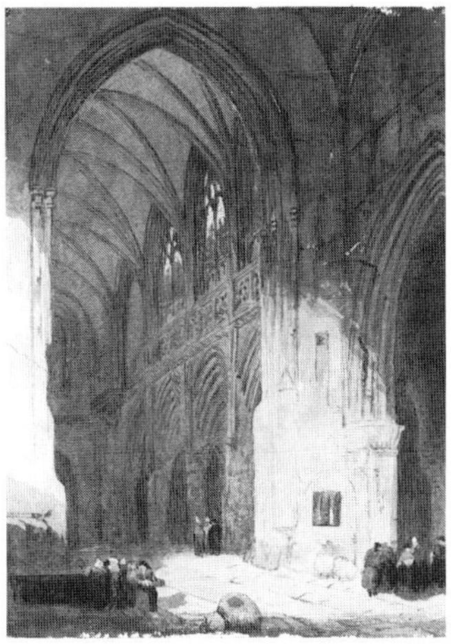
63c

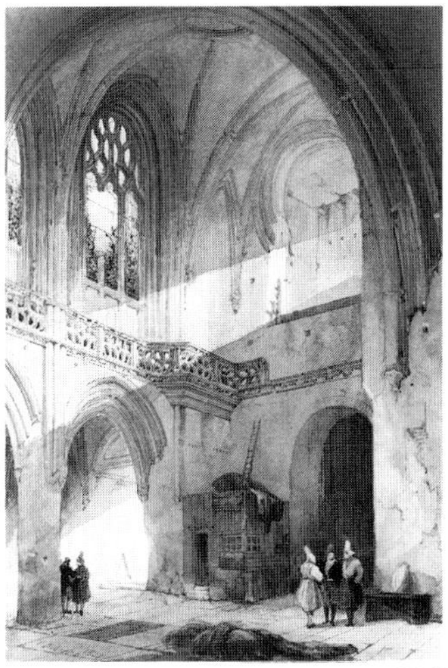
63d

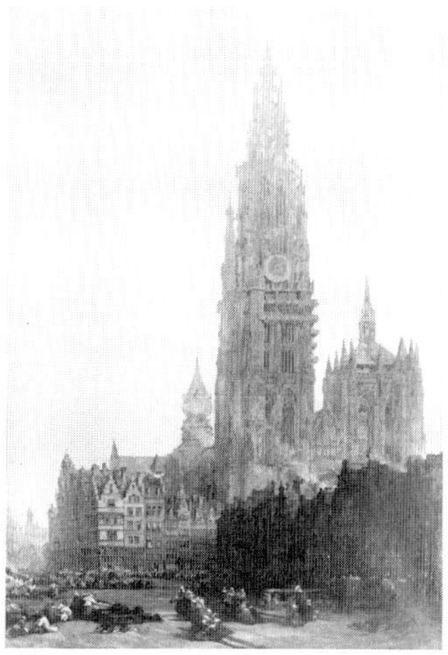

69

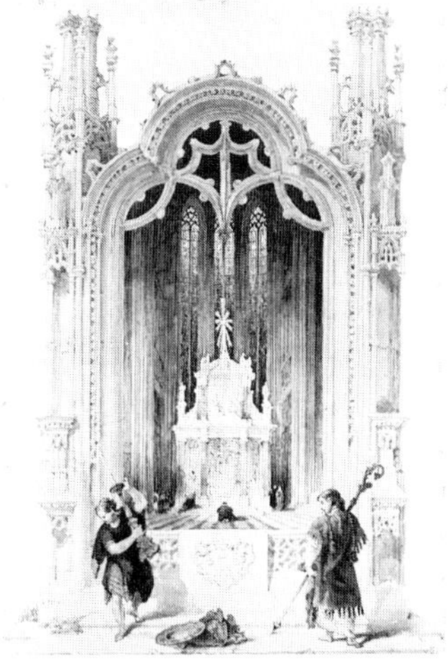

72

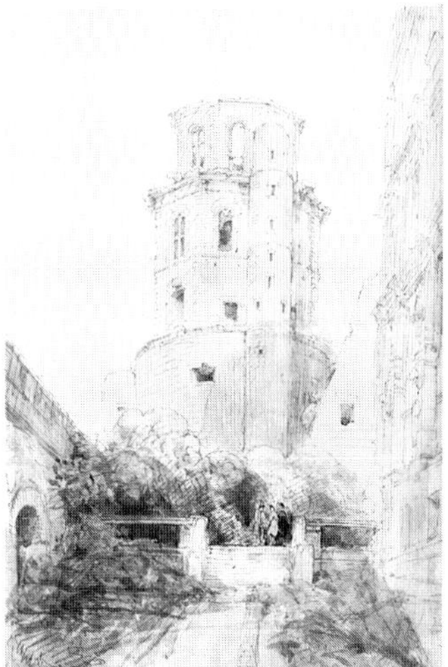

73

Belgium, Holland and Germany

Roberts went a number of times to Belgium. The first, unrecorded, visit was *c.*1825–6, based on the evidence of paintings (e.g. *Antwerp Cathedral*, 1827; Puerto Rico). Later visits were made in 1845, 1849, 1850 and 1861. His visits to Holland were more brief, the first being in 1830 on his way to the Rhine, and the second in 1849. An 1830 Rhine trip was his only sketching journey to Germany, although he went through the country on his way to and from Venice in 1851.

67 *Three Pages from an Antwerp Sketchbook*, 1845.
a. *Three Women Seated*. Pl. 29.
Pencil & wash, 5 × 7 (12.7 × 17.8); insc. *Antwerp*.
b. *Figures and Buildings*.
Pencil & wash, 5 × 7 (12.7 × 17.8); insc. *Antwerp Oct 17 45*.
c. *Figures*. Pl. 28.
Pencil & wash, 7 × 5 (17.8 × 12.7); insc. *Antwerp*.
Edinburgh, National Galleries of Scotland.

No complete sketchbook has yet been traced.

68 *Antwerp Cathedral*, (?)1845.
Pencil & wash, $13\frac{3}{4} \times 9\frac{3}{4}$ (34.9 × 24.8).
Cambridge, the Syndics of the Fitzwilliam Museum.

Drawn from the opposite side to Cat. 69. Probably HBS 1881 (241), bought by John Taylor, who was married to Rosa, one of Roberts's granddaughters.

69 *West Front of Antwerp Cathedral*, 1847.
Oil, $55\frac{1}{2} \times 39\frac{1}{2}$ (141 × 100.3); s. & d.
Preston, Harris Museum and Art Gallery.

Roberts wrote to his daughter that he was making a careful study from a window, of the tower of the Cathedral with the old houses around it (13 Oct. 1845, Ballantine, p. 161). The houses have now gone and one can better see the main elevation. The south tower of the Cathedral has never been completed.

Painted for Lord Northwick, it was exhibited RA 1847 (57), and Liverpool Academy 1847 (28), where it was bought by Richard Newsham, as Lord Northwick had decided that he already had too many paintings by Roberts, including another of Antwerp.

There are four other versions of the exterior of Antwerp Cathedral: Lord Northwick's, 1827 (Museo de Arte e Ponce, Puerto Rico), and ones dated 1829 (Cooper Art Gallery, Barnsley), 1860 (Guildhall Art Gallery, City of London), and 1852 (untraced).

70 *Collegiate Church of St. Paul, Antwerp*, 1848. Pl. 53 (colour).
Oil, $55\frac{1}{2} \times 44$ (141 × 111.8); s. & d., insc. verso *High Altar of the Church of St. Paul, Antwerp. Painted for Robert Vernon Esq*.
London, Trustees of the Tate Gallery.

Vernon was one of the great Victorian philanthropic art collectors; he presented 157 paintings to the nation in 1847. Exhibited RA 1848 (252), Cat. 70 was engraved by E. Challis for the *Vernon Gallery*, 1849, Vol. I, p. 41.

Shows the main altar from the choir, the stalls of which are much foreshortened; the altar and altarpiece are in reality wider; two box-shaped marble tombs flank the steps. Another version, 1861, is in a family collection; an undated oil in Sweden appears to be a study for Cat. 70; a third version (untraced), 1860, was described as very small (RB).

71 *Chapel in the Cathedral of Notre Dame, Bruges*, 1862. Pl. 54 (colour).
Oil, 48 × 36 (122 × 91.4); s. & d.
The Earl of Shelburne.

Exhibited RA 1862 (236), but poorly hung. Roberts noted that it was painted in a very short time (RB). It shows the side-aisle chapel of Notre Dame (which is not the Cathedral of Bruges); the paintings still hang there but Roberts made some alterations to the altar and windows.

72 *Tomb of the Three Kings, Cologne*, 1832.
Watercolour, $11\frac{1}{2} \times 8$ (29.2 × 20.3); s. & d.
Preston, Harris Museum and Art Gallery.

Engraved: W. Deeble, *Pilgrims of the Rhine*, 1834, facing p. 92. Another watercolour of the subject, *Shrine of the Kings*, 1831, is in the Whitworth Art Gallery, Manchester.

73 *Tower at Heidelberg*, 1830.
Pencil & wash, $13\frac{3}{4} \times 9$ (34.9×22.9); s. & d.
Leeds City Art Galleries.
Probably the preliminary drawing for the engraving by W. T. Willmore, *Literary Souvenir*, 1833, facing p. 218. Roberts went to the Rhineland in 1830 but did not stay long because of the 'Three Days Revolution', the overthrow of the monarchy in France, followed by unrest in Paris.

74 *By the Moselle, Koblenz*, (?)1830.
Watercolour, $14 \times 8\frac{3}{4}$ (35.6×22.2); insc. *Coblentz*.
Mrs Elizabeth Ochiltree Forbes.
This lively watercolour may have been drawn in 1830 when Roberts went to the Rhine, or in 1851 on his journey to or from Venice, when he went through the same part of Germany.

75 *Malines Cathedral*, 1831.
Watercolour, $12\frac{7}{8} \times 8\frac{7}{8}$ (32.7×22.5); s. & d.
Private collection.
Engraved: J. Carter, *Pilgrims of the Rhine*, 1834, facing p. 21. Malines (Mechelen) lies between Brussels and Antwerp; the Cathedral, St. Rombaut, was painted several times by Roberts (see Cat. 76).

76 *Malines Cathedral*, 1831.
Watercolour, $12\frac{1}{8} \times 8\frac{7}{8}$ (30.8×22.5); s. & d.
Michael Appleby.

77 *Mayence* (Mainz), 1831.
Watercolour heightened with white, $12\frac{3}{4} \times 8\frac{3}{4}$ (32.4×22.2); s. & d., insc. *Mitternachtsgasse*.
Ingram Family Collection.

78 *Scene on the Rhine*, 1831.
Watercolour with touches of white, $8 \times 11\frac{3}{4}$ (20.3×29.8); s. & d., insc. *ON THE RHINE*.
Miss Jane Wykeham-Musgrave.

79 *St. Laurence, Rotterdam*, 1831.
Watercolour heightened with white, $9 \times 12\frac{5}{8}$ (22.9×32.1); s. & d.
Private collection.
A similar drawing (untraced) engraved: J. Carter, *Pilgrims of the Rhine*, 1834, facing p. 62. Roberts painted the church twice, and sent one oil to D. R. Hay (both untraced).

Spain

Roberts went to Spain 1832–3. He was particularly struck by the Moorish architecture of southern Spain, and by the climate, so different to that of northern Europe. Morocco gave him an insight into yet another world, and may well have stimulated his wish to travel to Egypt and the Holy Land. He brought back numerous sketches, which he used for oils and drawings for lithographs and engravings; it was probably some of his earnings from these works that financed his eastern journey.

80 *Alcala da Guadaira, near Seville*, 1833.
Pencil & watercolour heightened with yellow bodycolour on grey paper, $9\frac{3}{4} \times 14$ (24.8×35.6); s. & d., insc. *The castle Alcala the banks of the Guadaira*.
Bill Thomson, Albany Gallery.

81 *Interior of the Cathedral at Burgos*, 1835. Pl. 7 (colour).
Oil on panel with shaped top, $21\frac{3}{4} \times 12$ (55.2×30.5); s. & d.
London, Trustees of the Tate Gallery.
'A portion of the Cathedral of Burgos with the fantastically decorated staircase and other rich details, is extremely picturesque, while the skill with which the greater portion is thrown into shade lends a peculiar mystery to the scene.' (Dr Waagen, *Treasures of Art in Great Britain*, 1854, Vol. I, p. 387.) The fine double staircase, *Escalera Dorada*, is at the end of the cathedral's north transept.
Exhibited RA 1835 (359) as *Entrance to the North Transept, Cathedral of Burgos*, it was bought by Robert Vernon (see Cat. 70), who gave it to the nation in 1847. Engraved: E. Challis, *Vernon Gallery*, 1849, Vol. I, pl. 15. Roberts wrote to Hay, 29 May 1835: 'As to my Picture now at the Academy I am very far from being satisfied with it . . . it wants vigor, add to which the disadvantage of not being allowed to paint upon it after being hung . . . still the subject is a good one.' (NLS.)

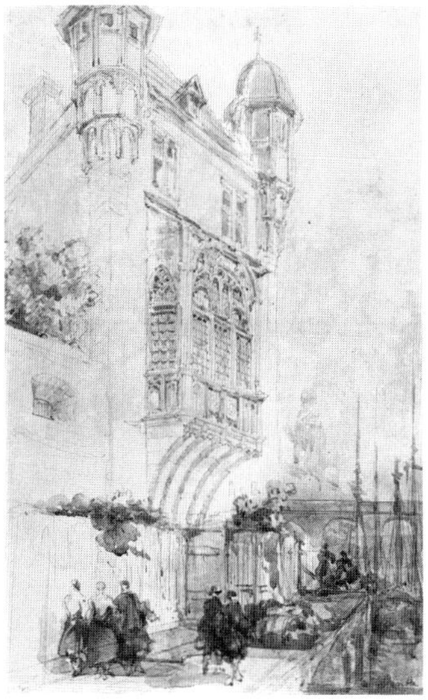
74

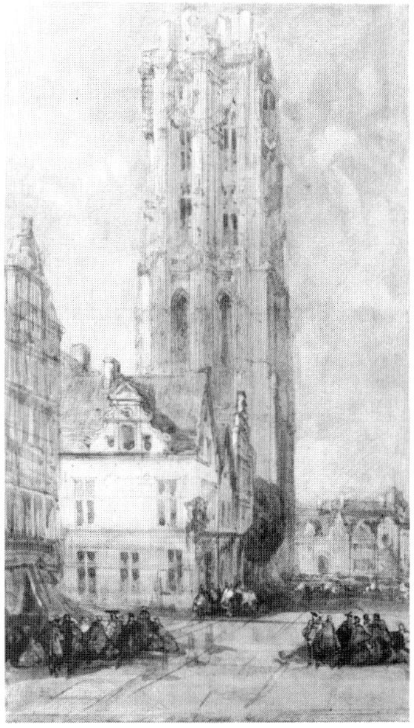
75

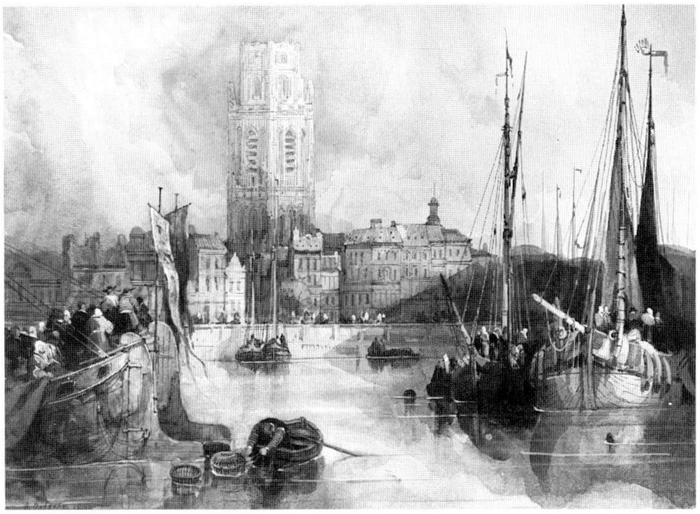
79

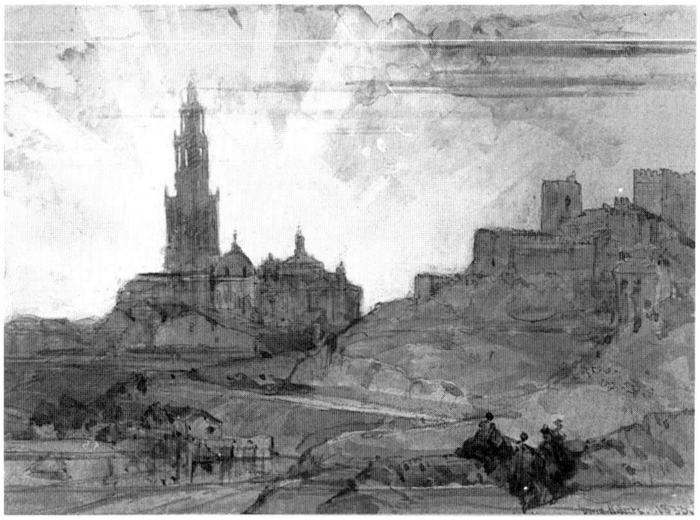
85

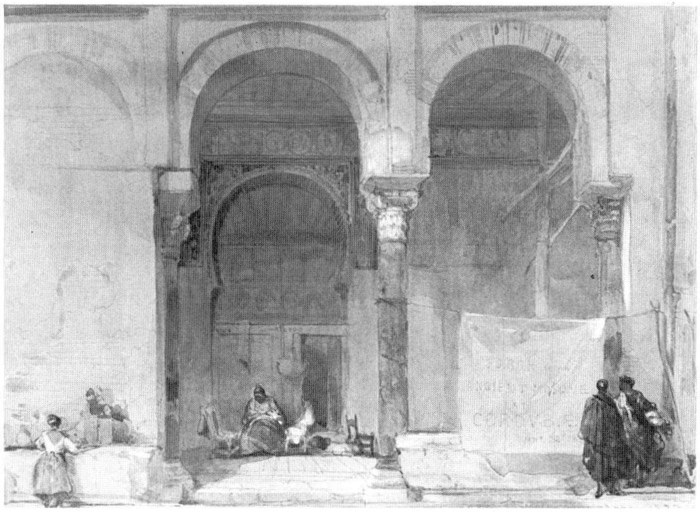
88

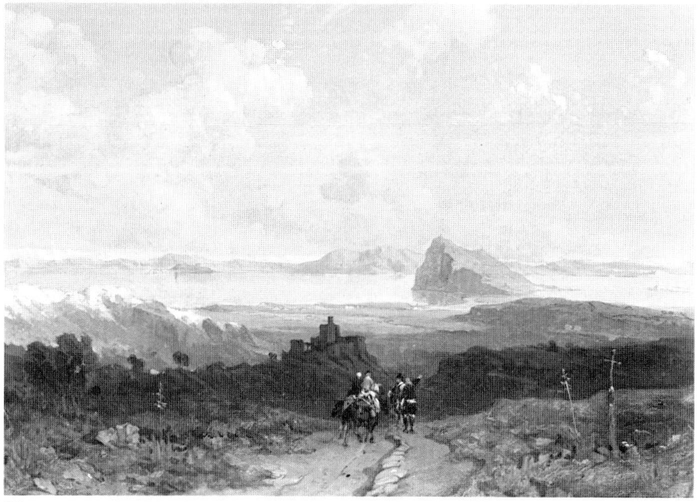
90

82 *Grand Staircase, Burgos Cathedral*, 1836.
Watercolour heightened with white, 14 × 11 (35.6 × 27.9); s. & d.
University of Manchester, Whitworth Art Gallery.
Engraved: E. Challis, *Landscape Annual*, 1837, facing p. 82. There are variations between this and Cat. 81 in the figures, the detail of the balustrade, and the omission of the framed painting. Light and shade are more dramatic in the oil.

83 *Exterior of Burgos Cathedral*, 1836.
Watercolour heightened with white, $15\frac{1}{2} \times 10$ (39.4 × 25.4); s. & d.
London, Trustees of the British Museum.
Engraved: E. Challis, *Landscape Annual*, 1837, facing p. 81. Another, slightly smaller version (private collection) is the on-the-spot version, dated 10 Dec. 1832; only the thatched building on the left is different. The latter no longer stands, but otherwise the view is little changed today.

84 *Chapter House, Burgos Cathedral*, (?)1836. Pl. 48.
Pencil & wash heightened with white, 17 × 11 (43.2 × 27.9).
Private collection.
Lithographed: T. S. Boys, *Picturesque Sketches in Spain*, 1837, pl. VII, as *Part of the Cathedral, Burgos*.

85 *Carmona, Sunset*, 1833.
Watercolour over black chalk on grey paper, heightened with yellow bodycolour, $7\frac{1}{4} \times 10\frac{1}{2}$ (18.4 × 26.7); s. & d., insc. *Carmona*.
Bill Thomson, Albany Gallery.
A similar watercolour (untraced) engraved: S. Fisher, *Landscape Annual*, 1836, facing p. 157, as *Entrance to the Town of Carmona*. Cat. 85 was incorrectly titled *Seville Cathedral, Sunset* when sold Christie's, 19 March 1985 (143).
A small oil, dated 1853, which appears to be similar, was presented by Roberts to his dentist, Mr Mereweather (untraced).

86 *The Alcazar or Palace of the Moorish Kings, Cordoba*, 1833. Pl. 52.
Watercolour with touches of white, $9\frac{1}{2} \times 13\frac{1}{2}$ (24.1 × 34.3); s. & d. 1832, insc. as title & d. 1833.
Dudley Museum and Art Gallery.
Roberts was mistaken in re-dating this watercolour 1832; he did not reach Cordoba until Jan. 1833. He made many drawings of the view of the Alcazar and Mosque from across the Guadalquiver; one, in the Whitworth Art Gallery, was engraved by J. C. Armytage, *Landscape Annual*, 1836, facing p. 43.

87 *Chapel of Mahomed in the Mosque at Cordoba*, 1833. Pl. 51.
Pencil & wash heightened with white, $13\frac{1}{2} \times 10$ (34.3 × 25.4); s., & insc. *Chapel of Mahomed in the Mosque at Cordova January 15th 1833*.
Private collection.
Roberts was fascinated by the interior of this enormous mosque; a painting, *The Sanctuary of the Koran*, 1849, is in the Museo de Arte de Ponce, Puerto Rico; another, 1837, was painted for Frank Hall Standish (untraced). 'The "*Lion*" of Cordova is the Mosque, once second only to that of Mecca.' (Roberts to Hay, 30 Jan. 1833, NLS.)

88 *Porch of an Ancient Mosque, Cordoba*, 1833.
Pencil & watercolour heightened with bodycolour on grey paper, $9\frac{5}{8} \times 13\frac{1}{2}$ (24.4 × 34.3); s. & d., insc. *PORCH OF AN ANCIENT MOSQUE CORDUBAE JAN 22 1833*.
Bill Thomson, Albany Gallery.

89 *The Church of St. Nicholas, Cordoba*, 1835.
Watercolour, $12\frac{1}{4} \times 7\frac{3}{4}$ (31.1 × 19.7); s. & d.
Cambridge, the Syndics of the Fitzwilliam Museum.
Engraved: Freebairn, *Landscape Annual*, 1836, facing p. 63. The on-the-spot version, 1833, is in the National Museum of Wales; an oil, 1834, is in Wakefield Art Gallery and Museum. The church and its tower are still there, but the building on the right has been replaced.
Roberts wrote to Hay, 30 Jan. 1833: 'Situation is the only glory of Cordova that remains . . . Modern Cordova is one of the most decayed & miserable Citys in Spain. But to the Antequary & the Artist rich beyond Measure.' (NLS.)

90 *Gibraltar from Ronda*, 1853.
Oil on panel, $15\frac{1}{2} \times 21\frac{3}{4}$ (39.4 × 55.2); s. & d.
Family collection.

Painted twenty years after Roberts's visit to Ronda (see Cat. 97). Given to his daughter, it was sold HBS 1881 (343), and later came back into the family.

91 *Granada*, 1833.
Watercolour, $13\frac{7}{8} \times 9\frac{3}{4}$ (35.2 × 24.8); s. & d., insc. *Granada Feb 14th 1833.*
London, Trustees of the British Museum.

A similar watercolour (Bradford Art Galleries and Museums) lithographed: W. Gauci, *Picturesque Sketches in Spain*, 1837, pl. 11. Shows the river Darro; an 1835 oil, *Granada*, is untraced. The painting *Old Houses on the Darro, Granada* (Victoria and Albert Museum) is from a different viewpoint.

92 *Tombs of Ferdinand and Isabella, Granada*, (?)1833.
Pen, ink & wash, squared up, $29 \times 35\frac{1}{2}$ (73.6 × 90.1).
London, Victoria and Albert Museum.

Probably the drawing for a painting exhibited RA 1836 (422), bought by William Beckford and much damaged by bitumen (whereabouts unknown). A similar watercolour lithographed: Thomas Allom, *Picturesque Sketches in Spain*, 1837, pl. 16; a section was engraved on wood for *Landscape Annual*, 1835, vignette p. 241.

The chapel, attached to the cathedral, is entered by a side entrance from the street; inside is 'a magnificent wrought iron *reja*. Here lie Ferdinand and Isabella in tombs of white marble, works of the full renaissance.' (James Stevens Curl, *A Celebration of Death*, 1980.) Roberts's view is taken from inside the *reja*.

93 *Tower of Comares, Alhambra, Granada.*
Watercolour heightened with white, 15 × 11 (38.1 × 27.9).
University of Manchester, Whitworth Art Gallery.

There are three known versions of this watercolour (there may be a fourth, for the engraving: J. Fisher, *Landscape Annual*, 1835, frontispiece). One (Princeton University Art Museum) was used with variations for the lithograph: *Picturesque Sketches in Spain*, 1837, pl. 10; another, dated 1833, is in a private collection. An oil, 1838, is in Indiana University Art Museum.

'Granada so far surpasses even the expectations I had previously formed of it great as these were. . . in a picturesque point of veiw it is perhaps unequalled in the World . . . Surrounding Scenery combines the wildest Mountain Views with the luxurent and fertile landscape.' (Letter to Hay, 2 Mar. 1833, NLS.) Roberts spent three weeks in Granada, and painted several oils of the Alhambra: one was *Fortress of the Alhambra*, 1836, for Lord Northwick (Fogg Art Museum, Harvard), another *General View of the Alhambra*, 1837, for the Marquis of Lansdowne, to hang at Bowood (untraced).

94 *Court of the Myrtles, Alhambra*, 1833.
Watercolour, $9 \times 11\frac{3}{4}$ (22.9 × 29.8); s. & d., insc. *ALHAMBRA*.
Manchester City Art Galleries.

The court derives its names (*Patio de la Alberca*, or *de los Arrayenes*) from the hedges of myrtle (*arrayenes*) and the pool (*alberca*). Another watercolour, 1834 (Eton College), engraved: J. Stephenson, *Landscape Annual*, 1835, facing p. 85; Roberts replaced the myrtle hedges with flowers.

95 *The Church of St. Iago, Jerez*, (?)1833.
Watercolour heightened with white, $14\frac{1}{4} \times 9\frac{3}{4}$ (36.2 × 24.8); s. & d., insc. indistinctly.
Cambridge, the Syndics of the Fitzwilliam Museum.

An undated version (Ulster Museum, Belfast) lithographed: T. S. Boys, *Picturesque Sketches in Spain*, 1837, pl. VI. Roberts wrote that Jerez 'is like most of the other towns of Andalusia of Moorish origin if not Roman . . . Some of the Churches, the Alcazar & City walls are most proment [prominent].' (Roberts to Hay, 4 May 1833, NLS.)

96 *Ronda*, 1834.
Watercolour, $9\frac{1}{4} \times 13$ (23.5 × 33); s. & d.
London, Trustees of the Tate Gallery.

Engraved: J. Cousen, *Landscape Annual*, 1835, facing p. 131. Roberts wrote to Hay of '*Ronda*, the situation of which Mountain town is one of the Most extraordinary of Spain if not in the world' (22 Apr. 1833, NLS).

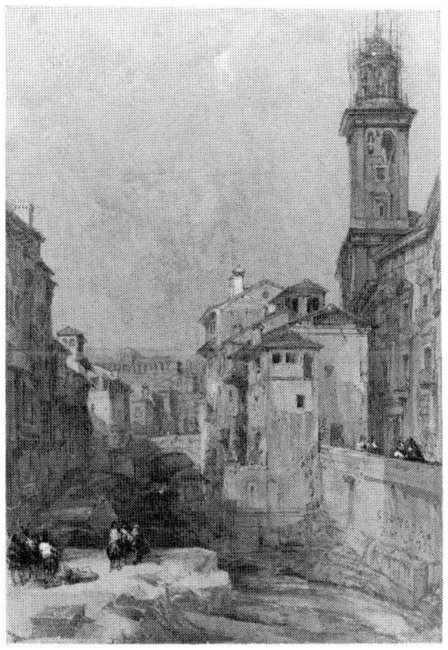
91

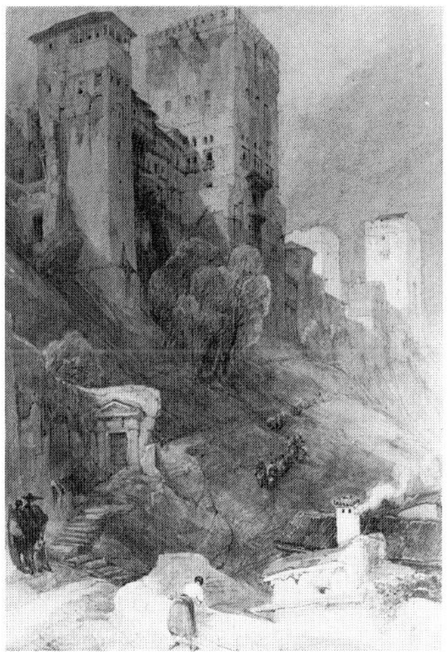
93

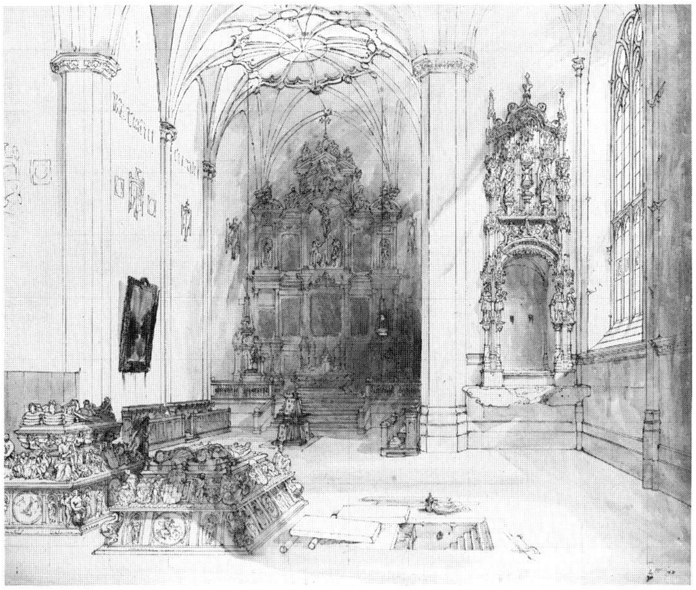
92

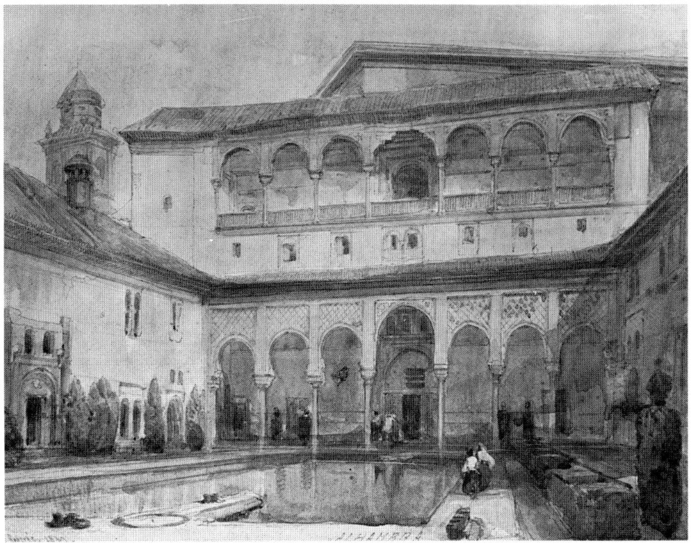
94

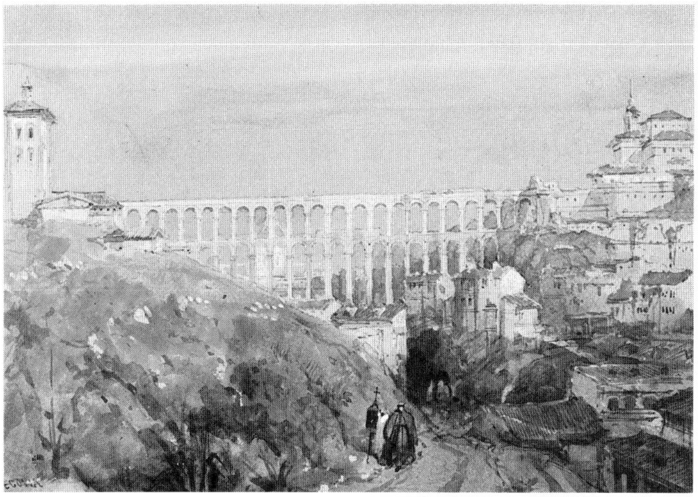

99

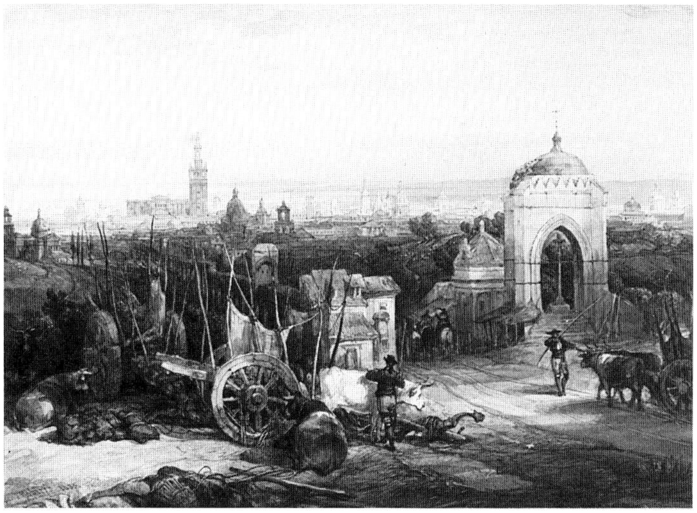

100

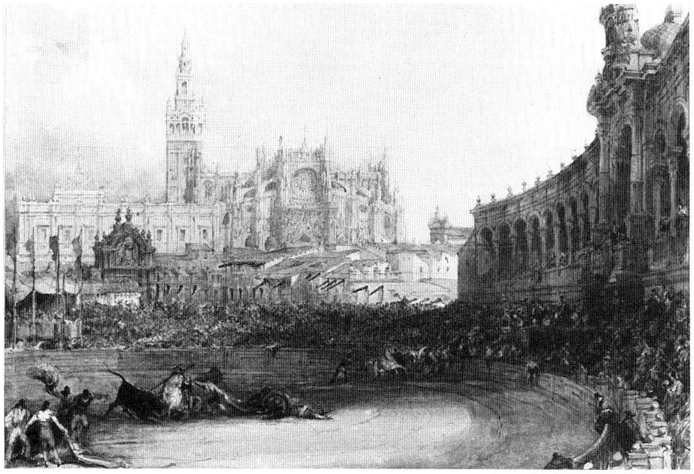

101

97 *Ronda*, c.1835. Pl. 42 (colour).
Oil, 35 × 45 (88.9 × 114.3).
Revd Canon Ivor Walters.

Roberts went to Ronda on his way from Malaga to Gibraltar in 1833. The oil and watercolour (Cat. 96) are from the same viewpoint, both worked up from the on-the-spot study (Huntington Library and Art Gallery, California).

98 *The Alcazar, Segovia*, 1836. Pl. 47.
Watercolour & bodycolour over pencil, $15\frac{5}{8} \times 10\frac{1}{4}$ (39.7 × 26); s. & d.
Birmingham City Museum and Art Gallery.

Engraved: J. Redaway, *Landscape Annual*, 1837, facing p. 111. The Alcazar, one of Segovia's greatest sights, is an old Castilian castle.

99 *The Roman Aqueduct, Segovia*.
Watercolour heightened with white, $6\frac{1}{2} \times 9\frac{1}{2}$ (16.5 × 24.1); insc. *SEGOVIA*.
London, Trustees of the British Museum.

The aqeduct, which still brings water to the town, is one of the finest structures surviving from Roman times. Another watercolour, 1836 (Whitworth Art Gallery) engraved: J. C. Armytage, *Landscape Annual*, 1837, facing p. 106.

There is some doubt as to whether Roberts went to Segovia. He noted that 'the cholera broke out in Seville and put a stop to all farther proceedings – my intention being to return again all through Spain' (RB, 1833). In a letter to Hay, 4 May 1833, he wrote that he wanted to go back to Madrid and visit Toledo and Segovia, Saragossa and Barcelona (NLS). He dd not reach the two latter, but may have meant that he wanted to *revisit* Toledo and Segovia. There are four known watercolours of Segovia (including Cat. 98 and 99), one of which was reproduced *Landscape Annual* 1838, and is the only one acknowledged as being after a sketch by another artist. None of the four known watercolours and two engravings have been attributed to another draughtsman.

100 *Seville from the Cruz del Campo*, 1835.
Watercolour heightened with white, $10\frac{1}{2} \times 15$ (26.7 × 38.1); s. & d.
Leeds City Art Galleries.

Engraved: Freebairn, *Landscape Annual*, 1836, facing p. 93. Like many watercolours that Roberts produced for the engraver, this is rather artificial.

101 *A Bull Fight, Seville*, c.1835.
Watercolour, $10\frac{3}{4} \times 16\frac{1}{4}$ (27.3 × 41.3); s. & d. (indistinctly), insc. as title.
The Provost and Fellows of Eton College.

Engraved: J. B. Allom, *Landscape Annual*, 1836, frontispiece. An untraced drawing with a different viewpoint lithographed: Louis Haghe, *Picturesque Sketches in Spain*, 1837, pl. 26. The bullring still stands; in the background are the cathedral and the Giralda.

102 *Interior of the Cathedral of Seville during the Ceremony of Corpus Christi*, 1833. Pl. 8 (colour).
Oil, 78 × 54 (198.1 × 137.2); insc. *Interior of Seville Cathedral by David Roberts 1833*.
The Abbot of Downside.

It was rare for Roberts to paint such large works on site. He wrote to Hay on 4 May 1833: 'The Moorish Tower . . . is worth a journey from London to see, but I must not say too much or you will be expecting more than a painter can carry away with him – indeed here alone is work for any Artist for a year or two . . .' On 10 Aug. he wrote again: 'I have been detained here longer than I expected, but the painting of two pictures each 6 feet 6 inches by 4 feet 6 inches, with a number of figures, all taken from the life, is no joke . . . I think the novelty of their having been painted in Spain will add to their value.' (Ballantine, p. 61.)

First shown BI 1834 (150), later bought by D. R. Hay. Like Cat. 104, belonged to Louis Loyd in 1852; exhibited Manchester Art Treasures Exhibition 1857 (535 and 588). Another version, *High Altar, Seville Cathedral*, is in the Art Gallery of Western Australia, Perth.

103 *Interior of Seville Cathedral,* 1833.
Watercolour, $14\frac{1}{4} \times 9\frac{3}{4}$ (36.2 × 24.8); s. & d., insc. *Seville Cathedral.*
Birmingham City Museum and Art Gallery.

Another watercolour (private collection) is nearer in viewpoint to Cat. 102. A third (sold Christie's, July 1984; whereabouts unknown) lithographed: Thomas Allom, *Picturesque Sketches in Spain*, 1837, pl. 5.

104 *The Moorish Tower at Seville, Called the Giralda,* 1833. Pl. 38 (colour).
Oil, 78 × 54 (198.1 × 137.2); d., & insc. *Sevillia.*
The Abbot of Downside.

First shown SBA 1834 (162); bought by G. G. Barrett; belonged to Louis Loyd by 1852. Exhibited Manchester Art Treasures Exhibition 1847 with Cat. 102 and 187.

The Giralda, the bell tower of the cathedral, takes its name from the weathervane (*giraldillo*) surmounting it.

105 *The Giralda, Seville,* (?)1835.
Watercolour, $9\frac{1}{2} \times 7$ (24.1 × 17.8).
Family collection.

Engraved: J. Redaway, *Landscape Annual*, 836, facing p. 121. There are several watercolours of the Giralda tower, a favourite subject for Roberts.

106 *Bridge of Toledo,* *c.*1836. Pl. 41 (colour).
Watercolour & brown ink heightened with white, $6\frac{3}{4} \times 9\frac{3}{4}$ (17.1 × 24.8); insc. *TOLEDO.*
Ingram Family Collection.

Study for the oil (Royal Collection) engraved: E. Goodall, *Royal Gallery of Art*, 1854, Vol. I, pl. 6, reproduced again *Art Journal*, 1855, p. 54.

In 1859 Roberts reworked 75 of his Spanish sketches for Ernest Gambart to exhibit at the German Gallery, 168 New Bond Street; they were sold at Christie's, 28 April 1860. A *Bridge of Toledo* was no. 151 in the sale, and in Roberts's catalogue note he wrote: 'I am indebted for the subject of this beautiful drawing to my friend Sir Edmund Head . . . we were in Spain together'; no sizes were given, so one cannot determine whether Cat. 106 is the version sold.

107 *A Moor* (Tangiers), 1833.
Watercolour, 12 × 9 (30.5 × 22.9); s. & d., insc. *A Moor, Servant to H M Vice Consul.*
Ingram Family Collection.

Roberts went to Tangiers from Gibraltar, and also to Tetuan. This was his first taste of Africa; he wrote to Hay from Tangiers: 'Here indeed I am in a New World. I thought Spain Nobell but this beggars all discription . . . Yesterday was the Market day – only fancy an African Market – I am so bewildered that I cannot trust myself to write about it.' (29 Mar. 1833, NLS.)

108 *Figure Studies at Tangiers,* 1833.
Pencil & watercolour eightened with white on grey paper mounted on card, $9\frac{3}{4} \times 6\frac{5}{8}$ (24.8 × 16.8); insc. *Tangiers 1833.*
London, Victoria and Albert Museum.

109 *Citadel of Tangiers,* 1833.
Watercolour heightened with white, 9 × 13 (22.9 × 33); s. & d., insc. *Tangiers March* (?) *9th.*
London, Trustees of the British Museum.

110 *Rabat and Salé, Morocco,* 1837.
Watercolour, $9\frac{5}{8} \times 14\frac{5}{8}$ (24.4 × 37.1); s. & d.
Sheffield City Art Galleries.

Engraved: J. T. Willmore, *Landscape Annual*, 1838, facing p. 248, from a sketch by Lieut. Smith, Royal Artillery. Rabat is on the west coast of Morocco, too far south for Roberts to have reached on his brief visit.

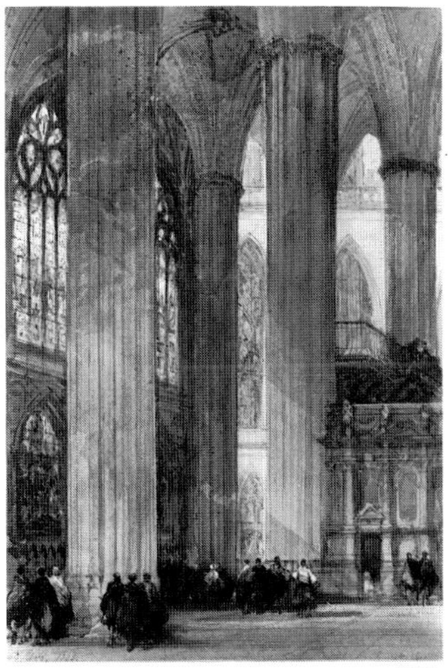
103

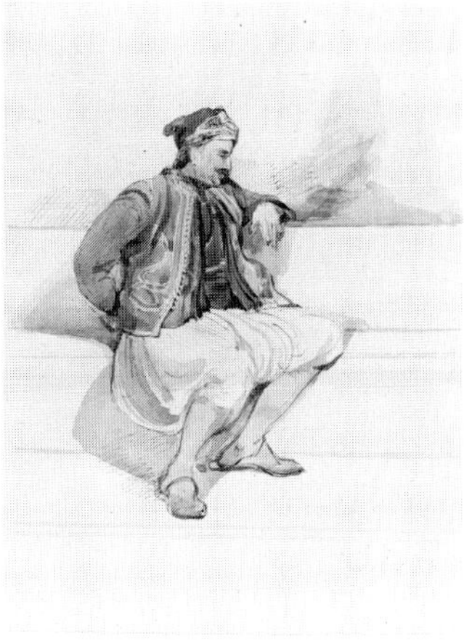
107

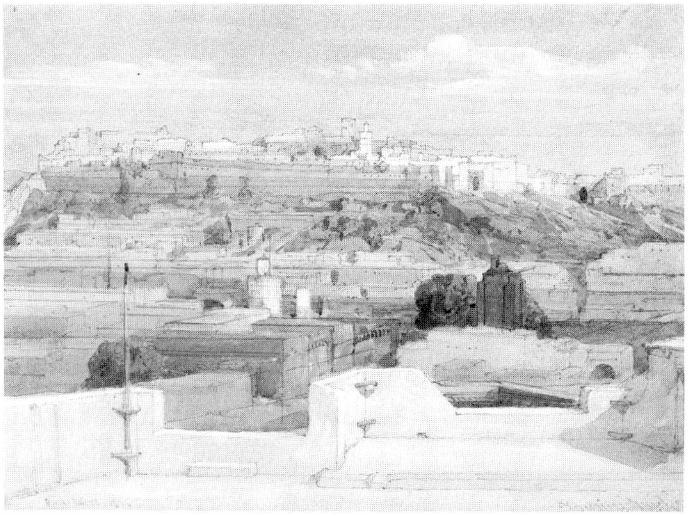
109

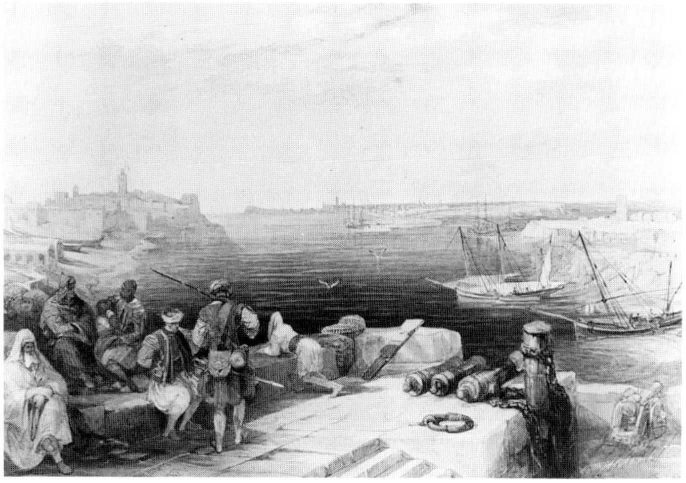
110

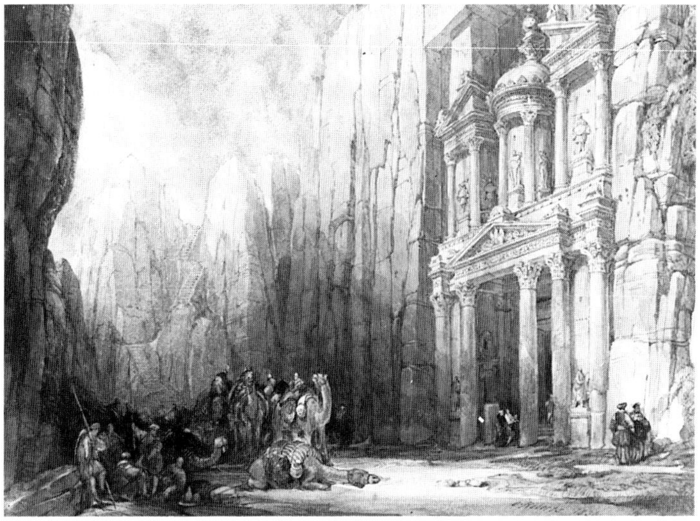
116

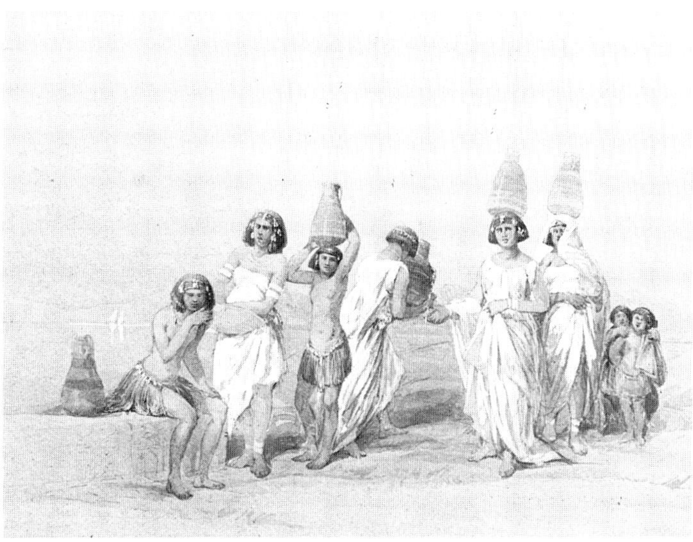
117

Indian Compositions

Although Roberts never visited India, he re-drew sketches by other artists for reproduction in print (as he did for other places).

111 *Hindoo Architecture: A Composition*, 1829. Pl. 78 (colour).
Oil on panel, $15\frac{3}{4} \times 11\frac{3}{4}$ (40×29.8); s. & d.
Private collection.
Commissioned by Captain Grindley, who also provided the drawing for it. Exhibited SBA 1830 (422). Reproduced in aquatint: Reeve, *Scenery, Costumes and Architecture chiefly on the Western Side of India* by Captain Grindley, R. Ackerman, London, 1826–30, frontispiece. Published as a colour print by George Baxter, 1831: 'engraved in mezotint but very badly' (Roberts, RB).

112 *Ghat and Temple at Gokul*, 1838. Pl. 36.
Sepia wash, 10×14 (25.4×35.6); s. & d.
Private collection.
Engraved: W. & E. Finden, *Oriental Annual*, 1839, facing p. 183. Roberts drew three other subjects for this issue: *Ruins at Futtepore, Sikri, The Moti Musjid, Agrah*, and *Ancient Temple at Kunkhull*, all based on drawings by Thomas Bacon. He also drew *View at Simla in the Himalayan Mountains* for *The Drawing Room Scrap Book of 1846*, from a drawing by G. F. White.

Near East

Roberts visited the Near East in 1838–9 (see p. 93 for details). Several eastern compositions were made before this trip.

113 *Study for 'The Israelites Leaving Egypt'*, 1827. Pl. 63.
Pen, ink & wash, $24\frac{3}{8} \times 16\frac{3}{4}$ (61.9×42.5); s. & d.
London, Trustees of the British Museum.
See Cat. 114.

114 *The Israelites Leaving Egypt*, 1829. Pl. 62.
Oil, 54×72 (137.2×182.9); s. & d.
Birmingham City Museum and Art Gallery.
Painted almost ten years before Roberts went to Egypt. Sold to Lord Northwick for 200 guineas, and exhibited SBA 1829, and Scottish Academy 1830. Also known as *Departure of the Israelites*.
Roberts chose the subject 'more as a Vehicle for introducing – That Grand allthough simple style of architecture the Egyptian and from which the other Three Greek orders have unquestionaly sprung – than from the object – by which the Picture is called'. Lord Northwick engaged another artist to alter the painting, which had 'the unpleasant effect of throughing the figures out of perspective as well as out of harmony' (RB, no. 33).
Several reviewers compared Roberts's grand conception with the work of John Martin, and referred to his early training in the theatre: the *Weekly Review* (1829) noted 'grave faults' in the work, but declared that 'as a piece of pictorial effect – as a specimen of *scene-painting* on a small scale – it is wonderful' (RB p. 58). See Cat. 113 for a preliminary study.

115 *Aaron Delivering the Message of the Elders of Israel*, c.1827. Pl. 21.
Pen, ink & watercolour, $9 \times 12\frac{1}{2}$ (22.9×31.8).
Wirral Borough Council, Dept. of Leisure Services and Tourism, Williamson Art Gallery and Museum.
A composition related to Cat. 114.

116 *Petra, Ruins of Selah*, 1834.
Pen, brown ink, watercolour & bodycolour, $8\frac{3}{4} \times 12\frac{1}{8}$ (22.2×30.8); s. & d.
Private collection.
Engraved: E. Finden, *Landscape Illustrations of the Bible*, 1836, Vol. I, pl. 33, after a sketch by Count Léon de Laborde. The latter visited Petra in 1826 and made numerous, fairly accurate, drawings of its principal monuments. They were reproduced as lithographs in *Voyage de L'Arabie Petrée*, published in 1830.

117 *Nubian Women at Kortie on the Nile*, 1846.
Watercolour & bodycolour, $9\frac{3}{4} \times 13\frac{1}{2}$ (24.8×34.3); s. & d., insc. as title.
London, collection of the Mathaf Gallery.
Lithograph: *Egypt*, Vol. I [pl. 39].

118 *Philae*, 1838.
Watercolour & bodycolour on grey paper, $11\frac{1}{2} \times 19\frac{1}{2}$ (29.1 x 49.5); d., & insc. as title.
Family collection.
Verso has pencil drawing of Baalbek. An oil painting showing 'Pharoah's Bed' from a slightly different angle was exhibited RA 1844 (368; whereabouts unknown).

119 *Under the Grand Portico, Philae*, 1838.
Pencil, watercolour & bodycolour on buff paper, $19\frac{1}{8} \times 12\frac{1}{2}$ (48.6 x 31.8); s. & d., insc. *Philoe Novr 18th 1838*.
Private collection.
Roberts spent three days sketching at Philae. Lithograph: *Egypt*, Vol. I [pl. 1], frontispiece.

120 *Portico of the Temple of Philae*, 1851. Pl. 65 (colour).
Oil, $43 \times 33\frac{1}{4}$ (109.2 x 84.5); s. & d.
Private collection.
Shows part of the Hypostyle Hall of the Temple of Isis. Exhibited BI 1851 (62) with the incorrect title, *Interior of the Portico of the Temple of Osiris at Philae, Nubia*. A watercolour and lithograph (see Cat. 118) are similar, but with a lower viewpoint and different reliefs and hieroglyphs on the walls and columns. This is strange as Roberts was impressed with their state of preservation: 'The remains of the brilliant and tasteful colouring of the walls and pillars still testify the exquisite taste and finish of the whole.' (EJ, 19 Nov. 1838.)

121 *Island of Philae, Nubia*, 1843. Pl. 60 (colour).
Oil, $30\frac{1}{2} \times 60\frac{1}{2}$ (77.5 x 153.7); s. & d.
Private collection.
Jens Pell, who bought this painting in 1843 for £100, accompanied Roberts from Cairo to Petra, Jerusalem and the Dead Sea, and is known to have had also a 'beautiful sketch of Philae', given to him by the artist (B. Barton to Roberts, 30 Aug. 1856). The watercolour (Sotheby's 1981) and lithograph (*Egypt*, Vol. I [pl. 26]) of this view are slightly less extended on each side.
The Island of Philae lay just beyond the first cataract of the Nile, and was a popular destination among nineteenth-century travellers. For Roberts it was 'a paradise in the midst of desolation' (EJ, 30 Oct. 1838); another described it as 'the most unearthly, strange, wild, beautiful spot, I ever beheld. No dreamer of the mystical old times, when beauty, knowledge, and power, were realized on earth, ever pictured to himself a scene of wilder grandeur and more perfect loveliness.' (Warburton, Vol. I, p. 279.) Flooded after the construction of the first Aswan dam in 1902, its buildings were dismantled and re-erected on a nearby island above the water level. The neighbouring island of Bigah, which Roberts took as his viewpoint, was also submerged.

122 *Temple of Edfou, Ancient Apollinopolis, Upper Egypt*.
Watercolour, & bodycolour, $13\frac{3}{8} \times 19\frac{3}{4}$ (34 x 50.3); s., & insc. as title.
London, Victoria and Albert Museum.
Lithograph: *Egypt*, Vol. I [pl. 34].

123 *View from under Portico of Temple of Edfou*, 1838.
Watercolour, $12\frac{5}{8} \times 19\frac{1}{8}$ (32.2 x 48.6) s., & insc. *Edfou, Novr 23 1838*.
London, Victoria and Albert Museum, on loan from H. M. Treasury.
There is another watercolour of this subject (Yale Center for British Art). Lithograph: *Egypt*, Vol. I [pl. 32].

124 *Dromos, or Outer Court of the Great Temple at Edfou in Upper Egypt*, 1840. Pl. 70.
Oil, $43\frac{1}{2} \times 56$ (110.5 x 142.2).
Family collection.
Sold to Frank Hall Standish in 1840 for £200. Exhibited RA 1840 (292) and International Exhibition, South Kensington, 1874 (177). A sketch is recorded (RB 1850, 145) for a second oil of this view, exhibited RA 1850 (378). There are also two watercolours of the subject (see Cat. 123).
Shows the view from the hall of the Ptolemaic Temple of Horus, looking out over the court towards the entrance pylon. Roberts considered Edfou to be one of the most beautiful temples in Egypt. 'True, it is not of the magnitude of Karnac nor is it in such preservation as Dendera but it has all that these want – In every situation in which it is viewed it is a picture. It has breadth in its parts, the pillars are large massy and in form exquisite. Though half buried it is more beautiful than if laid open and reminds me of Piranesi Etchings of the Forum of Rome.' (EJ, 26 Oct. 1838.) In the 1860s the temple was cleared of sand by the French Egyptologist Auguste Mariette.

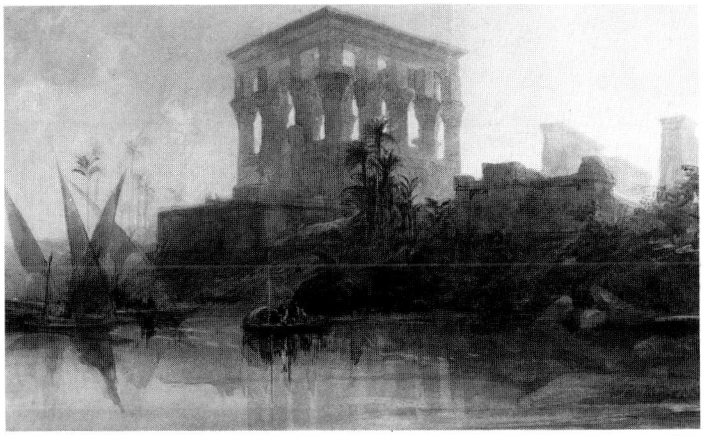
118

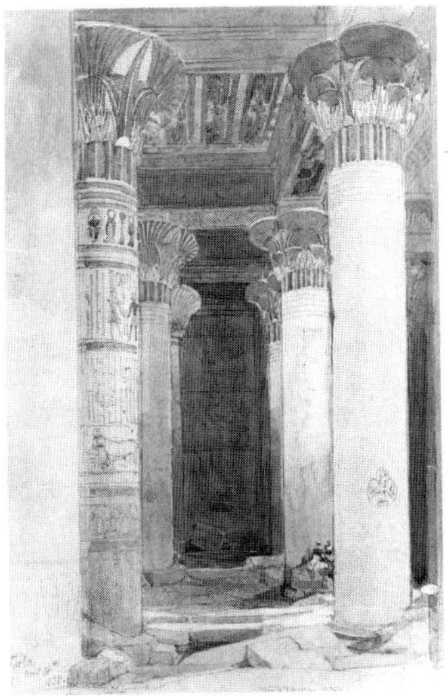
119

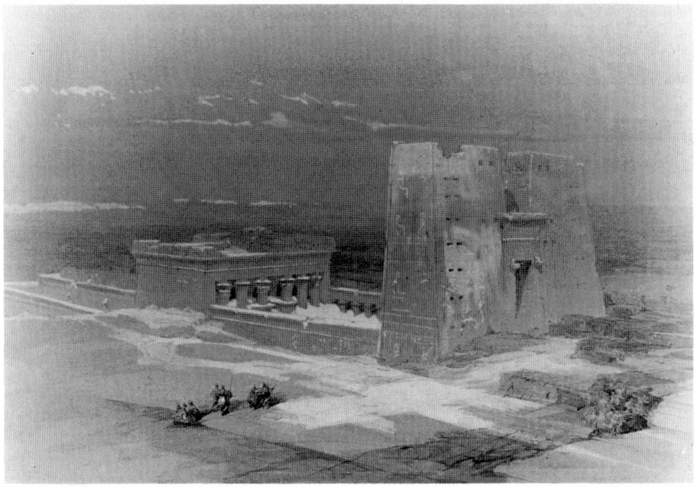
122

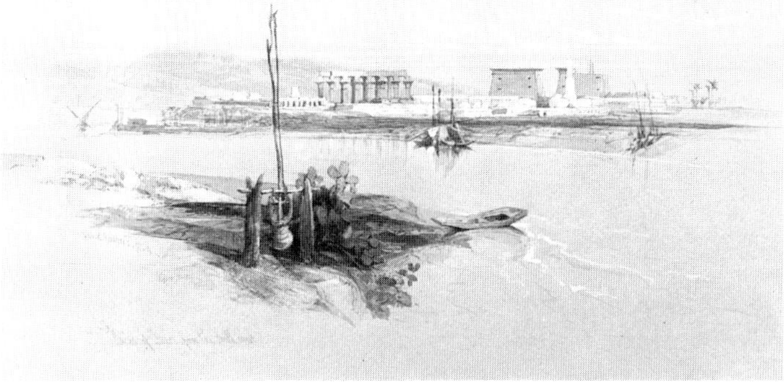

127

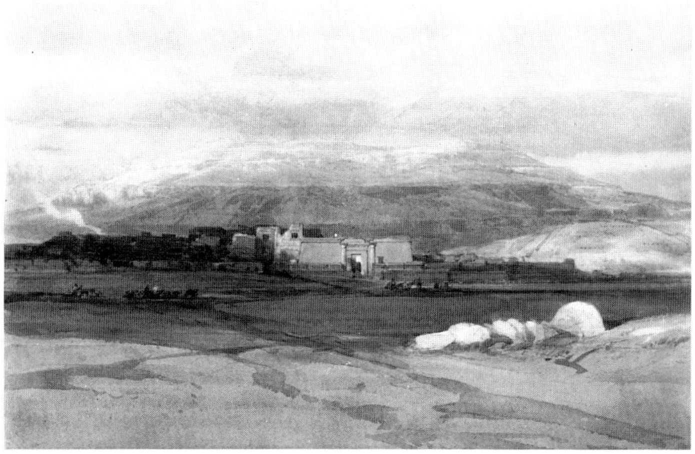

129

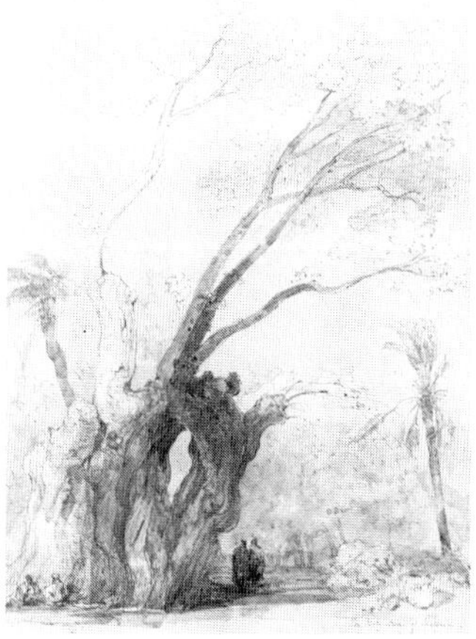

132

125 *Ruins of the Temple of Hermonthes in Upper Egypt*, 1848. Pl. 68 (colour).
Oil, $39\frac{3}{4} \times 55\frac{3}{4}$ (101×141.6); s. & d., insc. on stretcher with title and *Painted for James Foster, Esq., Stourton Castle.*
Private collection.

Exhibited RA 1848 (201), it received favourable reviews (see p. 80). Roberts made only brief reference to the ruins, which were 'as picturesque as most in this country, naked! They possess little interest.' (EJ, 26 Nov. 1838.) The site was traditionally believed to be the birthplace of Moses (letterpress to lithograph, *Egypt*, Vol. II [pl. 84]). The place is now known as Armant; little remains of the temple as it was largely dismantled later that century to provide some stone for a sugar factory nearby. Another version (private collection) is less elaborate, and closer to the lithograph.

126 *Thebes, Karnac*, 1838.
Pencil, watercolour & bodycolour, $19 \times 12\frac{3}{4}$ (48.3×32.4); s. & d., insc. as title & *Nov 29th 1838.*
Manchester City Art Galleries.

Lithograph: *Egypt*, Vol. II [pl. 73]. Roberts considered Karnak to be one of the most impressive of Egyptian temples. 'If Luxor struck me with its magnitude, what shall I say of Carnac? Its grandeur cannot be imagined. Were I to write what I think it would be mere rhapsody. It is so far beyond everything I have ever seen that can draw no comparison.' (EJ, 23 Oct. 1838.)

127 *Ruins of Luxor from the South West.*
Pencil, watercolour & bodycolour on buff paper, 10×14 (25.4×35.6); s., & insc. as title.
The Earl of Shelburne.

Lithograph: *Egypt*, Vol. I [pl. 15].

128 *Statues of Memnon in the Plain of Thebes*. Pl. 71.
Watercolour, $12\frac{1}{2} \times 19$ (31.7×48.2); s. & insc. as title.
Ingram Family Collection.

Roberts made several drawings of these statues, called the Colossi of Memnon after the hero of the Trojan War who is supposed to have fled from the city and died in Egypt.

129 *Medinet Habou, Thebes*, 1838.
Watercolour over traces of pencil heightened with bodycolour, $12\frac{3}{4} \times 15\frac{1}{4}$ (32.4×38.7); s., & insc. as title & *Dec. 8th 1838.*
London, Frost & Reed Ltd.

Engraved: *Egypt*, Vol. II [pl. 63].

130 *Dendera*, 1848. Pl. 59.
Watercolour & bodycolour, $19\frac{1}{8} \times 13\frac{1}{2}$ (48.6×34.3); s. & d.
Aberdeen Art Gallery and Museums.

Lithograph: *Egypt*, Vol. II [pl. 69]. There is a second watercolour of this view in Leeds City Art Gallery. 'The Portico of the Temple stands so high above the surrounding ruins that it is seen from the river. Upon entering it I was struck with amazement first at the beautiful preservation in which I found every part . . . and secondly with the endless labour expended upon the carving.' (EJ, 19 Oct. 1838.)

131 *Siout, Upper Egypt, One of Nine Mosques*, 1838.
Watercolour heightened with white, $13 \times 9\frac{1}{2}$ (33×24.1); insc. as title & *Dec 14th 1838.*
Private collection.

Lithograph: *Egypt*, Vol. III [pl. 105].

132 *The Holy Tree of Materia*, 1839.
Pencil, watercolour & bodycolour, $13\frac{1}{4} \times 9\frac{1}{4}$ (33.7×23.5); s., & insc. as title & *Jan 20 1839.*
Private collection.

Lithograph: *Egypt*, Vol. III [pl. 101]. *'20th Sunday.* Today having lured a donkey and boy I visited the celebrated Sycamore tree under which the Blessed Virgin and infant Saviour are said to have taken shelter on their arrival in Egypt.' (EJ.)

133 *Pyramids of Geezah, from the Nile*, 1845.
Watercolour & bodycolour, $9\frac{3}{4} \times 13\frac{3}{4}$ (24.8×34.9); s. & d., insc. as title.
London, Victoria and Albert Museum.

Roberts visited the Pyramids on two occasions, once on his way up the Nile in October 1838, and a second time in early 1839. 'I cannot express my feelings on again visiting these vast monuments – to describe them would only be to say what has been said over and over again. They must be seen to be comprehended.' (EJ, 17 Jan. 1839.) Lithograph: *Egypt*, Vol. 1 [pl. 3].

134 *The Simoon*, 1850. Pl. 67.
Oil on panel, $13\frac{3}{4} \times 19\frac{3}{4}$ (34.9 × 50.2); insc. verso *Presented to Charles Dickens Esq as a mark of respect and admiration for his talent and work by his very sincere friend and admirer David Roberts 1850.*
Private collection.

The title refers to the desert wind, usually known as the *Khamsin* (Arabic for 50, the number of days for which the wind can last between March and May). 'This fearful scourge to the traveller in the East sometimes occurs so near to Cairo that its hot and oppressive effects extend to the city.' (Letterpress to lithograph, *Egypt*, Vol. III [pl. 114], after a similar watercolour [Sotheby's, 1974]).

One of Roberts's more imaginative renderings of Near Eastern scenery, with topographical accuracy compromised in the interest of dramatic impact. The Sphinx, the embodiment of Ra-Herakhti (the rising sun), actually faces east, and Roberts was criticized by William Holman Hunt for putting 'the orb of the setting or the rising sun immediately behind the profile of the Sphinx . . . a very unaccountable liberty, because it is destructive of the cardinal idea'. Dickens nevertheless admired it 'as a poetical conception all the same'. (W. H. Hunt, *Pre-Raphaelitism and the Pre-Raphaelite Brotherhood*, 1905, Vol. II, pp. 216–17.)

135 *Ferry to Ghizeh*. Pl. 74.
Pencil, watercolour & bodycolour, $13 \times 18\frac{3}{4}$ (33 × 47.6); signed.
Private collection, courtesy of Mathaf Gallery.

Lithograph: *Egypt*, Vol. III [pl. 116].

136 *Mosque of Sultan Hassan, Cairo*, 1838. Pl. 72 (colour).
Pencil & watercolour, $18\frac{7}{8} \times 12\frac{1}{2}$ (47.9 × 31.7); insc. as title & *Decr 26th 1838*, & *Mosque of Mahmodee* (?).
The Provost and Fellows of Eton College.

137 *Mosque of El Rhamree Cairo*, 1839.
Watercolour, $13\frac{1}{2} \times 9\frac{1}{4}$ (34.3 × 23.5); insc. as title & *Jany 1st 1838*.
Nottingham, Castle Museum.

Misdated 1838 by Roberts. Lithograph: *Egypt*, Vol. III [pl. 99].

There is an oil painting of a similar view, called *Street in Grand Cairo* (Royal Holloway College, Egham).

138 *Cairo*, 1838.
Watercolour & bodycolour, 13 × 9 (33 × 22.9); s., & insc. *Cairo* . . . (illeg.) *1838*.
Private collection, courtesy of Mathaf Gallery.

This watercolour shows the Bab Zuwaylah (see Cat. 146).

139 *Tombs of the Caliphs*, 1839.
Pencil, watercolour & bodycolour, $21 \times 13\frac{1}{2}$ (53.3 × 34.3); s. & insc. as title & *Jany 16th 1839*.
University of Manchester, Whitworth Art Gallery.

Lithograph: *Egypt*, Vol. III [pl. 98].

140 *Entrance to the Citadel, Cairo*, 1839.
Watercolour, wash & bodycolour, $12 \times 18\frac{1}{2}$ (30.5 × 47); s. & d.
Burnley, Towneley Hall Art Gallery.

Lithograph: *Egypt*, Vol. III [pl. 102].

141 *Preliminary Sketch for 'Grand Cairo'*, 1839.
Pencil heightened with white, $11\frac{1}{4} \times 20\frac{1}{4}$ (28.6 × 51.4).
London, Victoria and Albert Museum.

Roberts made three sketches of 'parts of the town as seen from the mounds outside the walls' of Cairo (EJ, 18 Jan. 1839). This is a preliminary study for Cat. 142.

142 *Grand Cairo*, 1839.
Watercolour & bodycolour over pencil, $12\frac{5}{8} \times 19$ (32.1 × 48.3); insc. as title & *Jany 27th 1839*, & very faintly *Gate of Citizenib* . . . (illeg.).
London, Victoria and Albert Museum.

Lithograph: *Egypt*, Vol. III [pl. 112]. The location *Citizenib* (Sayidah Zaynab), given by Roberts on the watercolour and transmitted to the title of the lithograph, is incorrect. The view is in fact taken from Tel Zaynhum to the south.

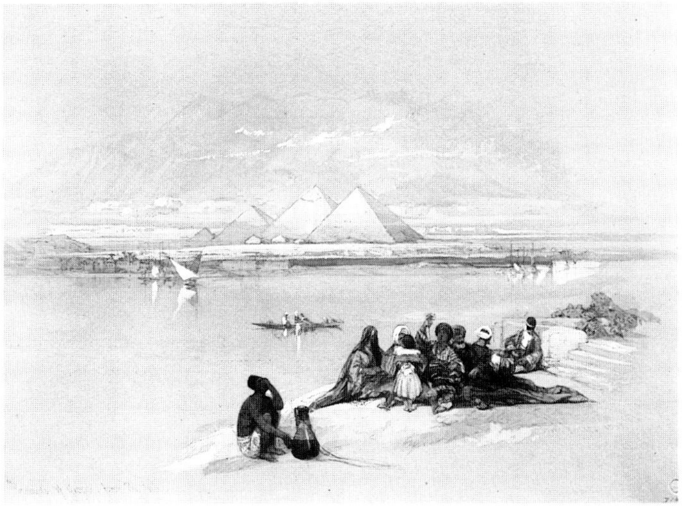
133

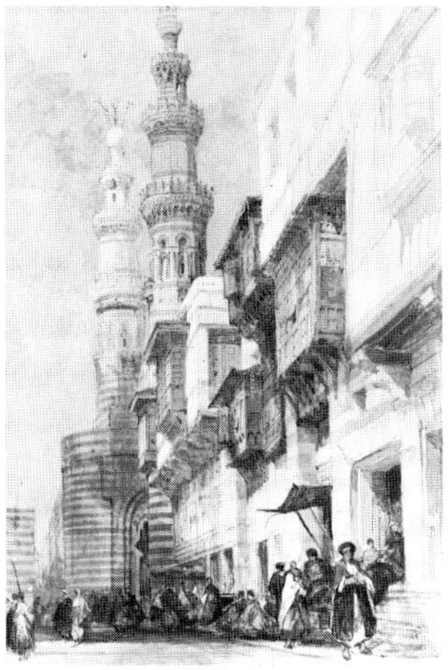
138

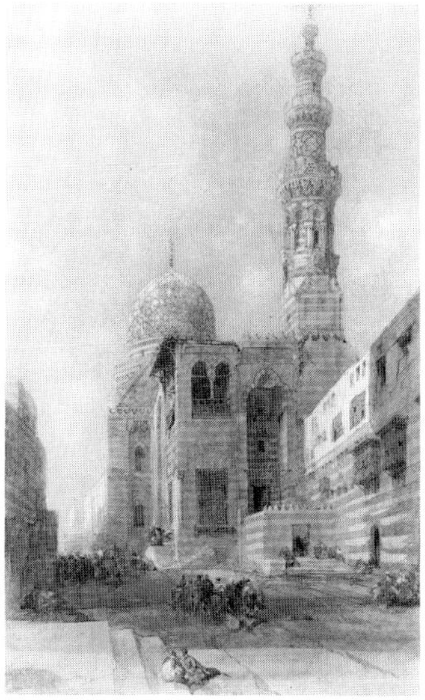
139

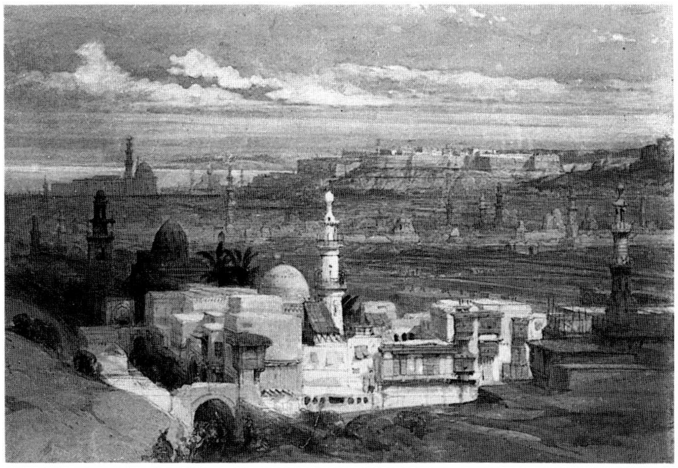
142

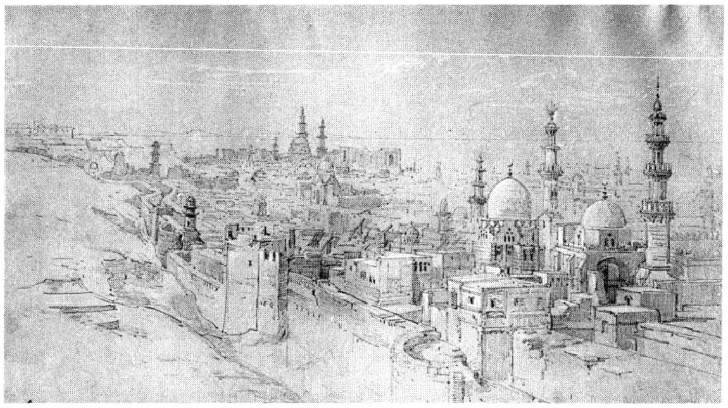
143

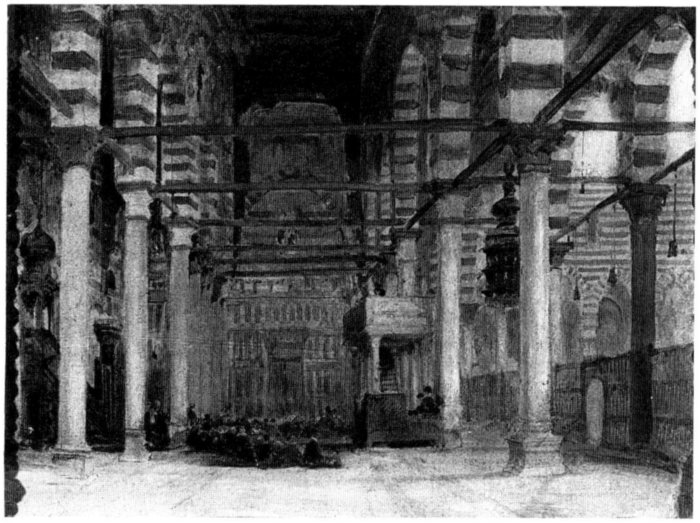
145

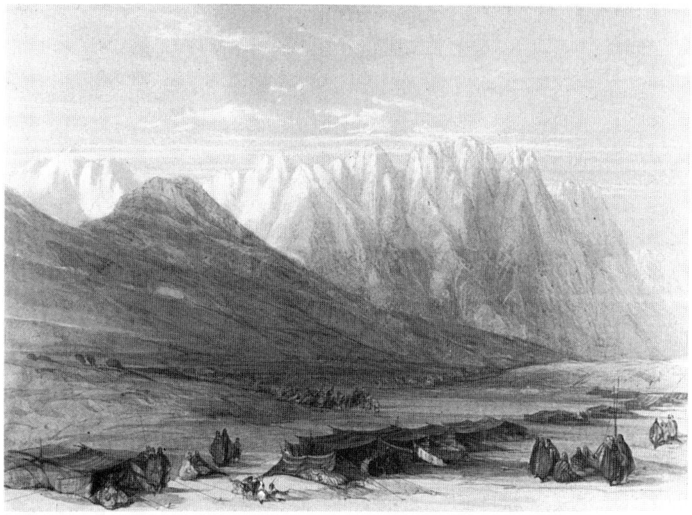
148

143 *Sketch for 'Cairo Looking West'.*
Pencil heightened with white, $11\frac{1}{4} \times 20$ (28.6×50.8); insc. verso with references to volumes of lithographs after sketches by S. Prout and L. Haghe.
London, Victoria and Albert Museum.
Shows the view from the other side of Cairo to Cat. 142 with the Pyramids in the background. Preliminary sketch for the watercolour, lithograph: *Egypt*, Vol. III, [pl. 100], incorrectly titled *General View of Cairo from the West.*

144 *In the Slave Market at Cairo.*
Pencil, wash, watercolour & bodycolour, $9 \times 13\frac{1}{2}$ (22.9×34.3); s., & insc. as title.
Manchester City Art Galleries.
Lithograph: *Egypt*, Vol. III [pl. 113].

145 *Interior of the Mosque of Metwalis.*
Oil, $11\frac{1}{2} \times 15\frac{1}{2}$ (29.2×39.4).
Private collection.
Roberts was granted the rare privilege of sketching inside the mosques in Cairo, provided he wore Turkish dress and shaved off his whiskers. 'This is too bad but I have taken too long a journey to stand now about trifles . . . my object can be accomplished in no other way, no Christian being allowed to enter these places at all. My object is to get at these remains of a bygone age all now fast hastening to decay many already being in total ruin. The day was, and that not long since, that a Christian life would have been forfeited for visiting them.' (EJ, 2 Jan. 1839.)
On 10 Jan. he 'made an Oil sketch of the Mosque of Metwalis', presumably the sketch exhibited here. The mosque is now more commonly known as that of Sultan Mu'ayyad Shaykh (see Cat. 146). No finished painting for this subject is known, but there is a lithograph in *Egypt*, Vol. III [pl. 106].

146 *Gate of Metwaley, Cairo,* 1843. Pl. 73 (colour).
Oil on panel, $30 \times 24\frac{1}{2}$ (76.2×62.2); s. & d.
London, Victoria and Albert Museum.
Sold to John Sheepshanks in 1843 for £105; exhibited RA 1843 (210) as *Gate of the Mosque of Metwalis, Grand Cairo.* Cat. 138, showing the same view, omits the building on the left.
Roberts spent one and a half months working in Cairo, intending to balance his coverage of Egypt's ancient temples with paintings of the country's Islamic architecture. Like many contemporaries, he was fascinated by Cairo's streets and bazaars. William Thackeray claimed that there was 'a fortune to be made for painters in Cairo, and materials for a whole Academy of them. I never saw such a variety of architecture, of life, of picturesqueness, of brilliant colour, and light and shade.' (Thackeray, p. 205.) Roberts found that the crowds made work difficult: 'I have stood in the crowded streets of Cairo jostled and stared at until I came home quite sick no one in looking over my Sketches will ever think of the pain and trouble I have had to contend with in collecting them.' (EJ, 1 Jan. 1839.) The Bab Zuwaylah was known locally as the Bab Mutwalli. The twin minarets above the gate in Roberts's picture are those of the Mosque of Sultan Mu'ayyad Shaykh.

147 *Temple on Gebel Garaba called Sarabit el Khadim,* 1839.
Pencil, watercolour & bodycolour on buff paper, $9\frac{3}{4} \times 13\frac{3}{4}$ (24.8×34.9); s., & insc. as title & *Feby 17th 1839.*
Leeds City Art Galleries.
Lithograph: *Holy Land*, Vol. III [pl. 118].

148 *Encampment of the Aulad Said, Mount Sinai,* 1839.
Pencil, watercolour & bodycolour on tinted paper, $13\frac{1}{2} \times 19$ (34.3×48.3); s. & insc. as title & *Feby 18th 1839.*
Southport, Sefton M. B. C., Atkinson Art Gallery.
Lithograph: *Holy Land*, Vol. III [pl. 109].

149 *Convent of St. Katrina, Mount Sinai*, 1839.
Pencil, watercolour & bodycolour, $9\frac{5}{8} \times 13\frac{5}{8}$ (24.4×34.6); s., & insc. as title & *Feby 20th 1839*.
Birmingham City Museum and Art Gallery.

Roberts spent five days on Mount Sinai in 1839 on his journey from Egypt to the Holy Land. He found the monks there very hospitable (see Cat. 150).

150 *The Chapel of the Convent of St. Catherine, on Mount Sinai*, 1842. Pl. 79 (colour).
Oil, $43 \times 59\frac{1}{2}$ (109.2×151.1); s. & d.
Private collection.

Sold to David Barclay M.P. for 200 guineas. Exhibited RA 1842 (228) with the above title (incorrectly titled RB as *Interior of the Chapel of St. Helena, Convent of St. Catherine, Mount Sinai*). There is a watercolour of the same subject (Huntington Library and Art Gallery, California); lithograph in *Holy Land*, Vol. III [pl. 111].

European visitors to the Near East often stayed at the Convent; one recalled that upon arrival, the monks immediately took him to the church, 'which is adorned with silver and gold lamps of costly workmanship, and rich and massive plate covers the high altar. The sides are hung with quaint old paintings of the most ancient, as well as modern times. The screen is a mass of gilding,—roof blue and gold.' (Castlereagh, Vol. I, p. 288.)

151 *Petra, Conference at Wady Moosa*, 1839.
Watercolour & bodycolour, $9\frac{1}{2} \times 13$ (24.1×33); s., & insc. as title & *March 6th 1839*.
Private collection.

Lithograph: *Holy Land*, Vol. III [pl. 100]. Roberts reached Petra on 6 March 1839, but was only allowed to explore the city after he and his companions had agreed to pay the Sheik of Wady Moosa 300 piastres. He spent several days drawing the principal monuments of the ancient Nabratean capital, unable to decide which was more spectacular, the city or its surrounding landscape. 'Although the ruins of this extraordinary place are immense they sink into insignificance when compared to these stupendous rocks. I often throw aside my pencil in despair of ever being able to convey my idea of it.' (EJ, 7 Mar. 1839.)

152 *El Khasne, Petra*, 1839.
Watercolour over pencil with touches of bodycolour on blue paper, $21\frac{1}{4} \times 13\frac{1}{4}$ (54×33.7); s., & insc. *Petra March 7th 1839*.
Private collection.

Lithograph: *Holy Land*, Vol. III [pl. 91]. Recto has studies of Petra with architectural details.

153 *Triumphal Arch, Petra*.
Watercolour & bodycolour, $13\frac{7}{8} \times 19\frac{3}{4}$ (35.2×50.2); signed.
Government Art Collection.

A similar watercolour was sold Sotheby's 1967. Lithograph: *Holy Land*, Vol. III [pl. 99].

154 *Gaza*, 1839.
Pencil, watercolour & bodycolour, $13\frac{3}{4} \times 19\frac{3}{8}$ (34.9×49.2); s., & insc. *Gaza, March 21st 1839*.
Glasgow Museums and Art Galleries.

Lithograph: *Holy Land*, Vol. II [pl. 58].

155 *Chapel of the Convent of Santa Saba*, 1839.
Pencil, watercolour & bodycolour, $13\frac{1}{2} \times 9\frac{1}{2}$ (34.3×24.1); s. & d., insc. as title.
Bedford, Cecil Higgins Art Gallery.

Study for a finished drawing (untraced) for the lithograph in *Holy Land*, Vol. II [pl. 50]. The monastery of St. Saba, founded in the 5th century AD, is located on the edge of the Kidron valley, south-east of Jerusalem. 'I asked permission to make a sketch of their beautiful chapel which was immediately granted and though they were about to begin the service long before I had finished they would not allow me to put my book away . . .' (EJ, 5 Apr. 1839).

156 *Bethlehem Looking Towards the Land of Moab*, 1839.
Watercolour, $13\frac{3}{4} \times 19\frac{7}{8}$ (34.9×50.5); s., & insc. as title & *April 6th 1839*.
Private collection.

There is a second, smaller watercolour of this view (private collection). Lithograph: *Holy Land*, Vol. II [pl. 84].

157 *Bethlehem, Looking Towards the Dead Sea*, 1853. Pl. 76 (colour).
Oil, $23\frac{5}{8} \times 47\frac{1}{8}$ (60×119.7); s. & d.
Private collection.

Sold to William Bicknell in 1853 for £165. Exhibited RA 1853 as *Bethlehem the city of David, looking towards the Dead Sea and the land of*

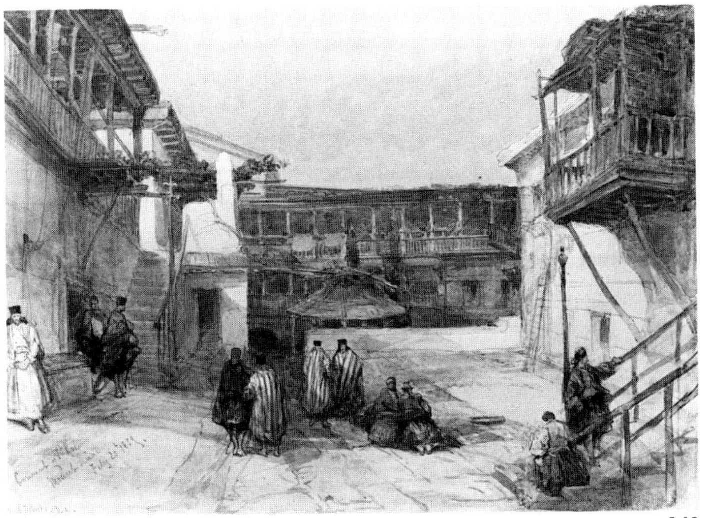

149

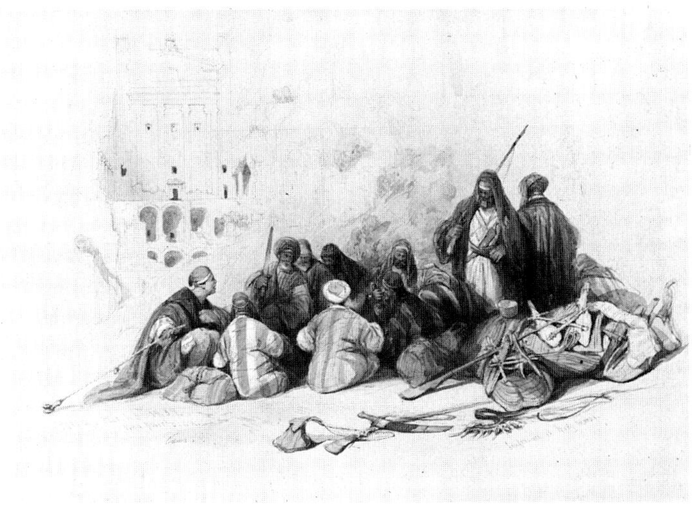

151

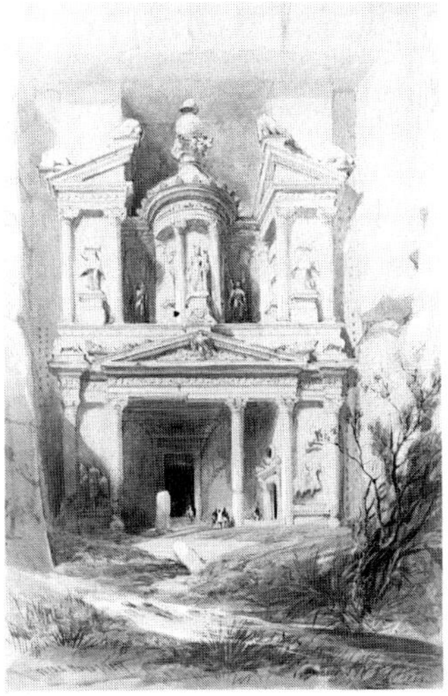

152

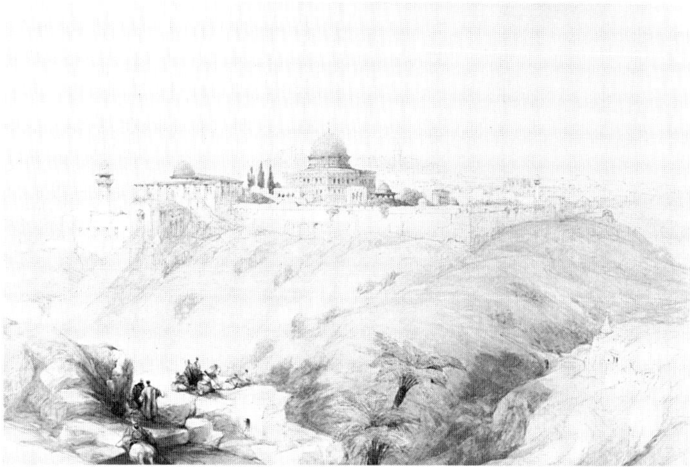

159

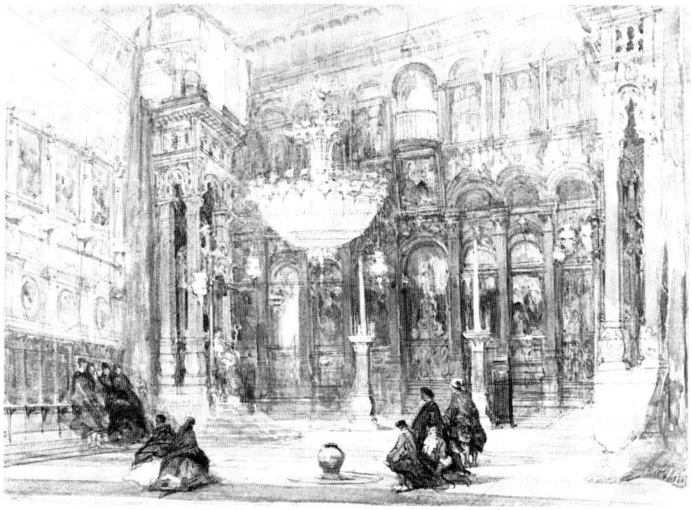

161

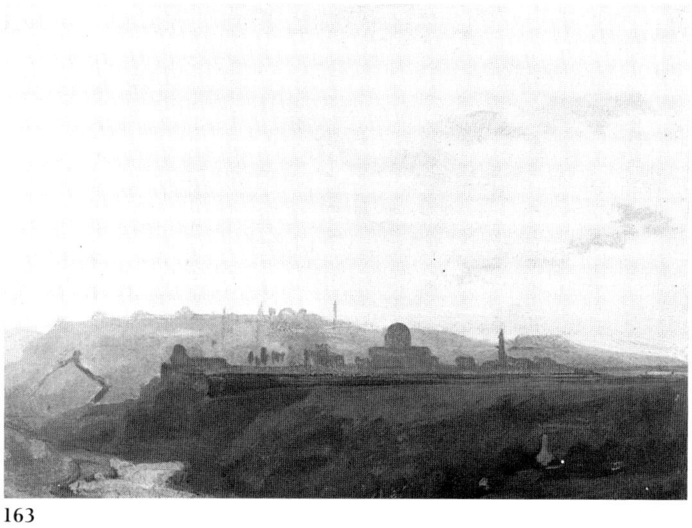

163

Moab. It was well received by critics: 'Mr Roberts never painted anything finer than this; it is in his grand picturesque style, remarkable for breadth and softness.' (*Illustrated London News*, May 1853, p. 385.)

158 *Jerusalem from the Mount of Olives*, 1839. Pl. 75.
Pencil, watercolour & bodycolour on light buff paper, $12\frac{3}{4} \times 19\frac{1}{4}$ (32.4×48.9); insc. *Jerusalem April 5th 1839*.
Private collection.

Lithograph: *Holy Land*, Vol. I [pl. 17]. Roberts made a number of drawings from outside the city walls, having found the interior 'a desert, two thirds of it being a mass of ruins and cornfields; the remaining third, with its Bazaars and ruined mosques being of such a paltry & contemptable character that no artist could render them interesting' (EJ, 13 Apr. 1839).

159 *The Dome of the Rock*, 1839.
Watercolour, $12\frac{3}{4} \times 18\frac{7}{8}$ (32.4×47.9); s., & insc. *Jerusalem April 9th 1839*.
Private collection.

Lithograph: *Holy Land*, Vol. I [pl. 15]. The Dome of the Rock, built in the 7th century, stands on the site of Solomon's Temple. Roberts reflected on the past with 'melancholy enjoyment', and derided 'the far famed mosque of Omer' (sic) as 'a tawdry piece of finery, fast hastening into ruin' (EJ, 13 Apr. 1839).

160 *Jerusalem from the North*, 1839.
Pencil, watercolour & bodycolour on light buff paper, $12\frac{3}{4} \times 19$ (32.3×48.2); s., & insc. *Jerusalem April 15th 1839*.
Private collection.

Lithograph: *Holy Land*, Vol. I [pl. 21].

161 *Church of the Holy Sepulchre, Jerusalem*, 1839.
Watercolour, $9\frac{1}{4} \times 13$ (23.5×33); insc. as title.
Preston, Harris Museum and Art Gallery.

The church of the Holy Sepulchre enshrines the traditional sites of the crucifixion, burial and resurrection of Christ. Built in the 12th century, it was almost destroyed by fire in 1810. Roberts criticized the restored church as the 'most monstrous jumble of walls, arches and domes that could be put together by people just emerging from Barbarism (EJ, 13 Apr. 1839). A version reproduced as a lithograph: *Holy Land*, Vol. I [pl. 3].

162 *The Holy Sepulchre, Jerusalem*, 1839.
Pencil, watercolour & bodycolour, 9×13 (22.9×33); insc. as title & *April 18th 1839*.
Private collection.

Lithograph: *Holy Land*, Vol. I [pl. 10].

163 *Jerusalem*.
Oil on board, $9\frac{7}{8} \times 14$ (25.1×35.6).
Private collection.

This painting passed by descent from Elhanan Bicknell to its present owner. It may be a study for one of the larger paintings of Jerusalem from the Mount of Olives (see Cat. 164).

164 *Jerusalem from the Mount of Olives with Pilgrims Entering from the River Jordan*, 1842. Pl. 77 (colour).
Oil, $32\frac{1}{2} \times 59\frac{3}{4}$ (82.6×151.8); s. & d.
Norfolk Museums Service, Norwich Castle Museum.

A smaller replica of a painting sold to Lord Monson in 1841 (Royal Holloway College, Egham); sold to Revd B. Hurnard for £100 in 1842. There are three other known paintings showing Jerusalem from the Mount of Olives, and an oil sketch (Cat. 163).

Roberts had observed the devotion of the thousands of pilgrims who visited the River Jordan each year: 'Such a scene could not be witnessed in any other country; young & old, male & feamal were in the stream in one promiscuous mass. Some of them wore slight dresses & these I was told are taken home and preserved that they may be wrapped in them when they are buried. Many of them narrowly escaped being drowned.' (EJ, 2 Apr. 1839.) The painting shows some of these pilgrims approaching Jerusalem on the road from Bethany.

Most travellers agreed that the city should be seen from the Mount of Olives, a vantage point which afforded the best possible view of the Dome of the Rock, site of the ancient Temple of Solomon. 'From that position, the city and the adjacent hill-country are spread out before you with map-like precision', evoking 'mingled sadness and admiration.' (Romer, Vol. II, p. 211.)

165 *Jerusalem*, c.1843.
Mezzotint, 21 × 37 (53.3 × 94).
Max Lightwood.

166 *Study for 'The Destruction of Jerusalem by Titus'*, 1848. Pl 20.
Oil, 44 × 72 (111.8 × 182.9); s. & d.
Wirral Borough Council, Dept of Leisure Services and Tourism, Williamson Art Gallery and Museum.

Study for one of Roberts's largest and most ambitious paintings (Christie's 1961, untraced; 84 × 144 [213.4 × 365.8]), and the second major example of his history painting (see Cat. 114). He worked on it from Aug. 1847 to Apr. 1849, and it was his only RA exhibit in 1849 (290). His frequent reference to the 'Siege' in letters reflected his regard for it as one of his most important projects.

The painting was well reviewed by critics: 'an exhibition in itself, and one of the most splendid pictures ever produced in our English school . . . The ruins of the battered city, the raging fires, the engines of war and fury of the combatants – all grandeur and desolation – are spread upon the canvas with consummate skill and wonderful effect . . . It is a work for a nation.' (*Literary Gazette*, 1849, p. 359.) Despite such praise, Roberts had difficulty selling it. In 1850 it toured Scotland and was exhibited in London to obtain subscriptions for the lithograph (Cat. 167). While on tour it was damaged, and sold to a dealer, Llewellyn of Bristol, who had it repaired before selling it.

167 Louis Haghe, after Roberts, *Destruction of Jerusalem by Titus*, 1850.
Colour lithograph, $27\frac{1}{2}$ × 42 (69.9 × 106.7).
Published with a key to the places shown and sold for four guineas (six guineas for proof copies).
Private collection.

Roberts was impressed with Haghe's reproduction, 'on a scale of magnitude never hitherto attempted in Lithography . . . the most rapid and extraordinary task in three weeks' (RB).

The destruction of Jerusalem by the Roman commander, Titus, occurred in A.D. 71, during the reign of Nero, after a Jewish revolt against Roman rule. 'The View is taken from the northside of The Mount of Olives showing the Temple with its various courts to great advantage whilst rising over all is Zion crowned with the Palace of Herod and its numerous Public buildings . . . In the foreground I bring in The Roman Soldiers with their captives. The whole composes much better than I at first had any idea of . . .' (to Henry Bicknell, 28 Aug. 1847). This view is similar to other Roberts paintings of Jerusalem from the Mount of Olives (see Cat. 164), but employs a very high vantage point to show the whole city, with prominence given to the enclosure of Herod's temple (site of the ancient Temple of Solomon and later of the Dome of the Rock, the dominant feature of many of Roberts's Jerusalem views).

168 *Sebaste, Ancient Samaria.*
Watercolour heightened with white, 12 × $19\frac{1}{2}$ (30.5 × 49.5); signed.
Ingram Family Collection.
Lithograph: *Holy Land*, Vol. I [pl. 43].

169 *Chapel of the Annunciation, Nazareth*, 1839.
Pencil, watercolour & bodycolour, $9\frac{1}{2}$ × $13\frac{3}{4}$ (24.1 × 34.9); s. & d.
Private collection.
A version reproduced as a lithograph in *Holy Land*, Vol. I [pl. 31].

170 *Cana of Galilee*, 1839.
Watercolour & bodycolour on tinted paper, $12\frac{1}{2}$ × 19 (31.7 × 48.3); s., & insc. as title & *April 20th 1839*.
Bury Art Gallery and Museum.
Lithograph: *Holy Land*, Vol. I [pl. 33].

171 *Tabarias from the Walls. Saffet in the Distance*, 1839.
Watercolour, $9\frac{3}{8}$ × $13\frac{1}{4}$ (23.8 × 33.7); s. & d., insc. as title & *April 22nd 1839*.
Leicester Museum and Art Gallery.
Lithograph: *Holy Land*, Vol. II [pl. 36].

172 *The Sea of Galilee*, 1850. Pl. 61 (colour).
Oil, $9\frac{3}{4}$ × 16 (24.8 × 40.6); s. & d.
Private collection.

Given to his daughter, Christine. A similar picture, *Town of Tiberias, Sea of Galilee, Mount Hermon in the Distance* (RB 1855, 171) may be one of the two other known versions (Leicester Museum and Art Gallery, and formerly Spink and Son Ltd.). There is also a watercolour (Cat. 171).

The columns in the foreground marked the site of ancient baths, about half an hour's walk south of Tiberias (letterpress to lithograph, *Holy Land*, Vol. I [pl. 34]). The town

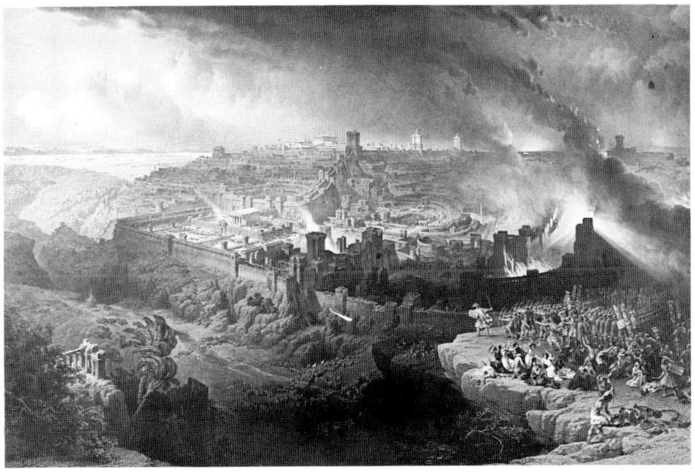
167

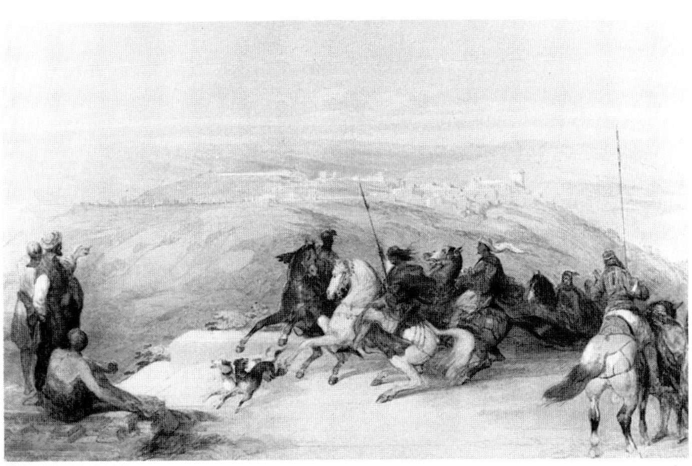
168

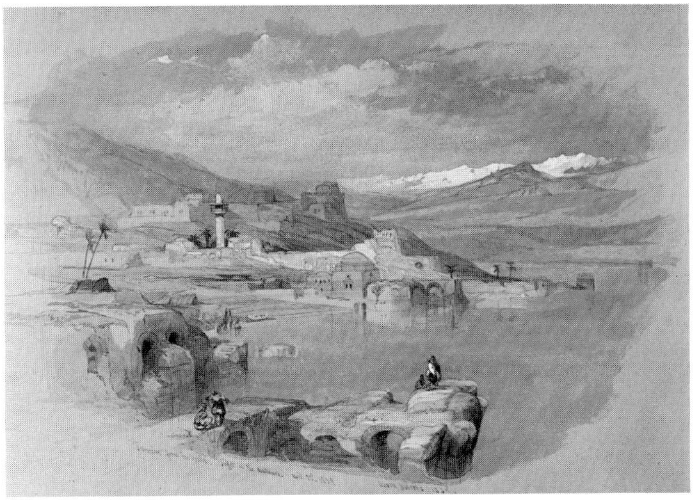
171

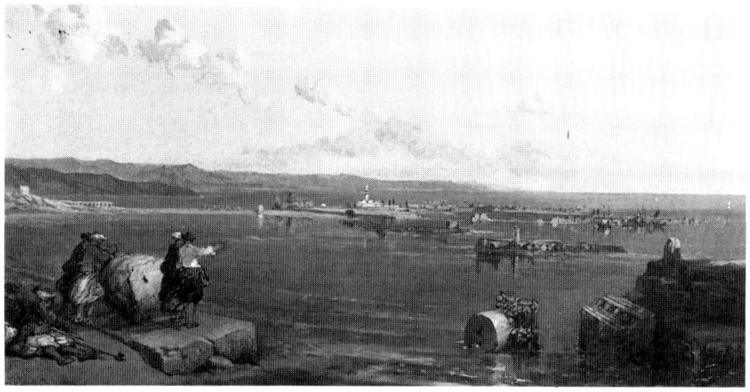
174

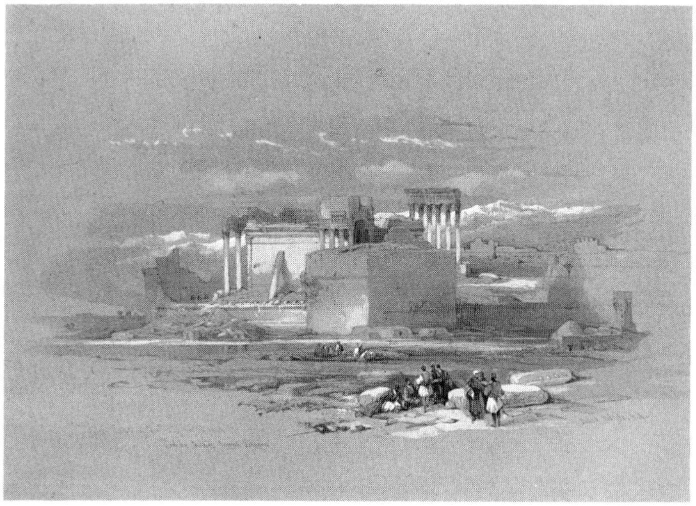
176

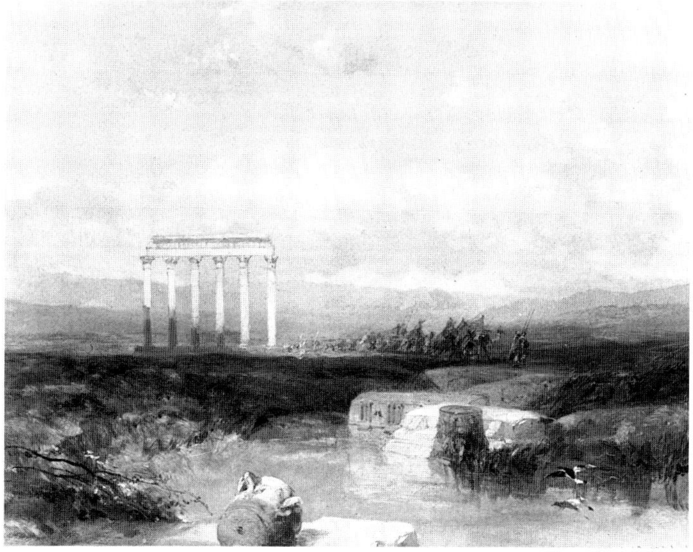
178

itself had been almost destroyed: 'the earthquake of 1835 left scarcely a house standing in the city, and the present habitations are miserable hovels raised upon the ruins.' (Romer, Vol. II, p. 320.)

173 *Tsur, Ancient Tyre, from the Isthmus*, 1839.
Pencil, watercolour & bodycolour on pale green paper, $13\frac{5}{8} \times 19\frac{3}{4}$ (34.6×50.2); s., & insc. as title & *April 27th 1839*.
Private collection.
Lithograph: *Holy Land*, Vol. II [pl. 70].

174 *Tyre*, 1858.
Oil, $22\frac{1}{2} \times 45$ (57.2×114.3); s. & d., insc. on stretcher *Ruins of Tyre from sketches made on the spot April 26th 1839. Painted for Elhanan Bicknell Esq.*
Sheffield City Art Galleries.
Painted for Elhanan Bicknell in 1858, with a companion, *Sidon* (private collection), £200 for the pair. Exhibited BI 1858 as *Tsur or Tyre of Phoenicia* (62).

Roberts had been hoping to find remains of ancient Tyre, but was disappointed: 'The present town is a mere village with a mosque rising in the centre, and the prophecy that it should become a rock for fishermen to dry their nets on is literally fulfilled . . . The harbour itself is choaked up with sand, only a few fishing boats were within it, their nets spread out to dry upon the ruins of the walls forcibly reminded us of the prediction of the prophet.' (EJ, 26 Apr. 1839.)

175 *Temple of the Sun at Baalbec*, 1839.
Watercolour & bodycolour, $20\frac{7}{8} \times 12$ (53×30.5); insc. as title & *4* (?) *May 1839*.
Government Art Collection.

176 *Lesser Temple of Baalbec, Looking towards Mount Lebanon*, 1839.
Watercolour & bodycolour, $9\frac{1}{8} \times 13\frac{1}{8}$ (23.2×33.3); s., & insc. as title & *May 5th 1839*.
Michael Appleby.
Lithograph: *Holy Land*, Vol. III, [pl. 79].

177 *Portico of the Great Temple at Baalbec*, 1840. Pl. 64 (colour).
Oil, $71\frac{3}{4} \times 52$ (182.2×132.1); s. & d.
Liverpool, National Museums and Galleries on Merseyside, Walker Art Gallery.

Sold to Elhanan Bicknell in 1840 for £250. Exhibited RA 1840 (944) as *Remains of the Portico of the Lesser Temple of Baalbec*, and in 1855 at the Paris Exposition Universelle (951). The Roman ruins at Baalbek impressed Roberts deeply: 'It would be difficult to convey even in drawing any idea of this magnificent ruin, its beauty of form, the exquisite richness of its decoration or the vast magnitude of its dimensions.' (EJ, 4 May 1839.)

Roberts considered this to be one of his best pictures (see RB 90). The low viewpoint and disproportionately small figures successfully accentuate the vast scale of the building. It was the first of at least seventeen oil paintings by Roberts of Baalbek. The watercolour of this view is also in the Walker Art Gallery, lithograph: *Holy Land*, Vol. II [pl. 78].

178 *Baalbec*, 1850.
Oil on panel, $11\frac{5}{8} \times 15\frac{1}{2}$ (29.5×39.4); s. & d., insc. verso *To Miss Newbury with David Roberts kind regards Janr 8th 1850.*
Private collection.

There are three other known views of Baalbec with the Temple of the Sun as their principal subject, one being the very large *Surprise of the Caravan, Baalbec* (Pl. 66), presented by Roberts to the Garrick Club, London. The temple greatly impressed contemporary travellers: 'Six lofty columns . . . tower above all the other ruins of Baalbec, and form the first object beheld from afar by the pilgrim . . . Egypt possesses nothing more imposing – nothing so harmonious – as these pillars, which, all-colossal as they are, have an airy lightness, an elegant richness of detail about them, that enchants even more than it astonishes.' (Romer, Vol. II, p. 381.)

179 *The Ruins of the Smaller Temple at Baalbec*, 1850. Pl. 69 (colour).
Oil, $24\frac{1}{4} \times 48$ (61.6 × 121.9).
Private collection.

Exhibited RA 1850 (277) as *Remains of the Eastern Portico of the Temple of the Sun at Baalbec, Mount Lebanon in the distance*; sold to Sigismund Rucker in 1851 for £157.10s. The *Athenaeum* considered it to be 'one more of those presentments of the ruined edifice in which Mr. Roberts stands unrivalled . . . The light and shade and colour are full of truth; and the distant mountains are expressed with that sense of aerial perspective which conveys the impression of great space as well as of purity of atmosphere.' (1850, p. 533.)

Another painting of this subject, *Eastern Portico of the Temple of Bacchus, Baalbec* (private collection), resembles more closely the lithograph in *Holy Land*, Vol. II [pl. 82].

180 *Valetta, Malta*, 1839.
Pencil, watercolour & bodycolour on four joined sheets, $12\frac{1}{2} \times 34\frac{1}{2}$ (31.8 × 87.6); s., & insc. *Valetta June 3rd 1839*.
Edinburgh, National Galleries of Scotland.

181 *Sheets from a Sketchbook Used by Roberts in the Near East*.
Pencil, or pencil & watercolour, mounted on card watermarked *J Whatman 1872*; average size $4\frac{1}{2} \times 6\frac{1}{2}$ (11.4 × 16.5).
University of London, Durning-Lawrence Library.

Selected from two portfolios of sheets from a dismembered sketchbook, all similarly mounted. They are the only survivals known from the 'three books filled' to which Roberts referred at the end of his long tour of the Near East (EJ, 16 June 1839). The subjects are mainly figure studies.

182 *Two Sheets of Tracings for 'The Holy Land' and 'Egypt'*.
a. Tracing for *Fountain of the Virgin, Nazareth* (*Holy Land*, Vol. I [pl. 28]).
Pencil on tracing paper, $8\frac{7}{8} \times 10\frac{1}{4}$ (22.5 × 26); insc. with numerous colour notes & instruction *Colours not too bright. Subdued.*
London, M. Z. Irani, the Connoisseur Gallery.
b. Tracings from studies for lithographs in *Egypt*, including *Approach to the Fortress of Ibrim-Nubia* (Vol. II [pl. 49]), *Ruins of the Temple of Kardeseh, Nubia* (Vol. II [pl. 70]), and *General View of the Ruins of Luxor from the Nile* (Vol. I [pl. 16]).
Pencil on tracing paper, $19\frac{3}{4} \times 20\frac{5}{8}$ (50 × 52.3); insc. *Ruins of Luxor from the Nile*, with colour notes.
London, M. Z. Irani, the Connoisseur Gallery.

Italy

Roberts made two visits to Italy, in 1851 to Venice (via Switzerland and back through Vienna), and in 1853 to Rome and Naples. He was very impressed with Venice, but found that 'the streets . . . are so crooked that the most cunning could never find his way in them, or, if in, out again. Secondly, from their narrowness & the great height of the houses, the stench arising from the Canals & the inate dirtiness of the Venitians, you can scarce breathe.' (26 Oct. 1851 to his daughter, PC.)

Ballantine is the main source of information for the Rome and Naples visit, as no MS letters or journals have been found. Roberts enjoyed Rome and produced a great many works as a result of his stay; only paintings of Paestum and Pozzuoli have been traced resulting from his Naples tour.

183 *Interior of Milan Cathedral*, 1863.
Oil, 50 × 41 (127 × 104.1); s. & d., insc. verso *Cathedral of Milan painted for Theophilus Burnand Esq.*
Rochdale Art Gallery.

Roberts went to Milan on his way to Venice. The cathedral 'in point of the picturesque I found beyond expectation so much so that I think I will get more than two or three subjects from it . . . I will commence painting in oil tomorrow . . . The Cathedral . . . is vile and corrupt in taste, overloaded with detail but splendid in colour . . . I think I will devote a week to it.' (16 Sept. 1851 to Henry Bicknell, PC.)

Exhibited RA 1863 (35) and sold to Theophilus Burnand. There are two other versions: one, undated, at the Victoria and Albert Museum; the other, dated 1857, in the Government Art Collection.

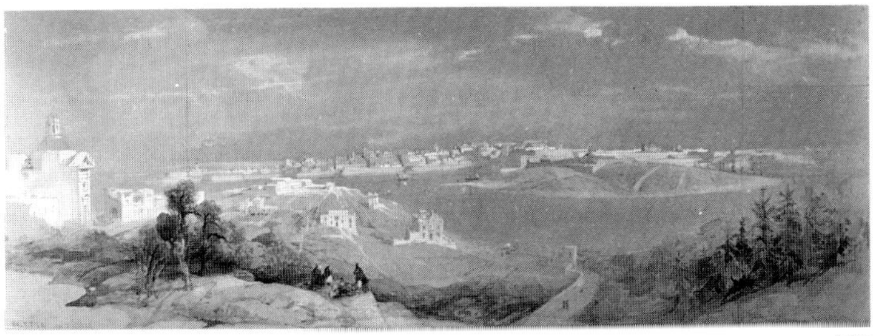
180

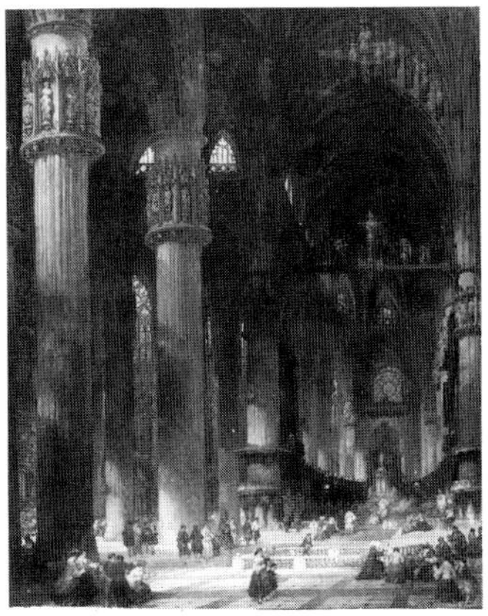
183

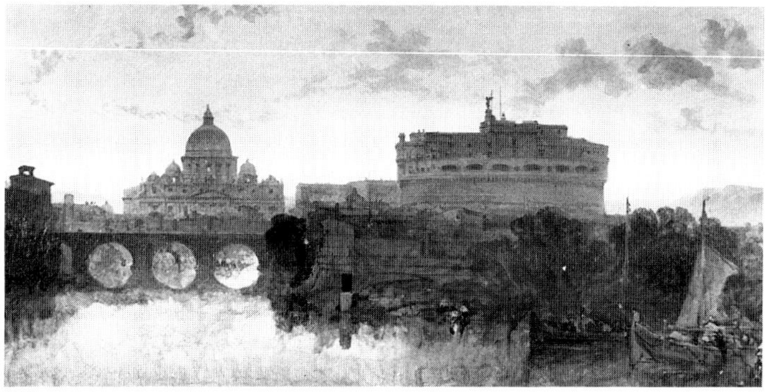

188

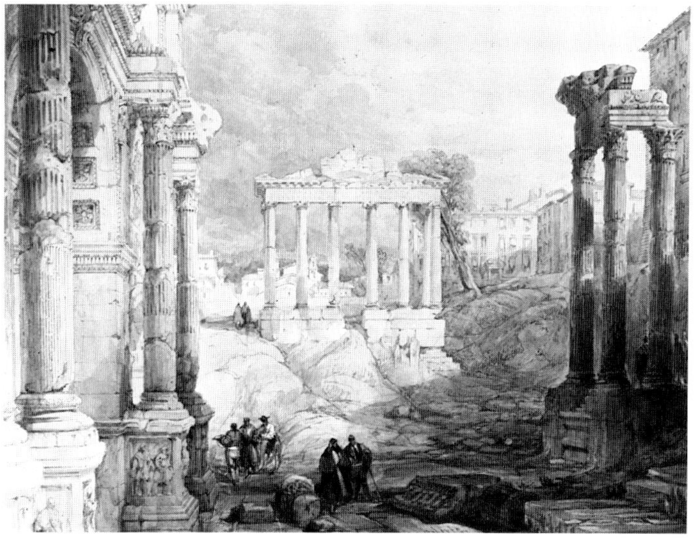

190

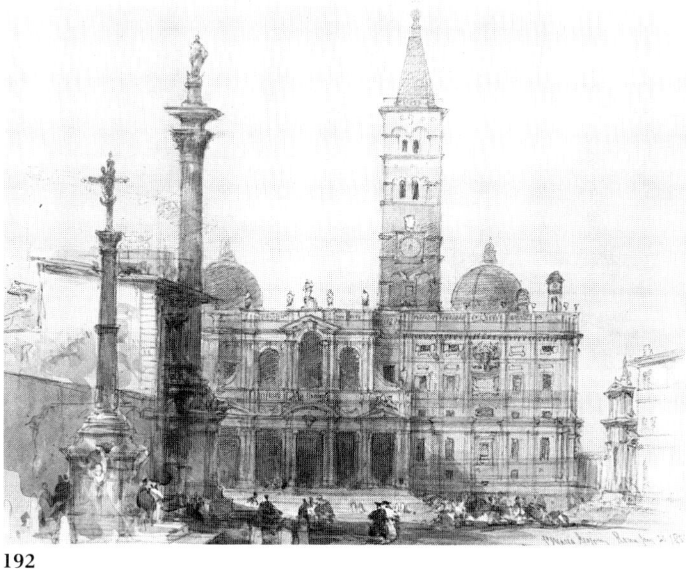

192

184 *Ruins of Paestum*, 1855.
Oil, $19\frac{1}{2} \times 49\frac{1}{2}$ (49.5×125.7); s. & d.
Private collection.

Exhibited *Royal Jubilee Exhibition*, Manchester, 1887 (758). One of three paintings of Paestum, all dated 1855. This version was bought by Richard Newsham; another is in the National Gallery of Ireland, and a third is untraced.

Shows the Basilica, or Temple of Hera, with the Temple of Neptune (Poseidon) behind. 'The Temples of Paestum I found so far superior to what I expected and so unlike all the drawings one has seen . . . that I strongly suspect the truth of those who have hitherto treated those magnificent ruins ever having seen them!! One Temple alone is worth the journey from England.' (25 Feb. 1854, to his son-in-law, NLS.)

185 *Santa Maria della Spina, Pisa*, 1855/6. Pl. 57 (colour).
Oil, $23\frac{1}{2} \times 47\frac{1}{2}$ (59.7×120.7); s. & d.
Private collection.

Roberts drew a space for *Pisa* in his *Record Book* (181) but did not fill it in; Cat. 185 may therefore be a study for another work that was not carried out. There is a pencil and wash drawing of 8 Oct. 1853 (Princeton University Art Museum) from the same viewpoint.

Roberts visited Pisa on his way to Rome. The church is named after its relic of a thorn (*spina*) reputed to come from Christ's crown of thorns.

186 *Ruins of the Temple of Neptune, Pozzuoli*, 1858. Pl. 49.
Oil, $20 \times 30\frac{1}{4}$ (50.8×76.8); s. & d., insc. verso *To the Revd James White Bonchurch with the Artists best wishes July 19th 1858*.
Private collection.

Pozzuoli is in the Bay of Naples. This work came to the present owners by direct descent from James White (see Cat. 36).

187 *Rome, from the Convent of St. Onofrio, Mount Janiculum*, 1856. Pl. 45 (colour).
Oil, 84×168 (213.4×426.7); s. & d.
Edinburgh, National Galleries of Scotland.

Presented by Roberts to the RSA in 1857, 'in order that it should be placed in the National Gallery'.

When exhibited RA 1855 (594), Ruskin was so critical that Roberts spent two months re-painting it, refusing to send it to the opening exhibition of the RSA's new Gallery in 1856. Ruskin felt that the rose-red effect was untrue, and that the warm light of sunset did not change the colour of roofs, trees, stucco or stone. Yet Ballantine recorded the account of a friend who was with Roberts and saw how 'the sun setting . . . shed a rich glow, lighting up the tops of every object with indescribable brilliancy, while the lower parts of the city were shrouded in gloom. The effect was extraordinary . . . Roberts commenced the studies first in pencil, then in watercolours, but could not catch the effect till he had recourse to oil colours, when he said . . . "I think I have got it at last . . ." His friend replied: "Yes . . . but the effect is so unusual, and you have rendered it so truthfully, that I doubt whether the critics will not say it is exaggerated and untruthful".' (Ballantine p. 181.)

Several studies are known: one in the National Gallery of Scotland ($8\frac{1}{2} \times 16$ [21.6×40.6]); one that belonged to Christine Bicknell, sold HBS 1881 ($13\frac{3}{4} \times 92$ [34.9×233.7], untraced); a third appeared recently at auction (24×48 [61×121.9], untraced).

188 *Castel San Angelo and St. Peter's, Rome*, 1860.
Oil, 23×47 (58.4×119.4).
Leeds City Art Galleries.

There are two smaller, almost identical paintings of the subject, dated 1860; one belonged to Roberts's daughter (private collection), the other was sold at Sotheby's, 1983 (untraced). A watercolour from a similar viewpoint is in the Huntington Library and Art Gallery, California.

189 *Interior of the Colosseum, Rome*, 1853.
Watercolour with touches of white on two joined sheets, $9\frac{1}{2} \times 27$ (24.1×68.6); s. & d.
Private collection.

Probably HBS 1881 (265). An untraced oil of this subject was left unfinished by Roberts when he died; according to Henry Bicknell, he found it difficult to compose pleasantly.

190 *The Forum, Rome*, 1835.
Watercolour, $11\frac{1}{2} \times 15\frac{1}{2}$ (29.2×39.4); s. & d.
Manchester City Art Galleries.

Made 18 years before Roberts went to Rome. Engraved: W. Finden, *Landscape Illustrations to the Bible*, 1836, Vol. II, pl. 69 (indexed as by J. D. Harding); *Landscapes of Interesting Localities mentioned in the Holy Scriptures*, n. d., p. 279, from a sketch by W. Page.

191 *At Rome*, 1859. Pl. 50 (colour).
Oil on panel, $15\frac{1}{8} \times 24\frac{5}{8}$ (38.4×62.5); s. & d.
Wolverhampton Art Gallery.

One of seven paintings of the Forum from Roberts's winter in Rome. Shows the three columns of the Temple of Vespasian, left foreground, SS Luca and Martina (the domed church), and the arch of Septimius Severus, right. Behind are the columns of the Temple of Antoninus and Faustina, with the Colosseum in the distance.

192 *Santa Maria Maggiore, Rome*. 1854.
Pencil & wash, $8 \times 10\frac{1}{2}$ (20.3×26.7); insc. *St Maria Majore Rome Jany 30 1854.*
Private collection.

193 *Tombs of the Popes, St. Peter's, Rome*, 1853.
Pencil & wash heightened with white, $9\frac{3}{4} \times 13\frac{3}{4}$ (24.8×34.9); insc. *St Peter Rome Decr 6th 1853*, with names of the Popes insc. on their tombs.
Cambridge, the Syndics of the Fitzwilliam Museum.

From the same sketchbook as Cat. 194, dated one day apart. Roberts wrote that he had completed two pictures in oil of St. Peter's and had made many sketches in watercolour (Ballantine p. 179).

194 *Interior of St. Peter's, Rome*, 1853.
Pencil & wash heightened with white, $13\frac{1}{2} \times 9\frac{3}{4}$ (34.3×24.8); insc. *St Peter's Decr 5 1853.*
Private collection.

See Cat. 193.

195 *Ruins of the Ponte Rotto, Rome*, 1853. Pl. 58 (colour).
Watercolour heightened with white, on two joined sheets, $9\frac{1}{4} \times 24\frac{3}{4}$ (23.5×62.9); s. & redated 1854, insc. *Ruins of Ponte Palatine or Rotto Rome Octr 31st 1853*, with three further insc.
Bedford, Cecil Higgins Art Gallery.

The Pons Aemilius, on the left, was damaged by a flood in 1598, hence its name Ponte Rotto (broken bridge). There are three oils of the bridge from another viewpoint (private collection; Beaverbrook Art Gallery, Fredericton, Canada; and untraced). A drawing, also from a different viewpoint, is in a private collection.

196 *Mausoleum of Plautius Lucanas near Tivoli*, 1858.
Oil, $17\frac{1}{2} \times 35\frac{1}{2}$ (44.5×90.2); s. & d., insc. verso *Painted for and presented to David Smith Esq. with the best wishes of his oblidged and ever sincere friend David Roberts.*
Barnsley, Cannon Hall Museum.

197 *Venice*, 1851. Pl. 40.
Oil on paper, $12\frac{1}{4} \times 20\frac{5}{8}$ (31.1×52.4); insc. *VENICE Oct 7 1851.*
Private collection.

This scene was expanded to show a wider view of the canal on the left in an oil of 1852 (RB 155, whereabouts unknown). Roberts also painted several versions of the Ducal Palace from a different viewpoint.

198 *SS Giovanni e Paolo, Venice*, 1861. Pl. 56.
Oil, $21 \times 29\frac{1}{2}$ (53.3×74.9); s. & d., insc. verso *To my dear Christine on her birthday 1861.*
City of London, Guildhall Art Gallery.

One of the most imposing churches in Venice, where the funeral services of the Doges were held. Roberts often gave his daughter, Mrs Henry Bicknell, paintings for her birthday; sold HBS 1881 (37), bought by Agnew, who sold it to Charles Gassiot. Exhibited International Exhibition, South Kensington, 1874 (180).

Another version from a different viewpoint is in the Manchester City Art Gallery.

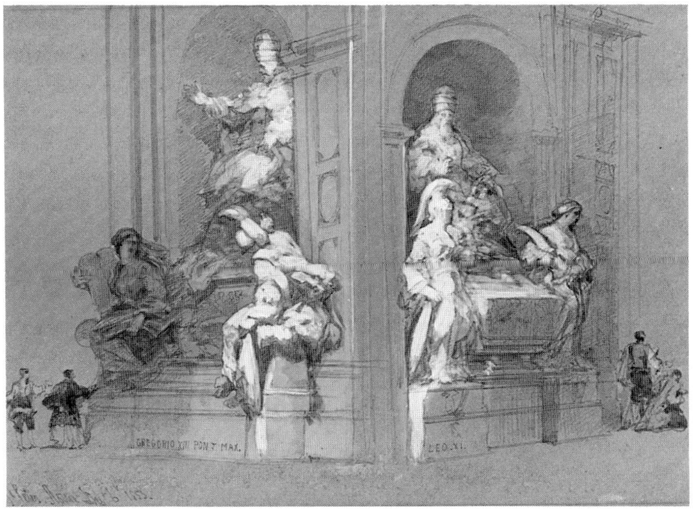

193

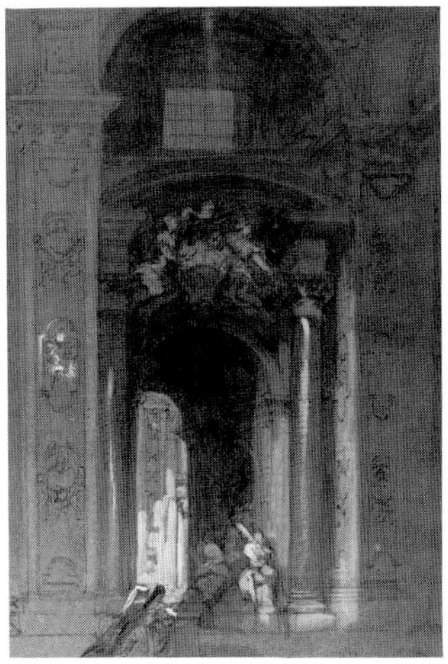

194

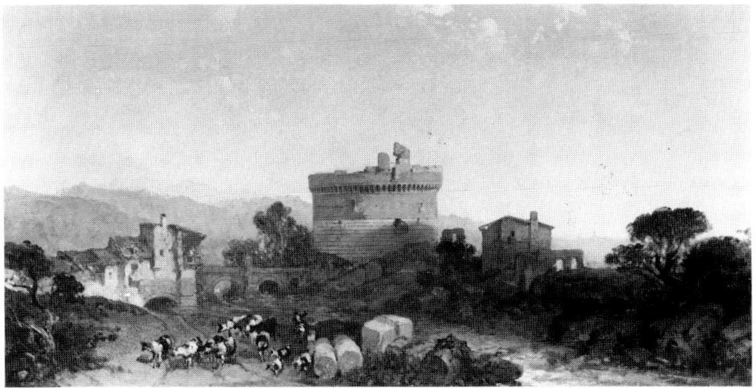

196

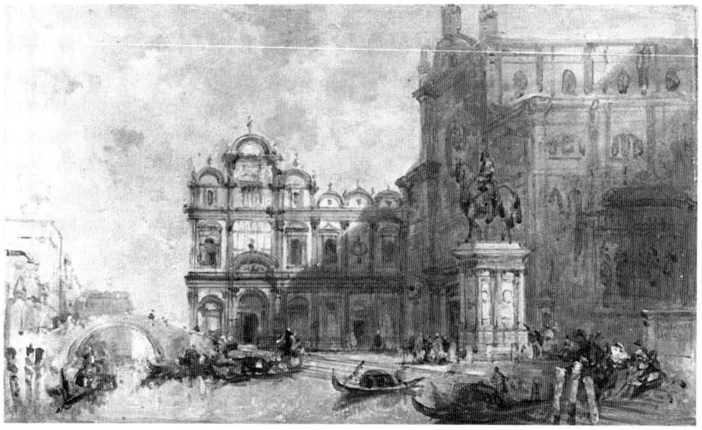
199

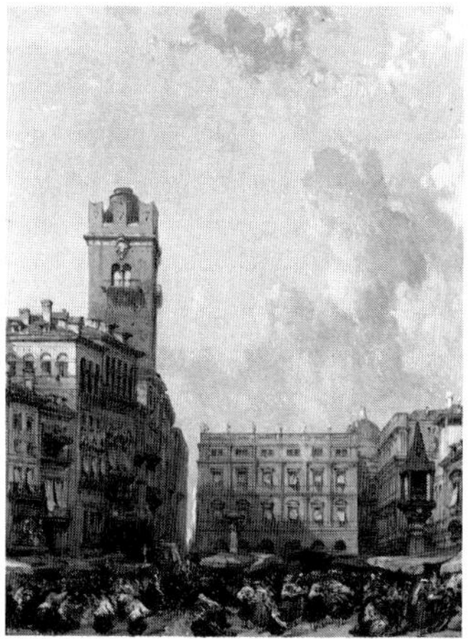
201

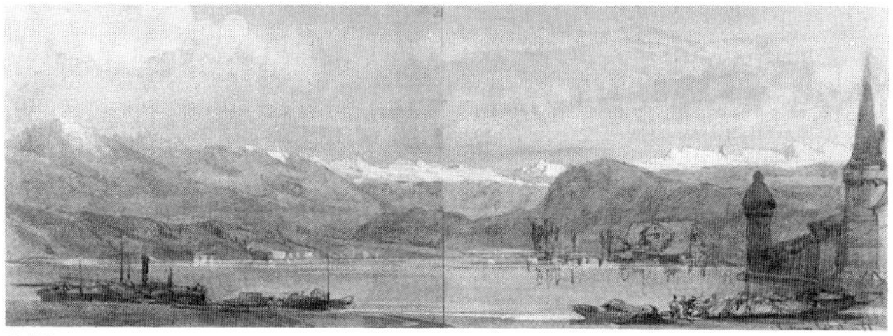
202

199 *SS Giovanni e Paolo with Statue of Colleoni, Venice,* 1851.
Oil on paper laid down on panel, $12\frac{1}{2} \times 20$ (31.8 × 50.8).
Private collection.

The church is on the right behind the statue; on the left is the Scuola di San Marco, now a hospital; the statue of Bartolomeo Colleoni is by Andrea Verrochio.

Sold HBS 1881 (363), bought Butler; a descendant sold it to Agnew. A larger version from a slightly different viewpoint, dated 1856, was sold at Phillips, 1977 (untraced).

200 *Santa Maria della Salute, Venice,* 1862. Pl. 39.
Oil, 28 × 45 (71.1 × 114.3); s. & d.
Sheffield City Art Galleries.

Roberts painted seven other views of Santa Maria della Salute, (all untraced), and many others of the Grand Canal. Ruskin scathingly criticized 'the gondoliers! still always where they couldn't possibly row! . . . I much regret Mr Roberts' abandonment of his old picturesque subjects for these severe ones. He had a great gift of expressing the ins and outs of Spanish balconies and roofs . . . and all his skill of this kind is now passing away with formal architectural drawing in brown and grey.' (*Academy Notes,* 1859.)

201 *Market Place of Verona,* 1859.
Oil, 36 × 27 (91.4 × 68.6); s. & d.
Wirral Borough Council, Dept. of Leisure Services and Tourism, Williamson Art Gallery.

Roberts found Verona 'a most interesting old town, with roman theatres, amphitheatres arches etc. The Streets, Churches etc. made for Painting.' (28 Sept. 1851 to his daughter, PC.) Bought by the art dealer, Ernest Gambart. A *Street Scene* of Verona was sold at Phillips, 1974 (untraced).

202 *Lucerne, Switzerland,* 1851.
Watercolour heightened with white on two joined sheets, $4\frac{3}{4} \times 13$ (12.1 × 33); insc. *Lucerne Sept 12th 1851.*
Private collection.

A pair to this watercolour of Como belongs to the same owner; both were drawn en route to Milan. Roberts wrote to his son-in-law that he had 'passed the day at Lucerne, making studies of the scenery of the Lake' (16 Sept. 1851, PC).

203 *St. Stephen's Cathedral, Vienna,* 1851. Pl. 55.
Pencil & wash, $9\frac{1}{2} \times 6\frac{3}{4}$ (24.1 × 17.1); insc. *St Stephens Vienna Oct 30 1851.*
Private collection.

204 *The Cathedral of St. Stephen, Vienna,* 1853.
Oil, 44 × 56 (111.8 × 142.2); s. & d.
Birmingham City Museum and Art Gallery.

Roberts visited Vienna on his way home from Venice: 'The Cathedral I found far better than I expected, indeed the interior is without exception the most beautiful thing of the kind I have ever seen . . . the weather was against me, cold, foggy and dark days . . . no permission could be gotten to paint & even drawings only from midday untill 3 Oclock. But as it was I got two very fine subjects which I will make much of; in doing these I was almost perished . . . they would not give me a seat . . .' (1 Nov. 1851 to his sister, PC.) Exhibited RA 1853 (89); Glasgow 1853; Manchester Art Treasures Exhibition, 1857 (187) as *Cathedral Interior.*

There are four other versions, dated 1851 and 1852 (both untraced), 1855 (South African National Gallery, Capetown), and 1863 (Guildhall Art Gallery, City of London.)

Books with Illustrations after Roberts

205 *Illustrations to the Waverley Novels,* Charles Tilt, 1832.
2 Vols.
Private collection.

206 *Illustrations Landscape, Historical and Antiquarian to the Poetical Works of Sir Walter Scott, Bart,* London 1834.
Private collection.

207 *Landscape Annual,* Robert Jennings & Co., London, 1835 and 1836.
Private collection.

208 *The Gallery of Modern British Artists, Consisting of a Series of Engravings from Works of the Most Eminent Artists of the Day,* London, Simpkin and Marshall, 1835.
Private collection.

209 *Landscape Illustrations of the Bible, Consisting of Views of the Most Remarkable Places Mentioned in the Old and New Testaments*, John Murray, 1836.
2 Vols.
London, Victoria and Albert Museum.
Appeared in small and large paper copies, first issued in parts. Plates dated 1834, 1835 and 1836.

210 *Picturesque Sketches of Spain*, Hodgson and Graves, 1837.
Private collection.

211 *The Holy Land, Syria, Idumea, Arabia, Egypt & Nubia. From Drawings made on the spot by David Roberts RA*, London, F. G. Moon, 1842–9.
Lithographed by Louis Haghe.
a. Unbound Monthly Parts.
Exeter College of Art and Design.
b. Bound Volumes.
University of London Library
Although published separately, *The Holy Land* and *Egypt* are actually two sections of the same work, planned by Roberts before his journey to the East. The expense involved made publishers reluctant to take on such an ambitious project, and Roberts was turned down by two firms before he found one willing to buy the copyright of his drawings. 'When having been much importuned by Mr Moon I told him the circumstances connected with it, then he [at] once offered to bring it out . . .' (RB 1839, p. 117.) Moon offered Roberts £3,000 for the use of his drawings, and in 1840 held exhibitions in London and the larger provincial towns to attract subscribers.

The Holy Land was originally issued in 20 monthly parts between 1842 and the end of 1845. *Egypt* appeared in 21 parts from 1846–9. Roberts was full of admiration for the work of the lithographer, Louis Haghe, responsible for all 248 plates: 'Haghe has not only surpassed himself – but has surpassed all that has been hithertoo done of a similar nature, in the masterly treatement of them [Roberts's watercolours], clear, simple – and unlaboured, add to which a vigour – and boldness, that only a painter like himself could transfer to Stone.' (RB 1842, p. 134.)

Roberts seems to have made a complete new set of drawings for the lithographer from the sketches made in the East. 'I have completed 132 finished drawings from the original Sketches . . . for Louis Haghe to engrave from,' he wrote on 23 Dec. 1844 (RB). He added that 25 of the drawings of Jerusalem and 57 of Syria had been sold to Lord Francis Egerton for a total of £1,400. The success of *The Holy Land and Egypt* between 1842 and 1849 led to its reproduction in England and abroad. In 1843 a French version of the work, containing 60 plates, appeared in Brussels, and in 1855–6 Day & Son published an edition in 6 volumes in England, with all the plates reduced photographically. There were also American editions of the work published in 1855 and 1879–84.

Portraits and Memorabilia

212 Robert Scott Lauder (1803–69). *Portrait of Roberts as a Young Man*, c.1820. Pl. 2.
Oil, $12\frac{1}{4} \times 9$ (31.1 × 22.9).
Mrs S. M. Fraser.
Lauder also painted a portrait of Roberts in eastern dress (Scottish National Portrait Gallery). Roberts wrote to Hay, 29 March 1836, 'Many thanks for your kind offer of the Sketch by Lauder, but my wife will not hear of it, she says . . . that it is *not half so handsome* as I am—and after all women are the best judges in these matters.' (NLS.)

213 John Ballantyne (1815–1897). *Roberts in his Studio*, c.1862. Pl. 1 (colour).
Oil, 28 × 36 (71.1 × 91.4); signed.
London, the Fine Art Society.
The child is probably Roberts's youngest grandson, Gilbert Elhanan Bicknell (b. 1859), a great favourite who often 'helped' Roberts with his paintings. The work on the easel is *St. Paul's from Fleet Street*, left unfinished at Roberts's death (now in the USA).
Ballantyne painted a series of portraits of artists in their studios, including Clarkson Stanfield, W. P. Frith, Daniel Maclise and Sir Edwin Landseer.

214 Sir Daniel Macnee (1806–82). *Portrait of David Roberts*, 1864.
Oil, $29\frac{1}{2} \times 24\frac{1}{2}$ (74.9 × 62.2).
London, the Royal Academy of Arts.
The last portrait painted of Roberts. Macnee was a friend of his, and another portrait by Macnee, dated 1863 and painted in one sitting, is in the Royal Scottish Academy.

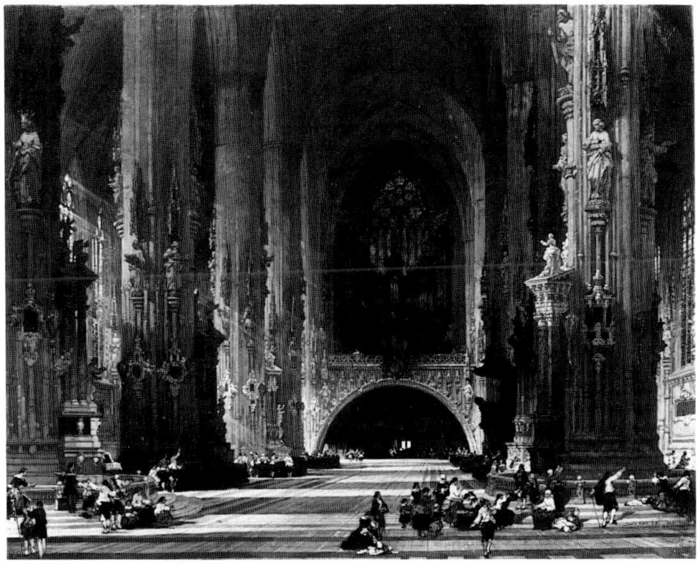

204

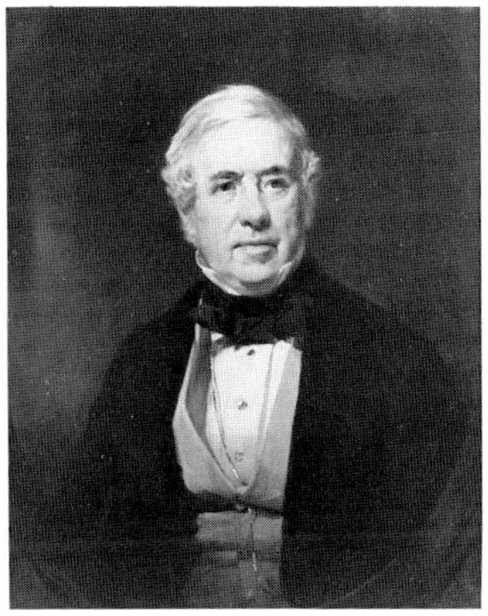

214

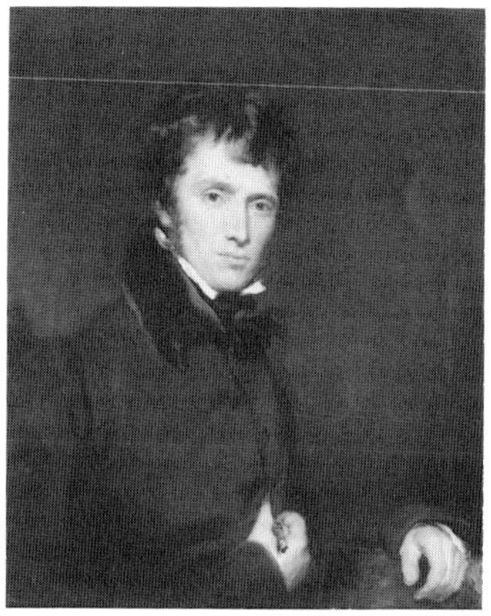
217

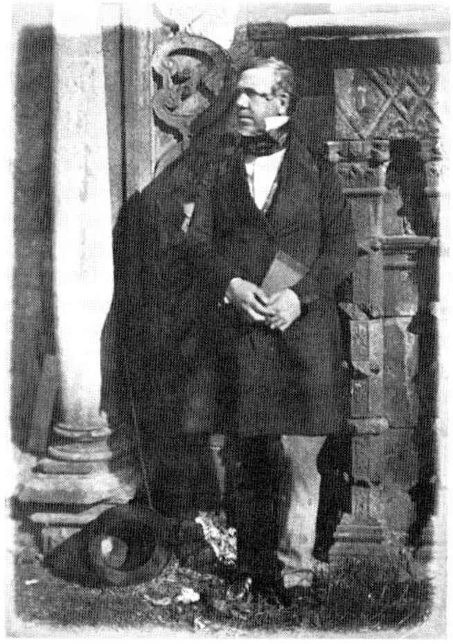
218a

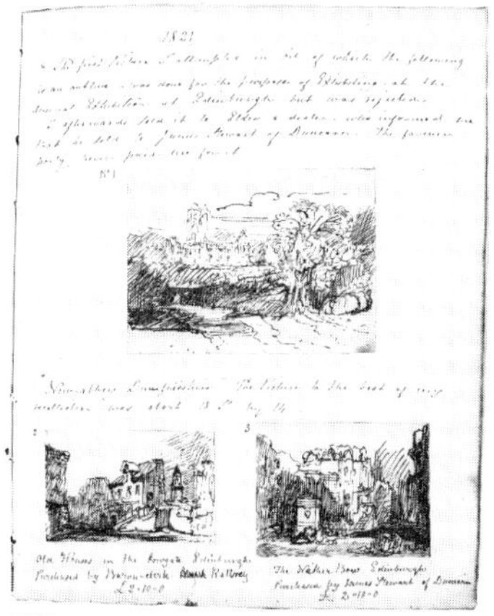
220

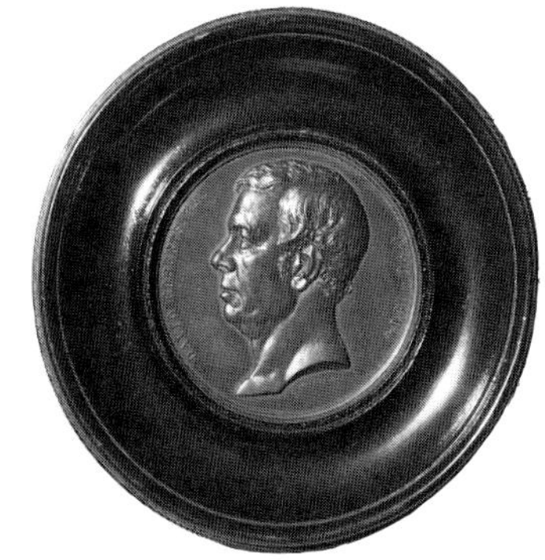
221 (recto)

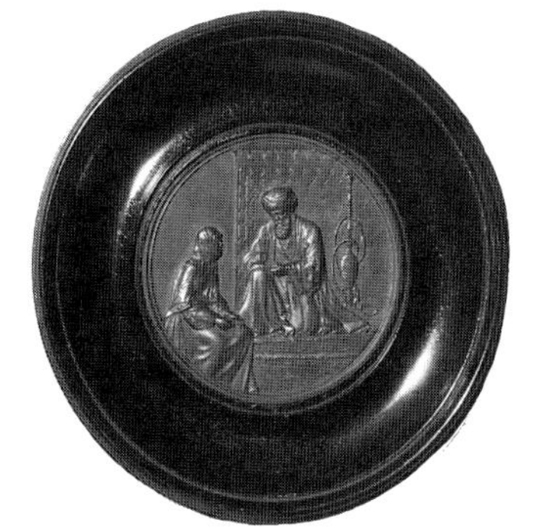
221 (verso)

215 Clarkson Stanfield (1793–1867). *David Roberts*. Pl. 37 (below).
Pen & ink, $7\frac{3}{4} \times 5$ (19.7×12.7); insc. *Roberts by Stanfield*.
London, the Royal Academy of Arts.

216 *Clarkson Stanfield*. Pl. 37 (above).
Pen & ink, $7\frac{1}{2} \times 6$ (19.1×15.2); insc. *Stanfield by Roberts* and *I Roberts fecit*.
London, the Royal Academy of Arts.

217 John Simpson (1782–1847). *Clarkson Stanfield, aged 35*.
Oil, 30×25 (76.2×63.5).
London, National Maritime Museum.

Stanfield was born in Sunderland of theatrical parentage. He went to sea in 1806, was press-ganged into the Navy, 1812–14, and then sailed to China in East India Company service. In 1816 he began scene-painting at the Royalty Theatre, Stepney and over the next 18 years became the most celebrated theatrical artist of his day, working with and in competition to, Roberts. An exhibitor of sea and landscapes at the RA from 1820, he was elected ARA in 1832 and RA in 1835, shortly after leaving the stage. Their rivalries over, he and Roberts became lifelong friends and Stanfield died the acknowledged doyen of English marine painting.

218 *Photographs of Roberts*.
a. David Octavius Hill (1802–90). David Roberts, Sept. 1844.
Edinburgh, Scottish National Portrait Gallery.
Taken in Greyfriars Churchyard.
b. with his granddaughter, Rosa, c.1860.
Family collection.
c. Family collection.
d. London, the Fine Art Society.
e. Private collection.

219 *Eastern Journal*.
a. Original pencil manuscript with entries from 7 May to 24 June 1839, the only remaining fragment of the original.
Family collection.
b. Transcription of the original manuscript by Christine Roberts (one volume of two).
Edinburgh, National Library of Scotland.

Roberts kept a journal throughout his eastern travels. When his daughter, then 18 years old, copied it at his request, she amended it; this is clear from the parallel parts of the original and the transcript. Ballantine, in quoting from it in his biography, further bowdlerized it, resulting in a loss of spontaneity.

Roberts wrote to Christine from Edinburgh, 30 Oct. 1839: 'Pray do get on with manuscript with what time you can spare, as immediately on my return I shall in all probability commence to some arraingement with Murray or someone else, and that [the manuscript] must be forthcoming with the sketches.' (PC.)

220 *Record Book*.
Two volumes.
Family collection.

Roberts recorded his oil paintings in small pen and ink sketches, numbered, with details of where they were first exhibited and who were the first purchasers. Sometimes later information about their history was added. There are some omissions, e.g. studies, sketches and repetitions of the same subject are generally not included, nor are any watercolours; nevertheless, it is an invaluable document for the art historian.

Roberts also pasted in press cuttings referring to his works, and contemporary topics such as architecture, archaeology, politics and religion. There are also essays written in 1837 on three of his fellow artists, Clarkson Stanfield, John Wilson and William Leighton Leitch. The early part of the *Record Book* is an important source of reference for Roberts's early life and scene-painting.

221 *Commemorative Medal*, designed by George T. Morgan. Issued by the Art Union, 1875.
Edinburgh, Scottish National Portrait Gallery.
Recto has a portrait of Roberts; verso *The Letter Writer, Cairo* from *The Holy Land and Egypt*, Vol. VI [pl. 117].

222 *Roberts's palette*.
Edinburgh, the Royal Scottish Academy.
Inscribed on silver plate: 'The favourite pallette of DAVID ROBERTS presented to the Royal Scottish Academy by Christine Bicknell in grateful remembrance of the honor in which her father was held by the artists in Scotland, June 1865'.

Bibliography

Abbey, J. R., *Travel in Aquatint and Lithography 1770–1860*, 2 Vols., London, 1956–7.
Altick, Richard D., *The Shows of London*, Cambridge, Mass., 1978.
Art Journal, 1858, 'British Artists, Their Style and Character: David Roberts'.
Ballantine, James, *The Life of David Roberts R.A.*, Edinburgh, 1866.
Brighton Museum and Art Gallery, *The Inspiration of Egypt*, 1983.
Castlereagh, Viscount, *A Journey to Damascus*, 2 Vols., London, 1847.
Caw, Sir James, *Scottish Painting Past and Present 1620–1908*, London, 1908.
[Edin. illus. guide] *Edinburgh, An Illustrated Architectural Guide*, Edinburgh, 1982.
Guiterman, Helen, *David Roberts R.A.*, London, 1978, reprinted 1981 and 1986.
— *The Old Watercolour Society's Club*, Vol. 59, 1985 and Vol. 60, 1986.
Hardie, Martin, *Watercolour Painting in Britain*, Vol. III, London, 1968.
Irwin, David and Francina, *Scottish Painters at Home and Abroad, 1700–1900*, London, 1975.
Leighton House, *Romantic Lebanon: The European View 1700–1900*, London, 1986.
Maas, Jeremy, *Victorian Painters*, London, 1967.
van der Merwe, Dr Pieter, *The Spectacular Career of Clarkson Stanfield*, Tyne and Wear County Council Museums, 1979.
The Old Watercolour Society's Club, Vol. 25, 1947.
Quigley, Jane, *Prout and Roberts*, London, 1926.
Redgrave, S., *A Dictionary of Artists of the English School*, reprinted 1970.
Redgrave, S. and R., *A Century of British Painters*, 1866, reprinted 1947.
Roberts, David, *Eastern Journal*, unpublished transcript by Christine Bicknell, 2 Vols., National Library of Scotland.
— *Record Book*, unpublished, 2 Vols., Family collection.
Robertson, David, *Sir Charles Eastlake and the Victorian Art World*, Princeton, 1978.
Romer, Isabella, *A Pilgrimage to the Temples and Tombs of Egypt, Nubia and Palestine, 1845–6*, 2 Vols., London, 1846.
Scottish Arts Council, *David Roberts: Artist Adventurer*, 1981.
Stevens, Mary Anne, ed., *The Orientalists: Delacroix to Matisse. European Painters in North Africa and the Near East*, Royal Academy, 1984.
Titmarsh, M. A. (W. M. Thackeray), *Notes on a Journey from Cornhill to Grand Cairo*, 2nd edn., London, 1846.
Walkers Quarterly Magazine, 1923.
Warburton, Eliot, *The Crescent and the Cross*, 2 Vols., London, 1845.

Lenders

Aberdeen Art Gallery and Museums, 130; Michael Appleby, 38, 76, 176; Barnsley, Cannon Hall Museum, 196; Bedford, Cecil Higgins Art Gallery, 26, 155, 195; Birmingham City Museum and Art Gallery, 59, 63c, 98, 103, 114, 149, 204; Blackburn Art Gallery and Museum, 35; Blackpool, Grundy Art Gallery, 65; Burnley, Towneley Hall Art Gallery, 140; Bury Art Gallery and Museum, 170; Cambridge, the Syndics of the Fitzwilliam Museum, 68, 89, 95, 193; The Abbot of Downside, 102, 104; Dudley Museum and Art Gallery, 86; Edinburgh, the Donaldson Trust, Donaldson's School for the Deaf, 14, 21; National Galleries of Scotland, 13, 20, 34, 37, 44, 67, 180, 187, 218a, 221; National Library of Scotland, 219b; the Royal Scottish Academy, 222; The Provost and Fellows of Eton College, 57, 101, 136; Exeter College of Art and Design, 211a; Family collections, 4, 5, 16, 22, 24, 51, 90, 105, 118, 124, 218b, 218c, 219a, 220; Mrs Elizabeth Ochiltree Forbes, 74; Mrs S. M. Fraser, 212; Glasgow Museums and Art Galleries, 154; University of Glasgow, Hunterian Art Gallery, J. A. McCallum Collection, 29; Government Art Collection, 47, 153, 175; Ingram Family Collection, 33, 49, 77, 106, 107, 128, 168; Leeds City Art Galleries, 52, 73, 100, 147, 188; Leicester Museum and Art Gallery, 171; Monica Bicknell Lightwood, 55; Max Lightwood, 165; Liverpool, National Museums and Galleries on Merseyside, Walker Art Gallery, 177; University of Liverpool, 64; London, Thomas Agnew and Sons Ltd., 27; Baring Brothers and Co. Ltd., 46, 63d; the Fine Art Society, 213, 218d; Frost and Reed Ltd., 129; M. Z. Irani, the Connoisseur Gallery, 182; Mathaf Gallery, 117; the Merchant Taylors Company, 58; National Maritime Museum, 39, 217; the Royal Academy of Arts, 214, 215, 216; Trustees of the British Museum, 2, 83, 91, 99, 109, 113; Trustees of the Tate Gallery, 66, 70, 81, 96; University of London Library, 6, 181, 211b; Victoria and Albert Museum, 30, 56, 92, 108, 122, 123, 133, 141, 142, 143, 146, 209; the Worshipful Company of Goldsmiths, 40, 42; City of London, Guildhall Art Gallery, 23, 198; City of London, Guildhall Library, 9, 10, 11; Manchester City Art Galleries, 60, 62, 94, 126, 144, 190; University of Manchester, Whitworth Art Gallery, 19, 82, 93, 139; Newcastle-upon-Tyne, Laing Art Gallery, 25; Newport Museum and Art Gallery, 50; New York, the Forbes Magazine Collection, 15; Norfolk Museums Service, Norwich Castle Museum, 164; Nottingham, Castle Museum, 137; Preston, Harris Museum and Art Gallery, 69, 72, 161; Private collections, 7, 12, 17, 18, 28, 32, 36, 43, 45, 54, 63a, 63b, 75, 79, 84, 87, 111, 112, 116, 119, 120, 121, 125, 131, 132, 134, 135, 138, 145, 150, 151, 152, 156, 157, 158, 159, 160, 162, 163, 167, 169, 172, 173, 178, 179, 184, 185, 186, 189, 192, 194, 197, 199, 202, 203, 205, 206, 207, 208, 210, 218e; Rochdale Art Gallery, 183; Sheffield City Art Galleries, 61, 110, 174, 200; The Earl of Shelburne, 48, 71, 127; Southport, Sefton M. B. C., Atkinson Art Gallery, 148; Bill Thomson, Albany Gallery, 31, 41, 80, 85, 88; Richard Walker, 53; Revd Canon Ivor Walters, 97; Wirral Borough Council, Dept. of Leisure Services and Tourism, Williamson Art Gallery and Museum, 115, 166, 201; Wolverhampton Art Gallery, 191; Miss Jane Wykeham-Musgrave, 78.

Photographic Acknowledgements

We are very grateful to the museums, art galleries and private owners detailed above for kindly supplying photographs of their loans, and for allowing us to reproduce them here. We would also like to thank the following: the Fine Art Society (Pl. 60); the Garrick Club (Pl. 66); Sotheby's (Pl. 69); the Royal Commission on the Ancient and Historical Monuments of Scotland (Pl. 18). Additional photography was done by: AIC Photographers; Dennis Assinder; Derek Balmer; Tim Bryce Photography; Prudence Cuming Associates; John Daniell; Mike Davidson; E. T. Archive Ltd.; Layland Ross Ltd.; Jonathan Morris-Ebbs; Godfrey New; Photographic Records Ltd.; Tony Scott; Studio D Photographers; Studio 62A.

Index

Abbotsford, 13, 93, Cat. 17
Abercairney Abbey, 12, 92
Abu Simbel, 73
Allom, Thomas, 47, 72, Cat. 103
Andrews, 'Old' Robert, and Thomas, 37, Cat. 1
Angus, George, 17
Antwerp Cathedral, Cat. 12, 68, 69
Arden, Joseph, 69
Artists' and Amateurs' Conversazione, 65
Astley's Theatre, and company, 29, 37
Baalbek (Baalbec), 77, 84, Cat. 118, 175–9
Bacon, Thomas, 61, Cat. 112
Ballantine, James, 21, 69, 89, 95, Cat. 13, 18, 40, 59, 69, 187, 193, 219
Ballantyne, John, Cat. 213
Bannister, James, 32, 33
Bartlett, William Henry, 47, 72, 76, 84
Barry, Charles, 16, 17, 93
Barrymore, William, 37
Baudelaire, Charles, 65
Beckford, William, Cat. 92
Beugo, Gavin, 9, 13, 16, 92
Bicknell, Christine (*née* Roberts), 92, 94, 95, Cat. 69, 90, 172, 187, 188, 198, 201, 219, 222
Bicknell, Elhanan, 69, 89, 94, 95, Cat. 163, 174, 177
Bicknell, Henry, Cat. 16, 30, 36, 42, 156, 167, 183, 184, 189, 199, 202
Billings, Robert, 23
Bonington, Richard Parkes, 61, 65
Britton, John, 47
Burn, William, 17, 21, Cat. 29
Byron, Lord, 53
Cairo, 72, 73, 76, 81, Cat. 134, 136–46, 221
Cattermole, George, 47
Christy, Samuel, M. P., Cat. 15
Clarke, John, 13
Cockburn, Lord, 21, 69, 94
Cockerell, Charles, 17
Cotman, John Sell, 65, Cat. 65
Covent Garden, Theatre Royal, 27, 28, 29, 37, 40, 41, 88 n.23 (PvdM), 92, Cat. 2–6, 9–11
Crace, J. G., 13
Craigcrook Castle, 12, 92
Danby, Francis, 41
Dearlove, 28, 33
Delacroix, Eugène, 41, Cat. 8
Dendara (Dendera), 73, 77, Cat. 130
Dickens, Charles, 44, 77, 94, 95, Cat. 134
Dioramas, 7, 40, 41, Cat. 63; see also Panoramas
Dixon, Cornelius, 33
Donaldson Hospital, 25, 94, Cat. 14, 20–1
Drury Lane, Theatre Royal, 27, 28, 29, 32, 37, 39, 40, 88 n.27 (PvdM), 92, Cat. 2, 4, 7, 8, 11
Dublin Theatre, 39
Eastlake, Charles, 16, 94
Edinburgh Theatre Royal, 32, 36, 39, 92, Cat. 3
Edfu (Edfou), 80, Cat. 122–4
Egerton, Sir Francis, 69, 94, Cat. 211
Egypt and Nubia, see *The Holy Land, Syria, Idumea, Arabia, Egypt and Nubia*
Elliston, R. W., 37
Finden, E. and W., 72, Cat. 32, 50, 112, 116, 190
French family, 28
Fry, Roger, 49
Fuseli, Henry, 48
Gambart, Ernest, 72, 89, 95, Cat. 106, 201
Garrick Club, 44, 94
Glasgow Theatre Royal, 36, 92
Graham, John, 9
Graphic Society, 65
Greenwood family, 28, 29
Grieve, John Henderson, Thomas, and William, 27, 28, 32, 40, 88 n.7 (PvdM), Cat. 6, 10, 11
Grindley, Captain, Cat. 111
Haghe, Louis, 69, 94, Cat. 167, 211
Hall, Samuel Carter, 53
Hamilton, Thomas, 17, 25, Cat. 12, 18
Harding, J. D., 47, 48, 61, 72, Cat. 190
Hay, David Ramsay, 9, 13, 16, 17, 23, 25, 88 n.6 (Gow), 89, 94, 95, Cat. 13, 14, 21, 37, 47, 51, 65, 79, 81, 87, 89, 93, 96, 99, 102, 107
Hermonthes, 80, Cat. 125
Holland, James, 53
The Holy Land and Egypt, see *The Holy Land, Syria, Idumea, Arabia, Egypt and Nubia*
The Holy Land, Syria, Idumea, Arabia, Egypt and Nubia, 7, 69, 72, 76, 81, 94, Cat. 117, 119, 121–3, 125–7, 129–35, 137–40, 142–5, 147–8, 150–6, 158–62, 168–73, 176–7, 79, 182, 211, 221
Horsley, J. C., 61
House-painting, 9–17, 32, 33, 92
Hunt, William Holman, 77, 81, Cat. 134
Illustrations . . . to the Poetical Works of Sir Walter Scott, Bart., Cat. 17, 206
Illustrations to the Waverley Novels, 93, Cat. 32, 50, 205
The Israelites Leaving Egypt, 41, 76, Cat. 113–14
Jerusalem, 73, 81, 85, Cat. 158–67
Jones, Owen, 65
Karnak (Karnac), 77, 80, Cat. 124, 126
Kemp, George Meikle, 17, 21, 88 n.11 (Gow), Cat. 13
Knox, John, 23, 25, 94, Cat. 12
Landscape Annuals, 47, 48, 49, 53, 61, 65, 93–4, Cat. 82–3, 85–6, 89, 92–4, 96, 98–101, 105, 110, 207
Landscape Illustrations of the Bible, 61, 72, Cat. 116, 190, 209
Lauder, Robert Scott, 94, Cat. 212
Lawrence, Sir Thomas, 53
Leitch, William Leighton, 9, 36, 41, Cat. 2, 220
Lewis, John Frederick, 48, 61, 65, 81, 85
Linnell, John, 61
Lithographs, technique, 61
de Loutherbourg, Philippe, 27, 28
Luxor, 76, Cat. 126–7, 182b
McCulloch, Horatio, 9
MacGregor, Joseph, Cat. 25
MacKinlay, Thomas G., Cat. 35
Macnee, Daniel, 95, Cat. 214
Marinari, Gaetano, 37, 39, 92
Martin, John, 76, Cat. 114
Moon, Francis Graham, 73, 89, 94, Cat. 211
Müller, William James, 76, 89, n.30 (BL)
Napier, Robert, 89
Nasmyth, Alexander, 21, 36, 94, 95
National Gallery, designs for, 23, Cat. 16
Nile, 73, 76, Cat. 133
Northwick, Lord, 89, 92, 94, Cat. 61, 65, 69, 93, 114
Oram family, 28
Oriental Annual, 61, Cat. 112
Palgrave, F. T., 53
Panoramas, 7, 39–40, 92, Cat. 4–5; see also Dioramas
Pantheon, Edinburgh, 33, 92
Pell, Jens, 94, Cat. 121
Petra, 77, Cat. 116, 151–3
Philae, 80, Cat. 118–21
Phillip, John, 9
Phillips, 'Old', 28, 29, 32, 33
Picturesque Sketches in Spain, 93, Cat. 84, 91–3, 95, 101, 103, 210
Pilgrims of the Rhine, 47, 93, Cat. 72, 75, 79
Playfair, William, 17, 21, 25, Cat. 14, 21, 23
Prout, Samuel, 47, 48, Cat. 66
Pugin, A. N. W., 53
Queen Victoria, 94, Cat. 48
Richards, John Inigo, 28
Roslin, 23, Cat. 34–6
Royal Coburg Theatre ('Old Vic'), 37, 92
Ruskin, 49, 80, 81, 89 n.30 (BL), Cat. 187, 200
Scene-painting, 12, 27–44, 92, Cat. 1–11
Scone Palace, 12, 92
Scotland Delineated, 94, Cat. 22
Scott Monument, 17, 21, 93, 94, Cat. 13, 23
Scott, Sir Walter, 13, 17, 53, Cat. 13
The Seraglio, 40–1, 88 n.25 (PvdM), Cat. 9
Sheepshanks, John, 69, 89, Cat. 146
The Simoon, 77, Cat. 134
Sinai, 77, 81, Cat. 147–50
Skene, James, 12, 13
Smirke, Sidney, 21
Stage scenery, see Scene-painting
Standish, Frank Hall, 89, Cat. 87, 124
Stanfield, Clarkson, 7, 27, 29, 32, 33, 36, 37, 39, 40, 41, 44, 47, 49, 61, 72, 92, Cat. 1, 7, 11, 213, 215–17, 220
Stark, William, 21
Thackeray, William, 49, 53, Cat. 146
Thornhill, James, 27
Turner, J. M. W., 47, 49, 53, 61, 65, 72, 84, 88 n.18 (MP), 92, Cat. 40
Venice, 49, Cat. 197–200
Vernon, Robert, 89, Cat. 70, 81
Views in India, Chiefly among the Himalaya Mountains, 61
Wallace (scene-painter), 33
Westminster, New Palace of, 16, 23, 94, Cat. 40
Wharncliffe, Lord, 65
White, Revd James, 89, Cat. 36, 186
Whitmore, 28, 29
Wilkie, David, 13, 61, 81, 94
Wilson, John 'Jock', 29, 39, Cat. 220